für Alfred und Ursula

ANDREAS ZYBACH

Herausgegeben von / edited by Aargauer Kunsthaus, Aarau

Interview: Daniel Baumann

Verlag der Buchhandlung Walther König, Köln

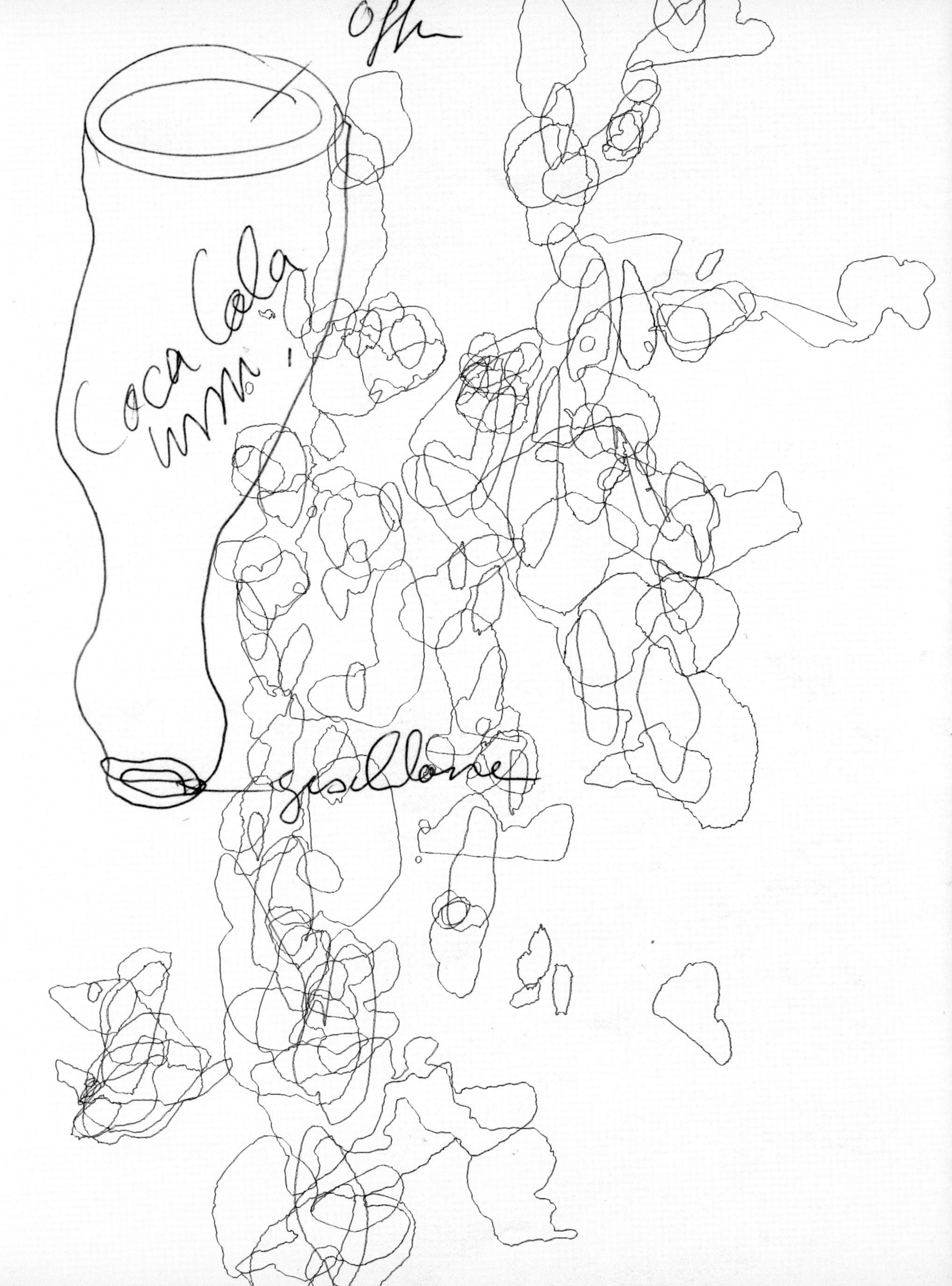

Coca Cola

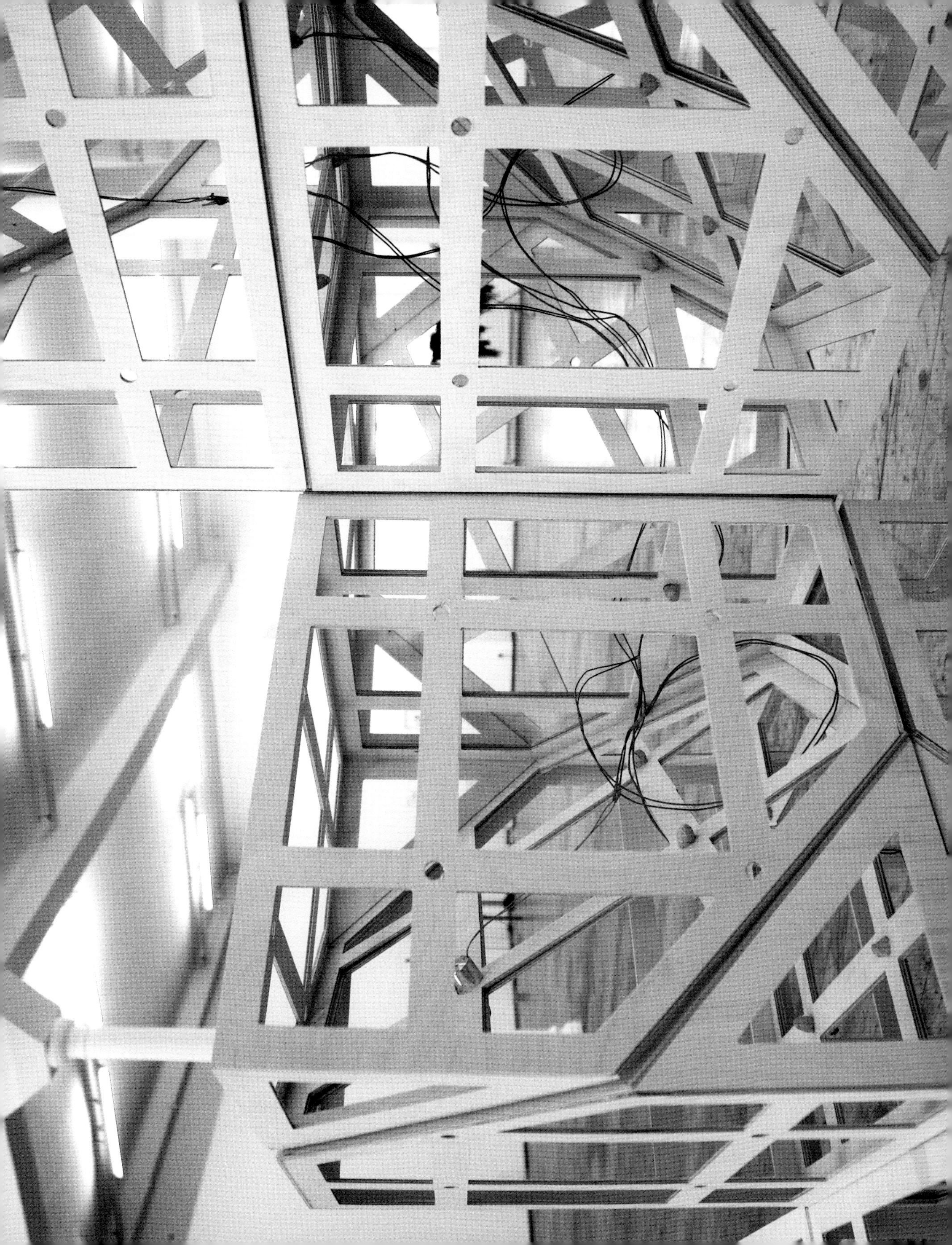

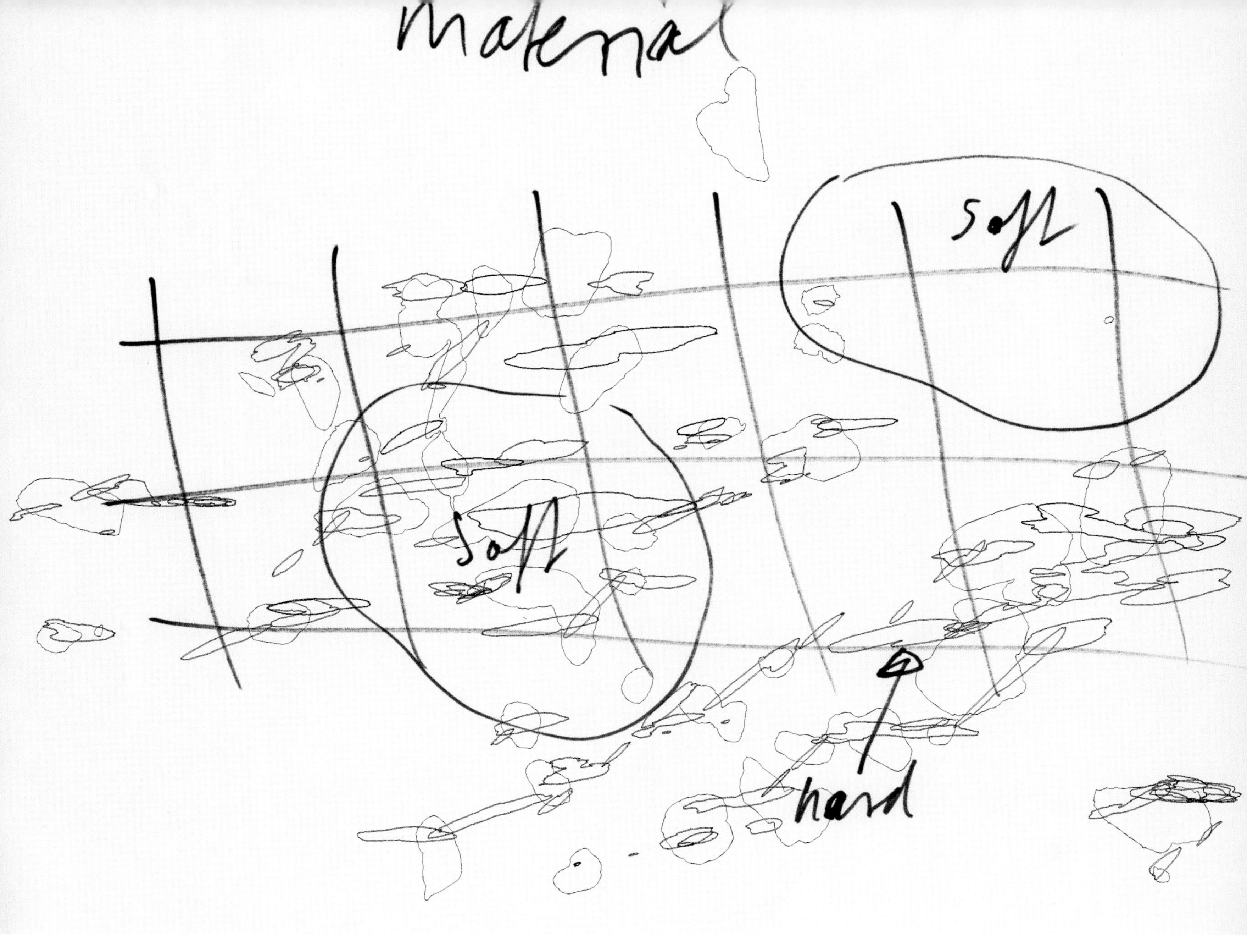

material
soft
soft
hard

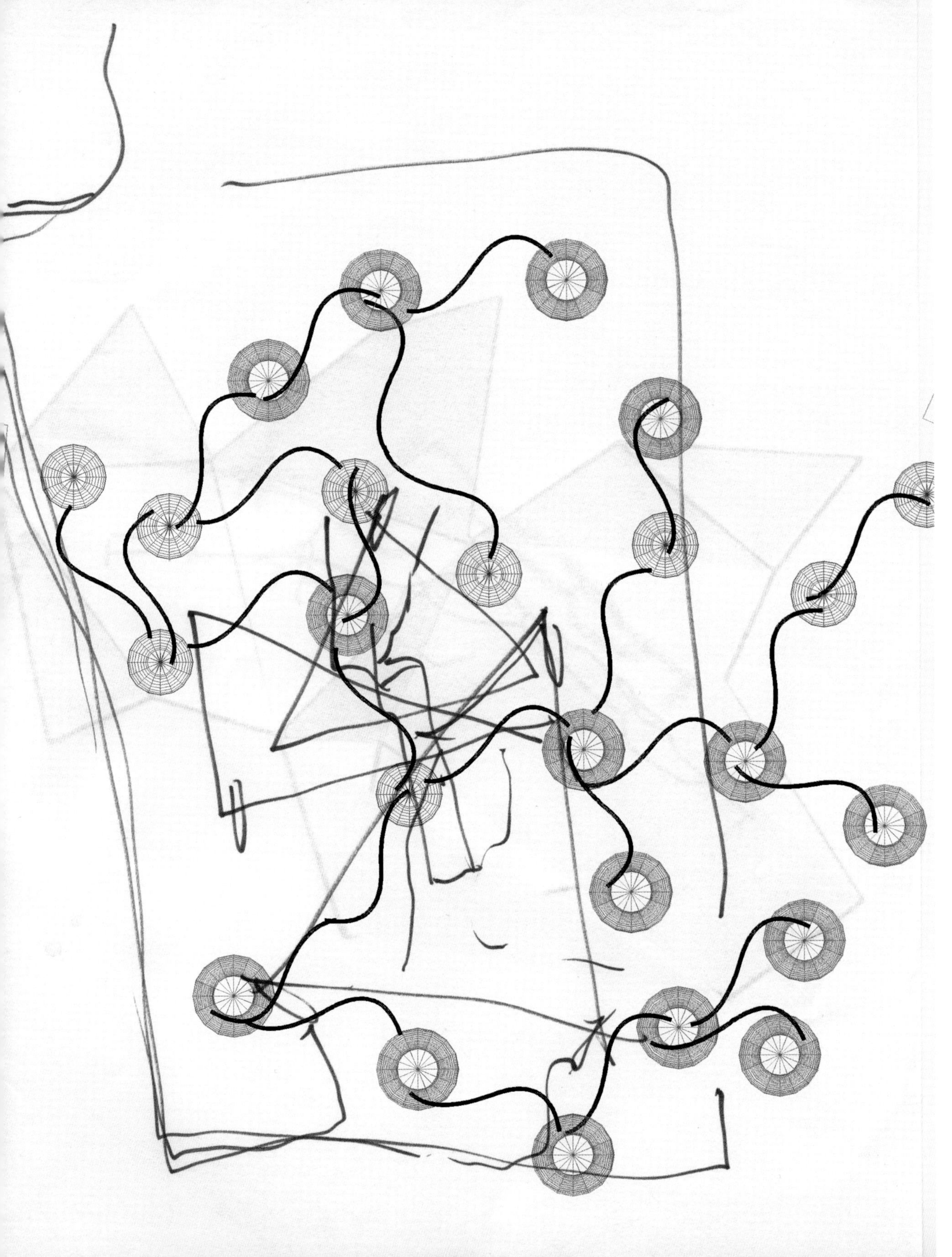

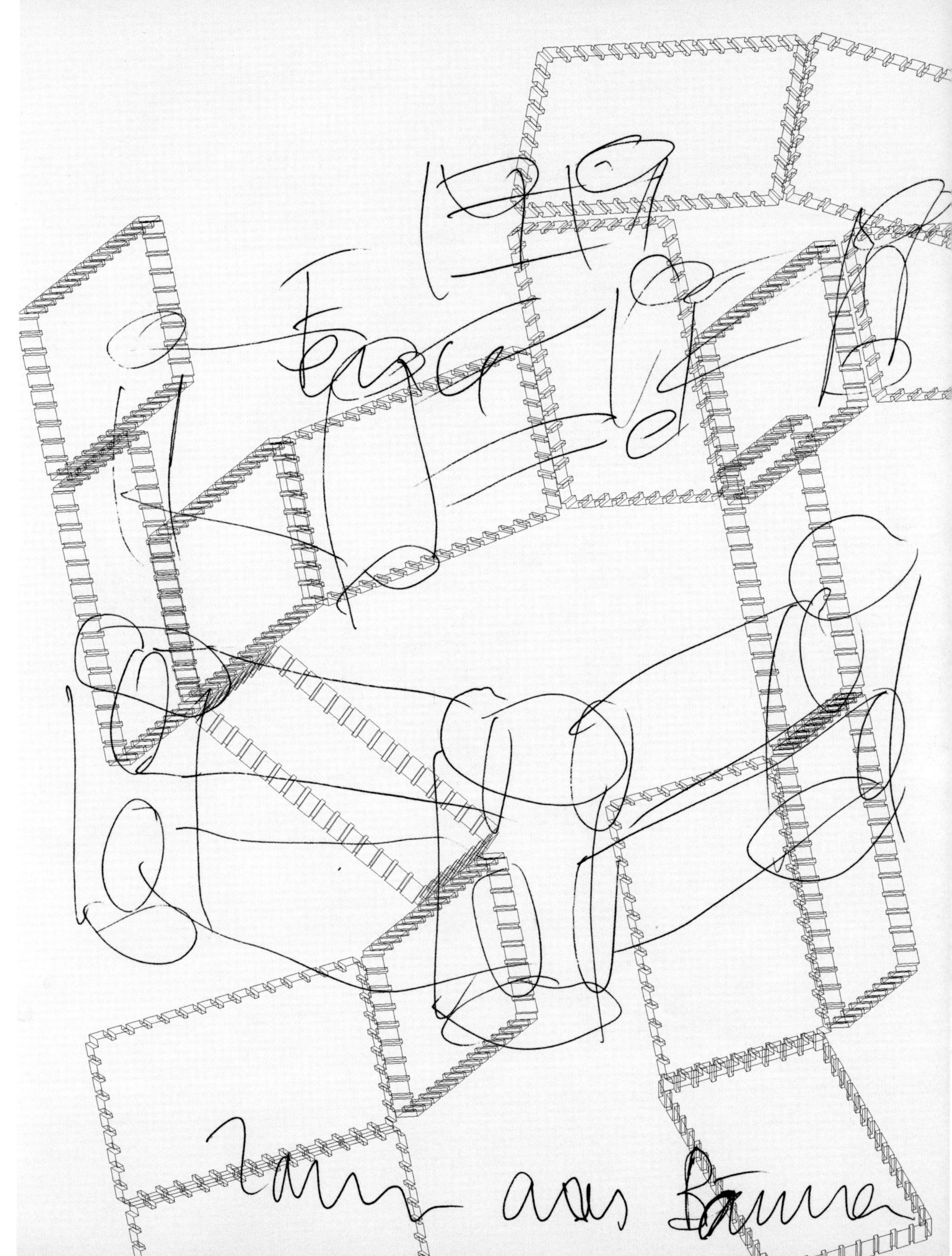

The New-York Times

PROF. BELL HAS NEW IDEAS

Believes Flying Machines Are Practicable—Also Geared Contrivances to Increase Horses' Speed.

Prof. Alexander Graham Bell, the inventor, who has been in France and Belgium four weeks, returned to this city yesterday on the French Line steamship La Bourgogne, and is staying at the Gilsey House.

To a reporter for THE NEW-YORK TIMES Prof. Bell last night talked of the rumor that he was engaged in the construction of a flying machine.

"That is not exactly correct," he said. "While I am greatly interested in flying machines, and have been making some experiments, I am not constructing any aerial machine. I am merely working up tables which will be of use to future inventors. I believe that the idea of a flying machine is practicable, but that balloons and butterfly wings must be discarded. I started on my experiment with the idea of having a machine of greater specific gravity than the air. I believe that is the only correct principle. I have experimented with a French design made of metal and of simple construction. I have also been much interested while in France by a machine called the helikoptea, invented by M. Trouvé, made of iron and metal, and which screws itself up into the air.

"I have not done anything further with the radiaphone. It is just as perfect as the

LAW PREVENTS FUNERAL

Bough's Widow Fighting His Sister for His Body and Fortune.

A MIDNIGHT INJUNCTION GRANTED

The Case to be Heard in the Superior Court To-day Before Judge Dugro—An Estate of $10,000 Is Involved.

A case, which the law records of fifty years show to be unprecedented, comes up this morning in the Superior Court, before Judge Dugro, when Mary Bough will be called on to show cause why an injunction granted by Judge McAdam Saturday night, restraining her from burying the body of her brother, George Bough, until further order of the court, should not be made permanent.

It was just a few minutes before midnight Saturday when the lawyers of Mrs. Grace Bough, the widow, after a long search, met Judge McAdam, at Thirty-first Street and Eighth Avenue, and, having hur-

RUSSIA WANTS OUR

An Order for Forty Mass received by the Baldwin Works of Philad

PHILADELPHIA, Penn., S creasing ability of America to compete successfully in the Old World has just be by the Baldwin Locomotive city, whose managers are large contract for engines f roads. For many years the have been able to sell t Central and South America, Japan, and in other distan they have never been able foothold in European coun English type of locomoti been preferred to the Amer

This prejudice has at been broken down. Contra by the Baldwin Works call motives, twenty each for freight service. They are with the least possible d the orders already in han big Baldwin establishment rest of the year.

The names of the Russi which the engines are to be withheld by the firm, but, meat controls practically of that country, the contra to have come from the Go order, taken in connection to the Bethlehem Iron Com

---

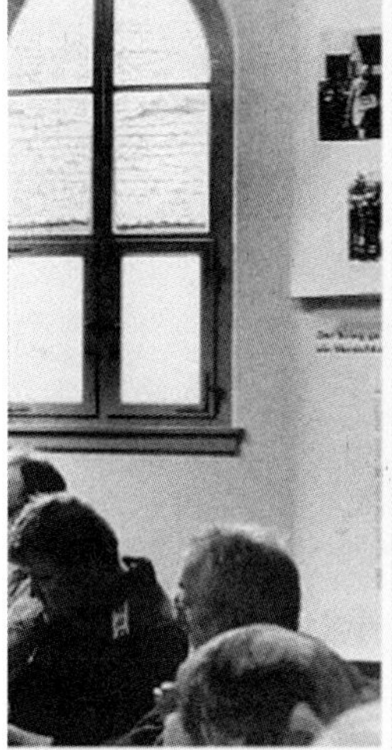

Foto Michael Kretzer

Mit geraubtem Auto in den Tod gefahren

wbr. MÜNSTER/FRANKFURT. Gestern in den frühen Morgenstunden hat ein noch nicht identifizierter Mann in Münster mit Hilfe einer Schußwaffe das Auto geraubt und ist zweieinhalb Stunden später damit auf der A 661 frontal gegen eine Wand gefahren. Der Unbekannte war sofort tot; die Polizei nimmt an, daß er Selbstmord begangen hat. Die Frau hatte gegen 4.30 Uhr mit ihrem Kleinbus an der Eduard-Vogel-Straße in Münster gehalten, als der Mann die Fahrertür öffnete und der Frau eine Waffe an den Kopf hielt. Er forderte sie auf, ihm das Auto zu überlassen, gestattete ihr aber noch, persönliche Dinge aus dem Bus zu nehmen. Anschließend fuhr er mit dem Wagen in Richtung B 45 davon. Kurz nach 7 Uhr verständigte ein Zeuge die Polizei in Frankfurt, daß auf der A 661 in Höhe des Seckbacher Tunnels ein Auto gegen eine Wand gerast sei. Wie sich herausstellte, handelte es sich um das zuvor in Münster geraubte Fahrzeug.

„Wochenende der Verständigung"

ziz. DARMSTADT. Am interkulturellen Wochenende von heute bis Sonntag in Darmstadt wollen verschiedene Vereine, Wohlfahrtsverbände und Initiativen mit einem umfangreichen Programm gegen Rassismus und Gewalt Stellung beziehen. Die Aktionen stehen unter dem Motto „Heiner kennen keine Grenzen". Schirmherr ist Oberbürgermeister Peter Benz (SPD). Der Kabarettist Sedat Pamuk eröffnet das Programm am Freitag abend um 20 Uhr im Gemeindesaal der Stadtkirchengemeinde, Kiesstraße 17, mit seinem Programm „Gastarbeiterlos". An den folgenden Tagen findet das Hauptprogramm in der Mornewegschule, Hermannstraße 21 statt. Kunstausstellungen, Diskussionen, Informationsstände, Workshops und eine Feier der Religionen sollen sich kritisch mit dem

Minensuchgeräte und Chips

Esa-Tagung zum Technologietransfer / Viele Anwendungen

ziz. DARMSTADT. Wie kommen die Kartoffelchips heil in die Tüte? Damit sie beim Einfüllen nicht zerbröseln, bedarf es einer besonderen Technik, und die haben sich die Chipshersteller bei der Raumfahrt beschafft. Technologietransfer nennt man die branchenfremde Nutzung von technologischen Entwicklungen, und kaum eine Technologie muß so ausgefeilt und ausgereift sein wie die der Raumfahrt.

Weil auf diesem Gebiet intensive und aufwendige Forschung betrieben wird, kam die Europäische Weltraumagentur Esa vor etwa zehn Jahren auf den Gedanken, diese Technologien für Parallelanwendungen in der Industrie zu vermarkten. Dazu wurde die MST Aerospace GmbH als Beratungsunternehmen mit Sitz in Köln gegründet, das bis zu dreimal im Jahr Foren unter der Fragestellung veranstaltet: „Haben Sie ein technisches Problem?" Jetzt fand ein solches Esa-Forum zum Thema „Sensoren und Meßtechniken" im Raumfahrtkontrollzentrum Esoc in Darmstadt statt, zu dem 65 Vertreter großer und vor allem mittelständischer Unternehmen angereist waren.

Ein herausragendes Beispiel, das auf dem Kongreß vorgestellt worden ist, war nach Darstellung des Tagungsleiters Hans-Peter Dworak ein für die Mars-Erforschung entwickeltes Tiefenradar. Das Gerät ist Bestandteil eines Roboters, der in einer unbemannten Rakete auf den Mars geschickt werden und Wissenschaftlern Einblick in die oberflächennahen Schichten unterhalb des Marsbodens ge-

ben soll. Ein solches Tiefenradar könne aus bis zu 50 Zentimeter Tiefe ein Bild mit sehr hoher Auflösung liefern, aus bis zu zehn Meter Tiefe ein immer noch verwendbares.

Dieses Tiefenradar eigne sich sehr gut für Minensuchgeräte und sei unter der Bezeichnung „Projekt Hope" vorgestellt worden, berichtete Dworak. Denn die Landminen bestünden heute kaum noch aus Metall und seien mit den Metalldetektoren kaum auffindbar. Mit dem Tiefenradar würden sie auf einem Bildschirm sichtbar und könnten auch an ihrer Form klassifiziert werden.

Besonders großes Interesse an der Weltraumtechnik hat die Medizin. Die Raumtechnik muß leicht, hoch belastbar und sehr zuverlässig sein, weil Reparaturen nur schwer vorgenommen werden können. Zudem muß sie sparsam im Energieverbrauch sein. Ähnliche Anforderungen haben beispielsweise Herzschrittmacher, deren Herstellung technische Erkenntnisse aus der Raumfahrttechnik übernimmt.

Auch Raumfahrtsoftware kann in der Medizin angewendet werden, wenn bei Krebsuntersuchungen Veränderungen über einen längeren Zeitraum beobachtet und abgeglichen werden müssen. Mit gleichen optischen Verfahren werden aus dem All Erdbeobachtungen gemacht. Die Kartoffelchips verdanken es einem Windkanal für die Entwicklung der Trägerrakete Ariane, daß sie unzerbröselt in die Tüte gelangen – durch einen Luftstrom nämlich. Für den Hersteller des Massenartikels Kartoffelchips ist der Einsatz dieser Windkanal-Technik bares Geld.

Künftig nur noch „Soziale Arbeit"

Neuordnung der Studiengänge an Evangelischer Fachhochschule

wbr. DARMSTADT. Die zukunftsweisende Arbeit der Evangelischen Fachhoch-

Unterstützung durch Sponsor

Gotteshaus unversehrt blieb, ist dem vorherigen Verkauf an einen „arischen" Nachbarn zu verdanken, der das Gebäude als Alterssitz für seine Mutter herrichtete. 1989 erwarb der Förderverein das Gebäude und sanierte es für 600 000 Mark. Erneuerungsbedürftig war auch der Tora-Vorhang. Metallborten und -stickereien hatten sich gelöst, der Stoff war verblaßt und abgegriffen. Eine Wiesbadener Exper-

habe die Studienordnung so geändert, daß das Studium mit seinen Semestern

Gebäude an

… der Natur …

Übersetzung in eine

— Form

Kohlenmuskelmalerei

Flucht aus der Schale

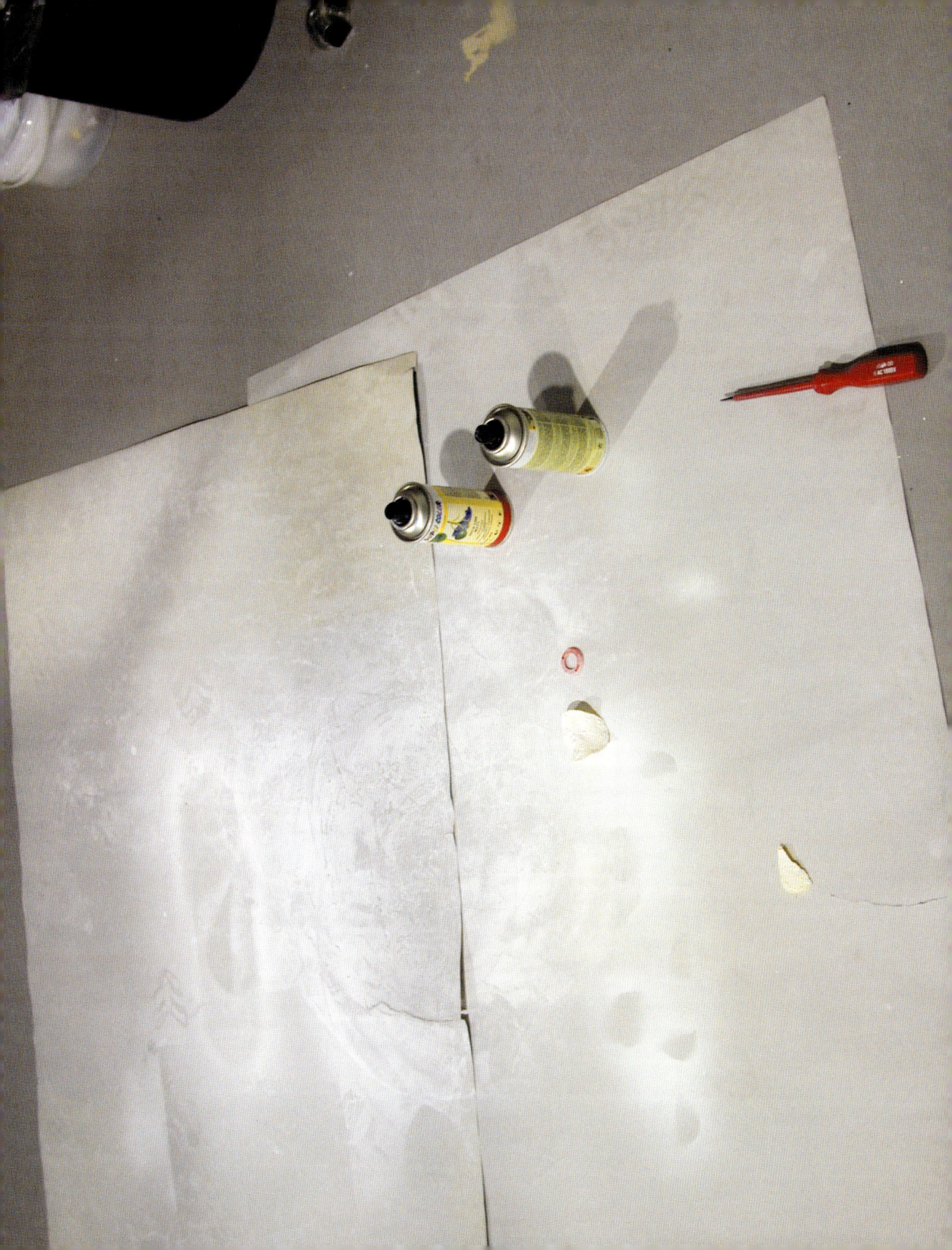

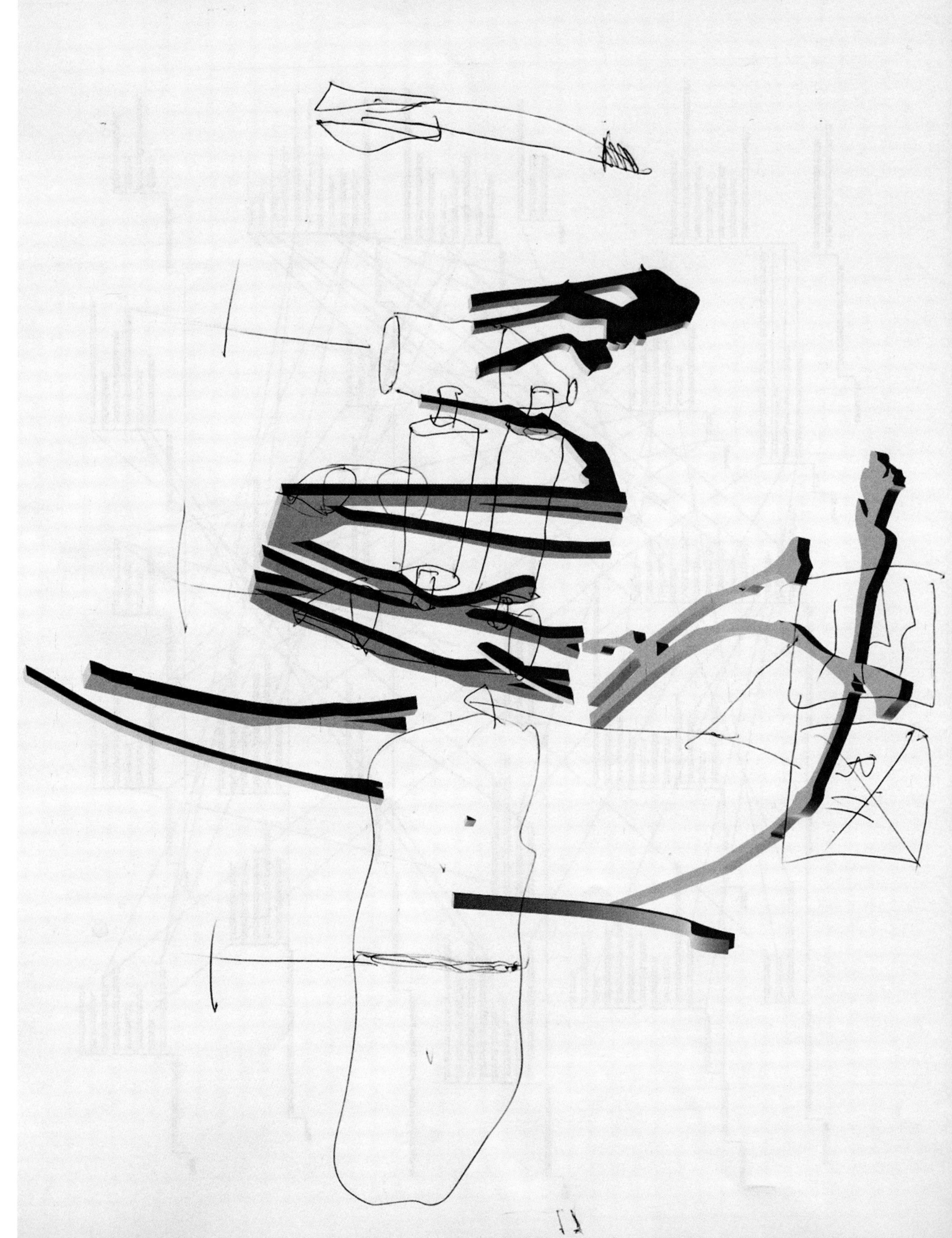

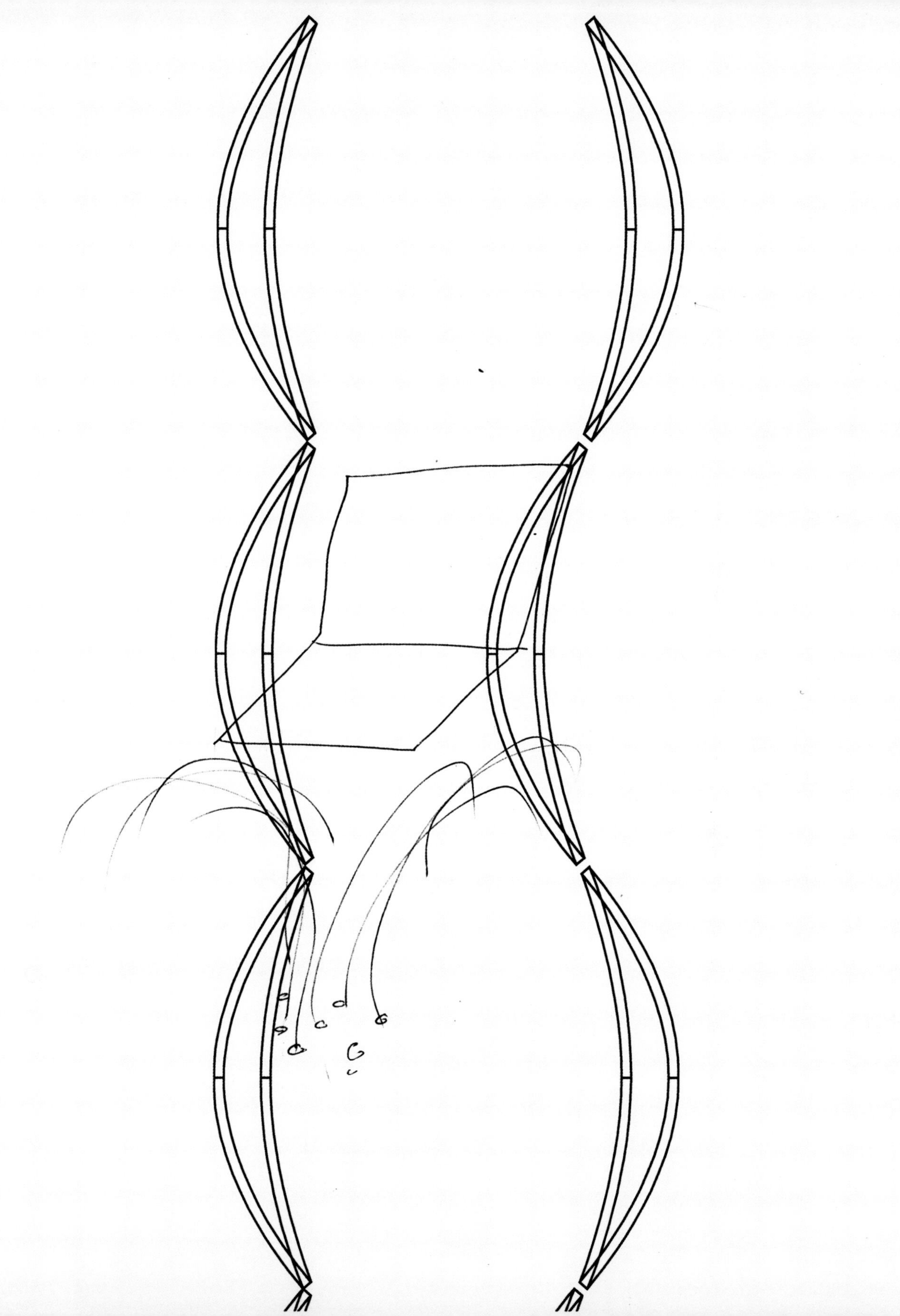

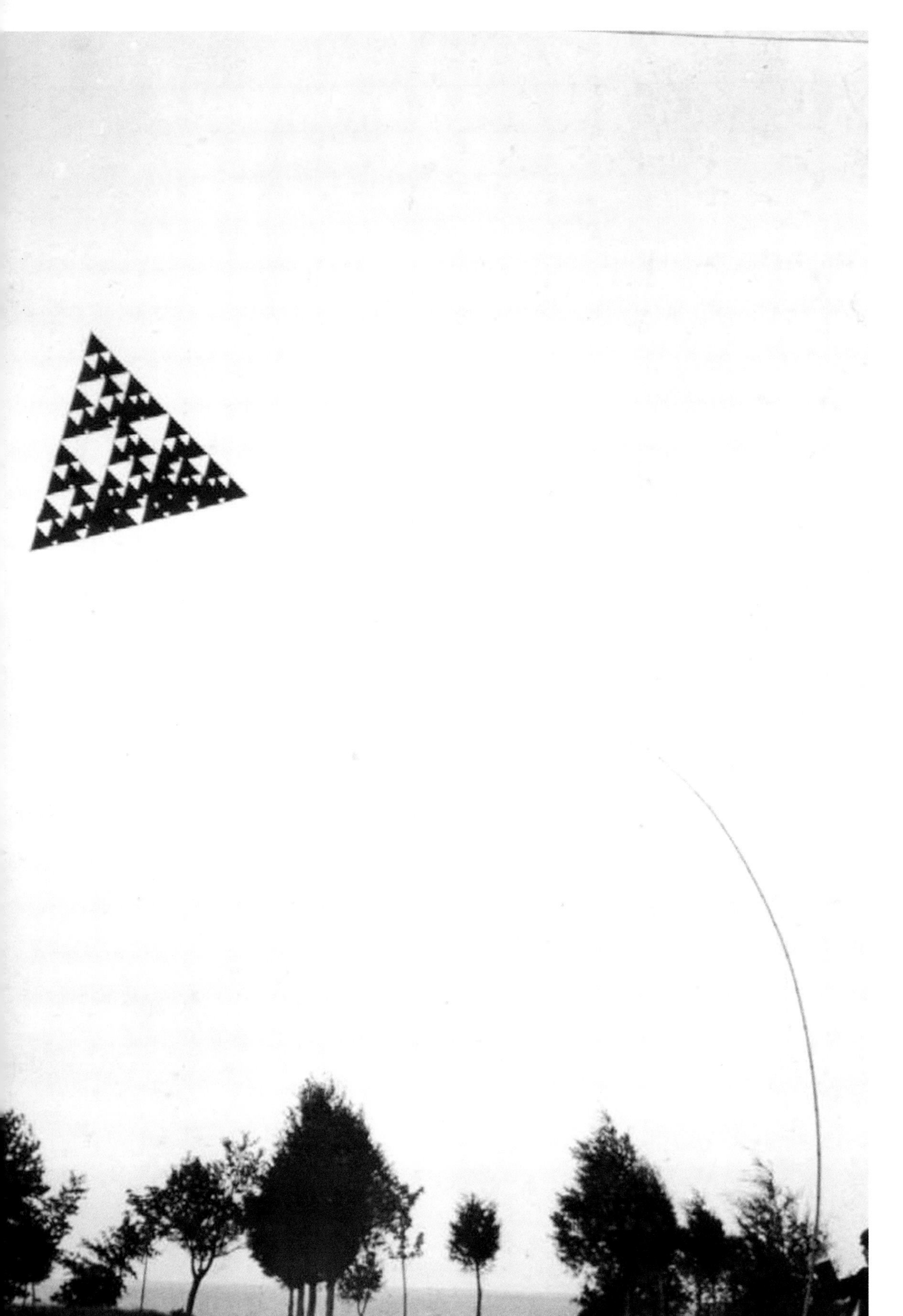

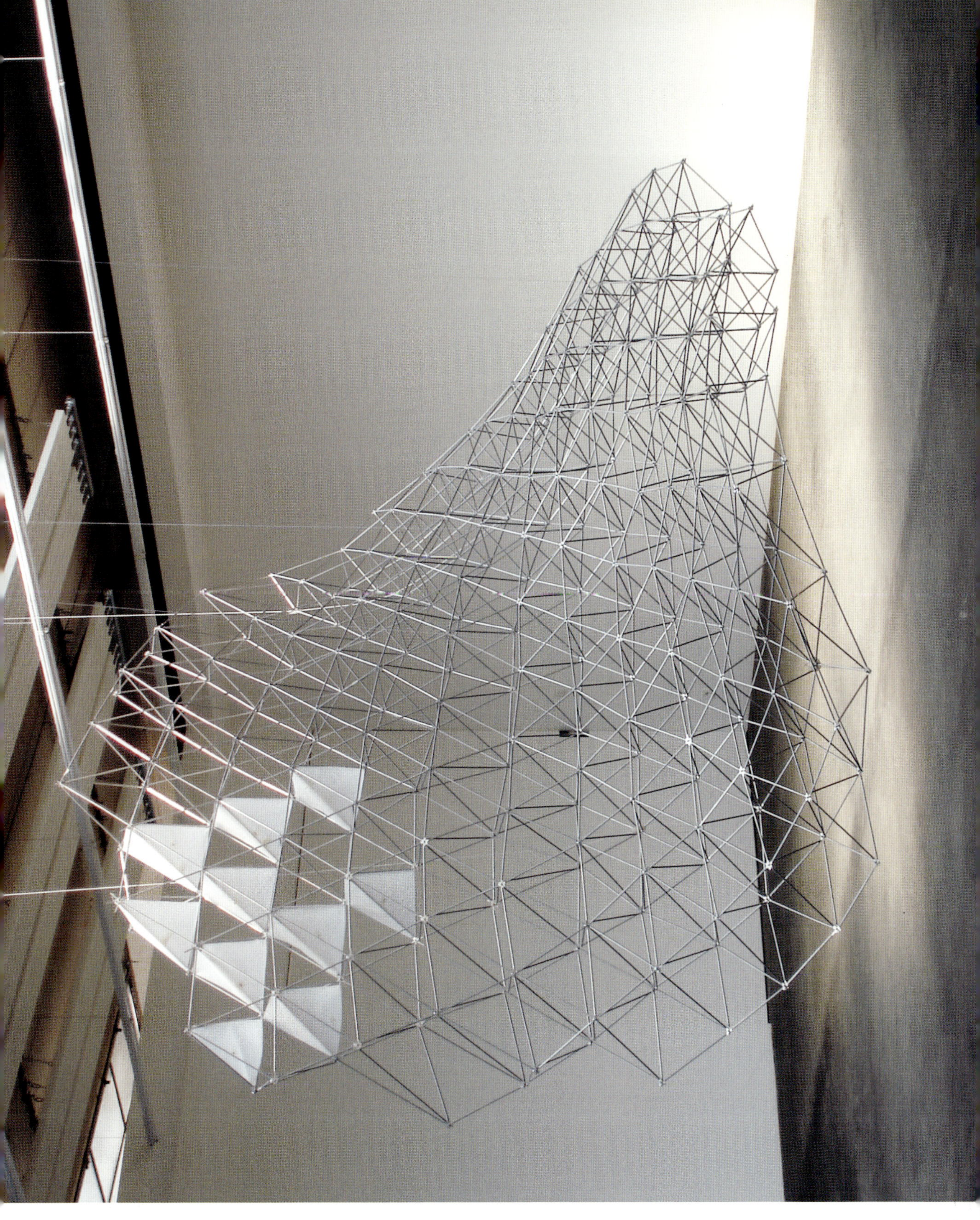

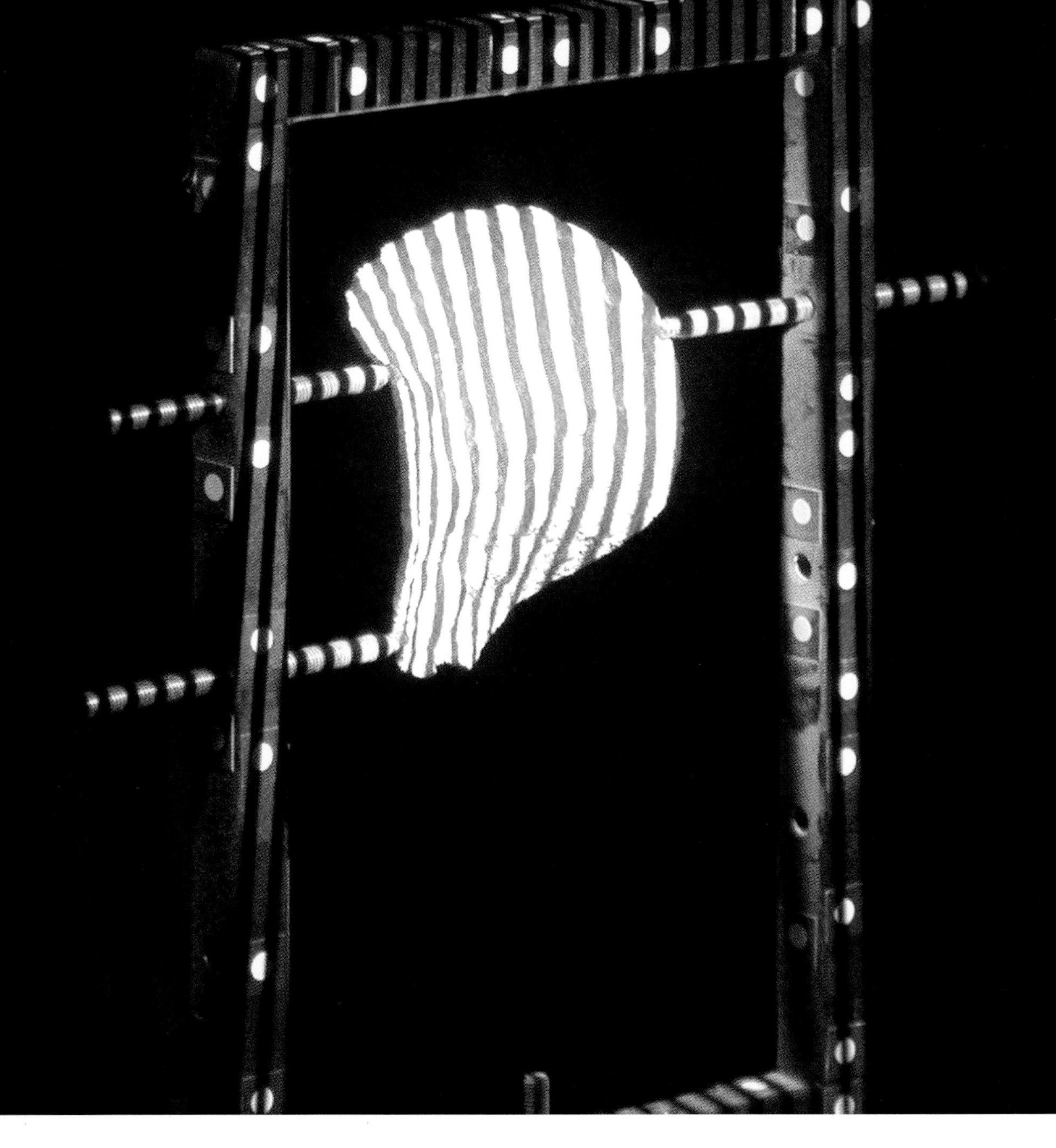

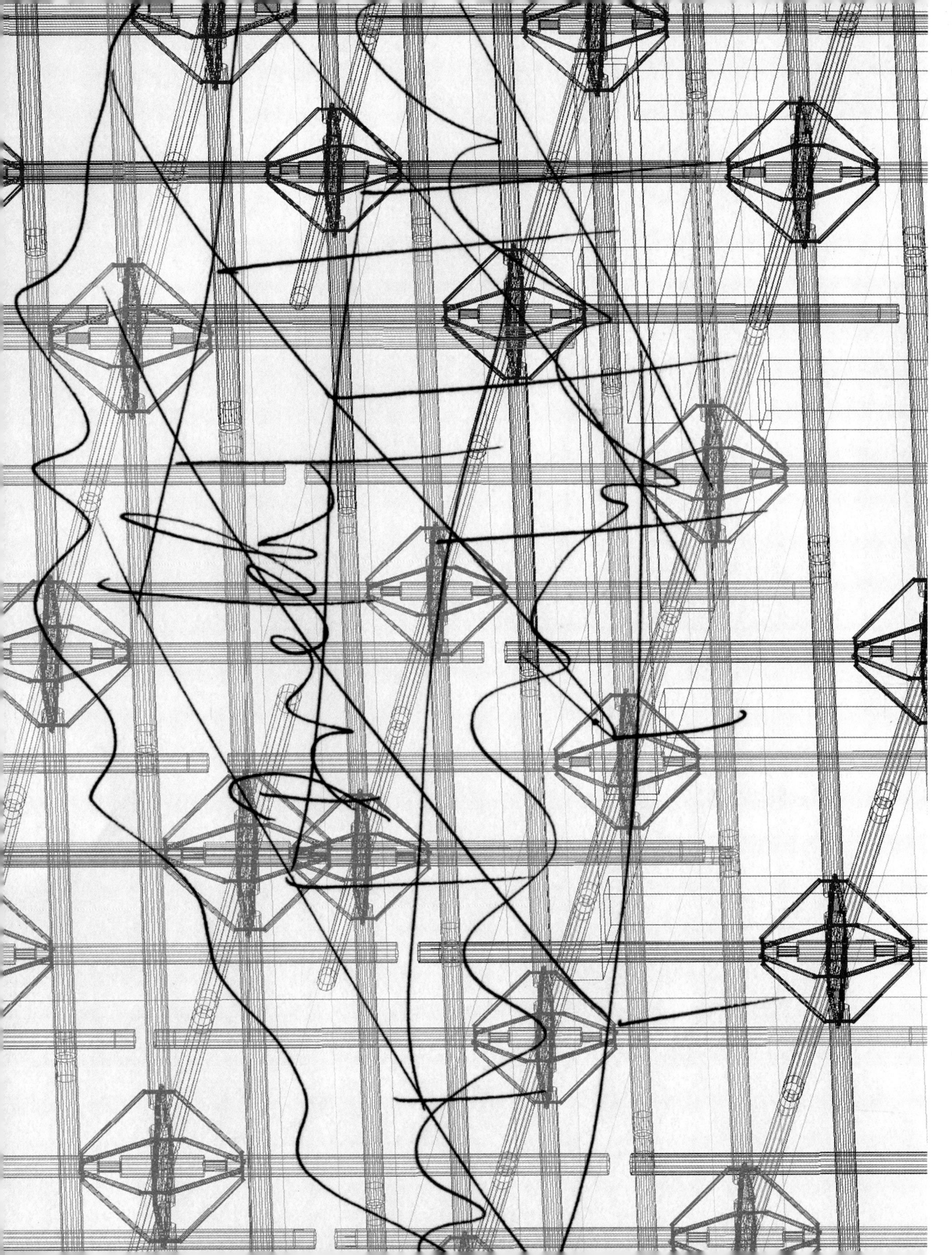

125:1

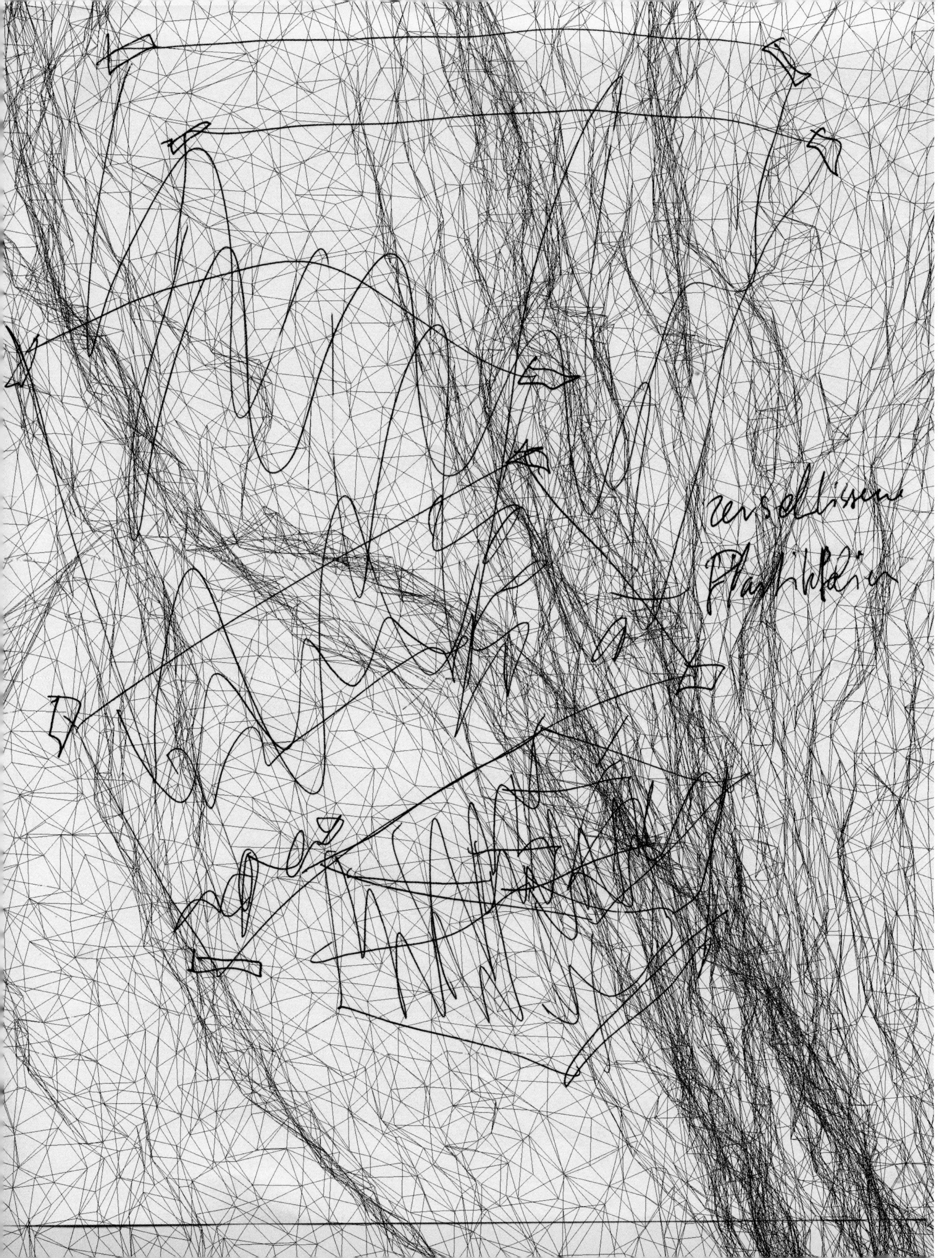

zerschlissene
Plastikfolien

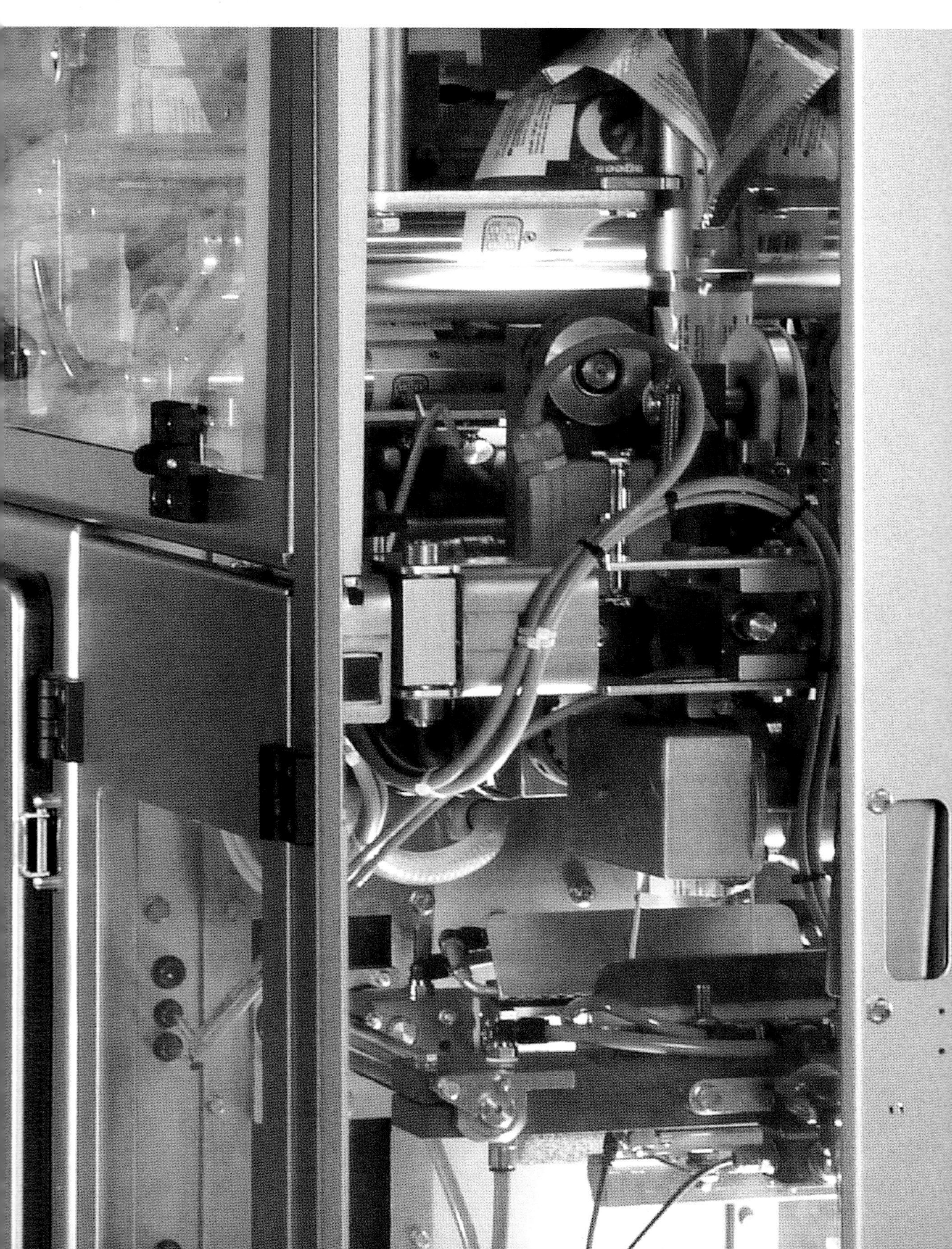

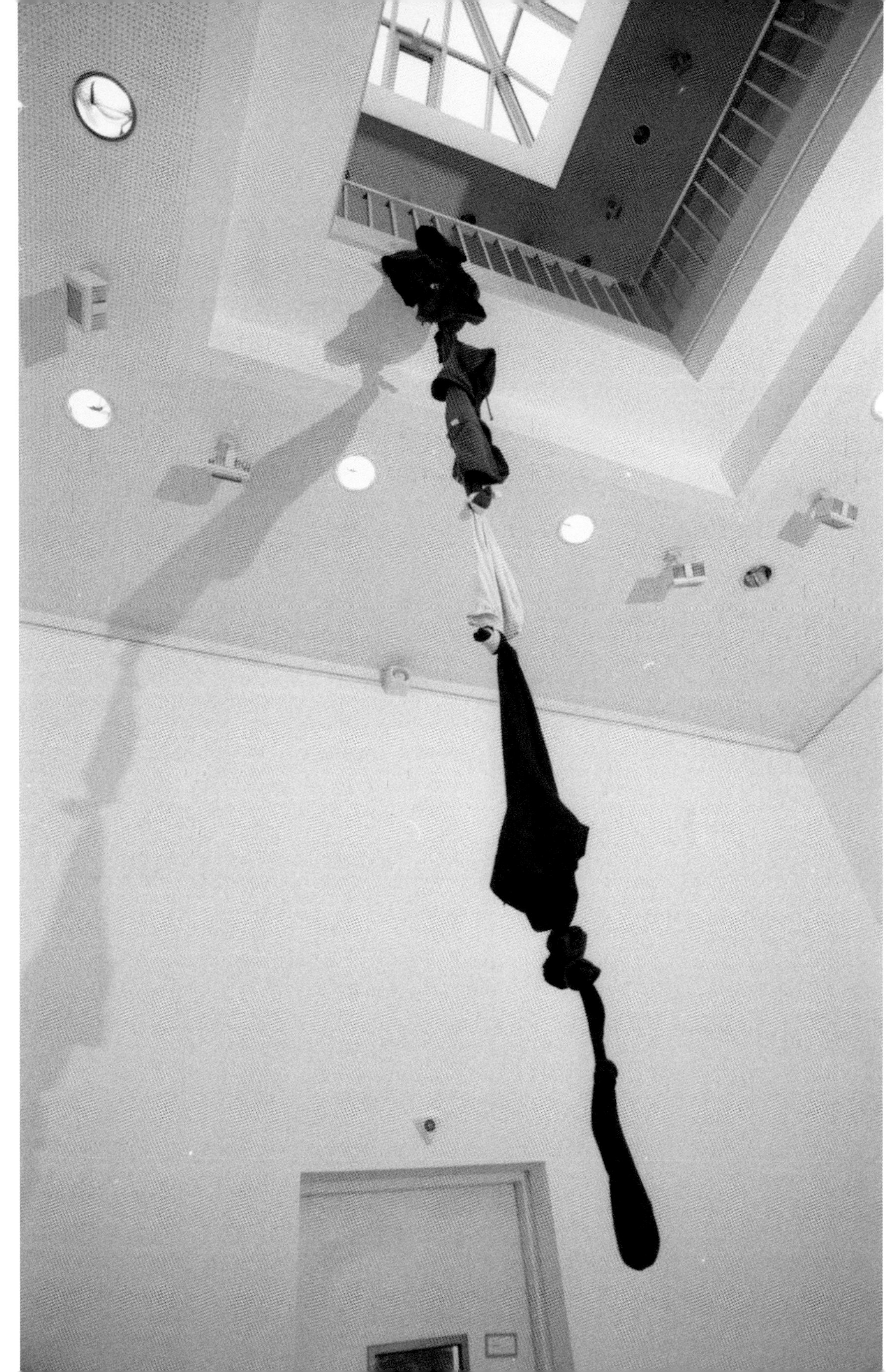

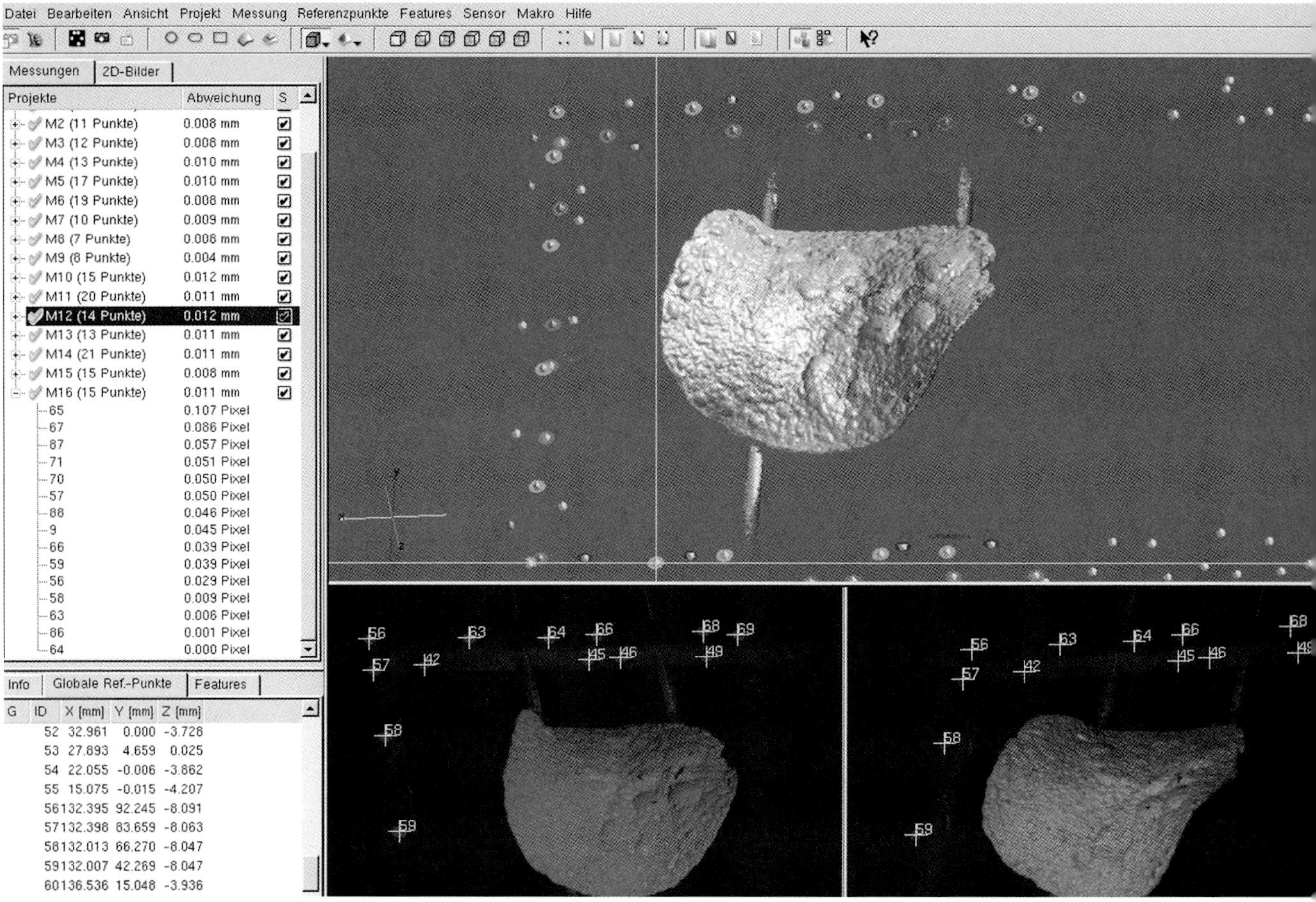

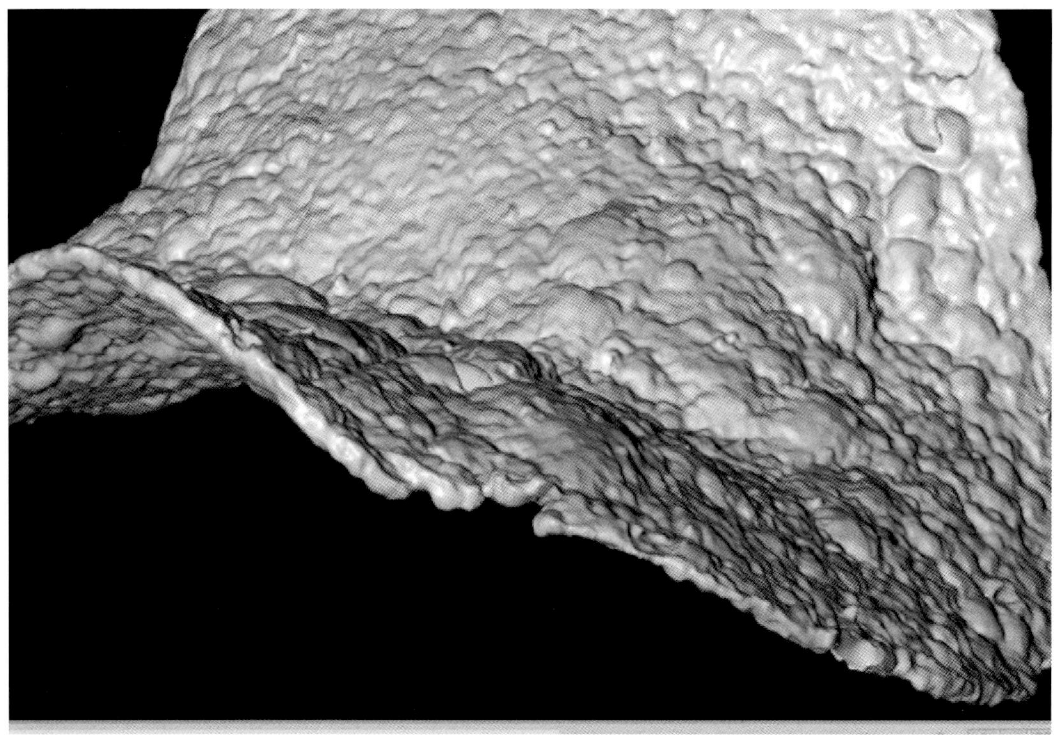

Datei Bearbeiten Ansicht Projekt Messung Referenzpunkte Features Sensor Makro Hilfe
Messungen   2D-Bilder
Projekte   Abweichung   S
M2 (11 Punkte)   0.008 mm
M3 (12 Punkte)   0.008 mm
M4 (13 Punkte)   0.010 mm
M5 (17 Punkte)   0.010 mm
M6 (19 Punkte)   0.008 mm
M7 (10 Punkte)   0.009 mm
M8 (7 Punkte)   0.006 mm
M9 (8 Punkte)   0.004 mm
M10 (15 Punkte)   0.012 mm
M11 (20 Punkte)   0.011 mm
M12 (14 Punkte)   0.012 mm
M13 (13 Punkte)   0.011 mm
M14 (21 Punkte)   0.011 mm
M15 (15 Punkte)   0.008 mm
M16 (15 Punkte)   0.011 mm
65   0.107 Pixel
67   0.086 Pixel
87   0.057 Pixel
71   0.051 Pixel
70   0.050 Pixel
57   0.050 Pixel
88   0.046 Pixel
9   0.045 Pixel
66   0.039 Pixel
59   0.039 Pixel
56   0.029 Pixel
58   0.009 Pixel
63   0.006 Pixel
86   0.001 Pixel
64   0.000 Pixel
Info   Globale Ref.-Punkte   Features
G ID   X [mm]   Y [mm]   Z [mm]
52 32.961   0.000   -3.728
53 27.893   4.659   0.025
54 22.055 -0.006   -3.862
55 15.075 -0.015   -4.207
56 132.395 92.245   -8.091
57 132.398 83.659   -8.063
58 132.013 66.270   -8.047
59 132.007 42.269   -8.047
60 136.536 15.048   -3.936

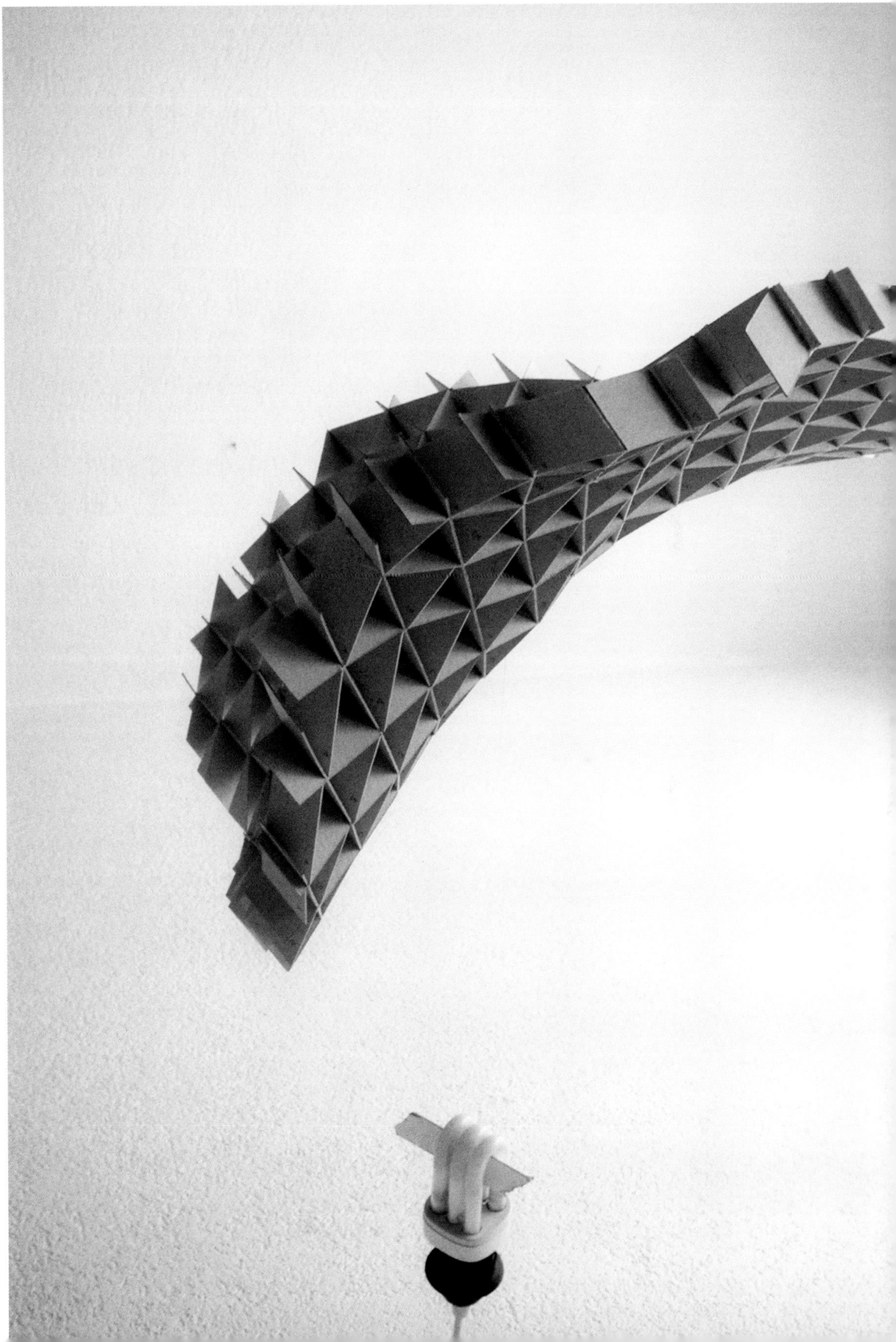

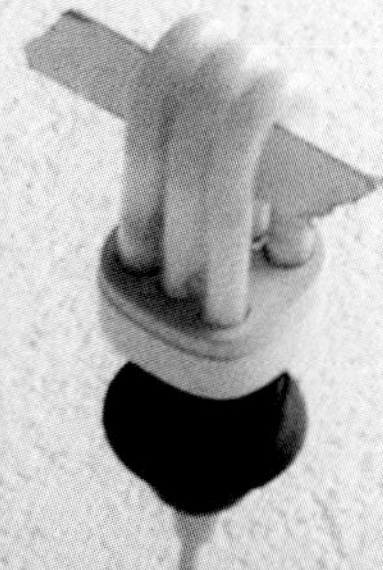

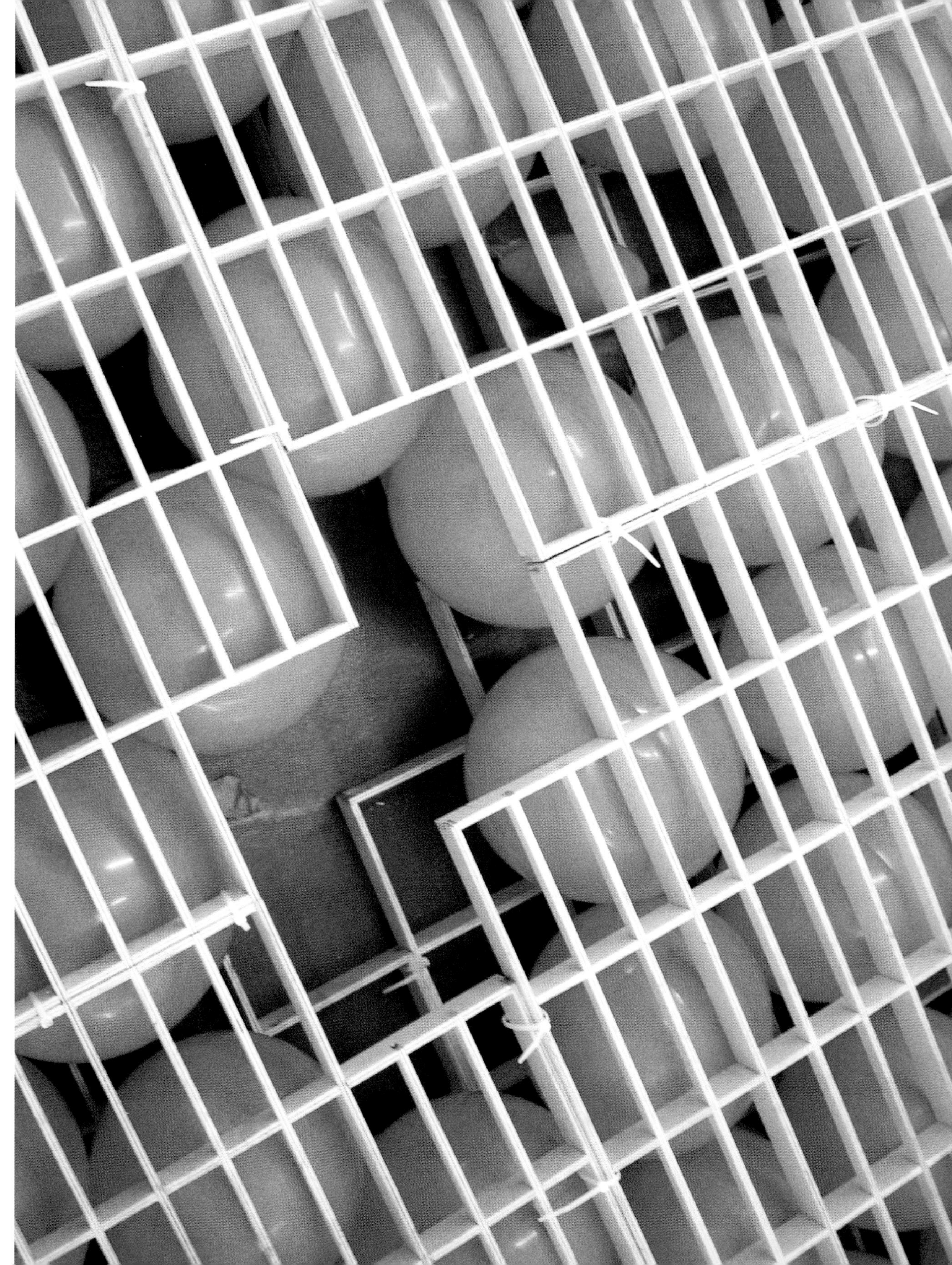

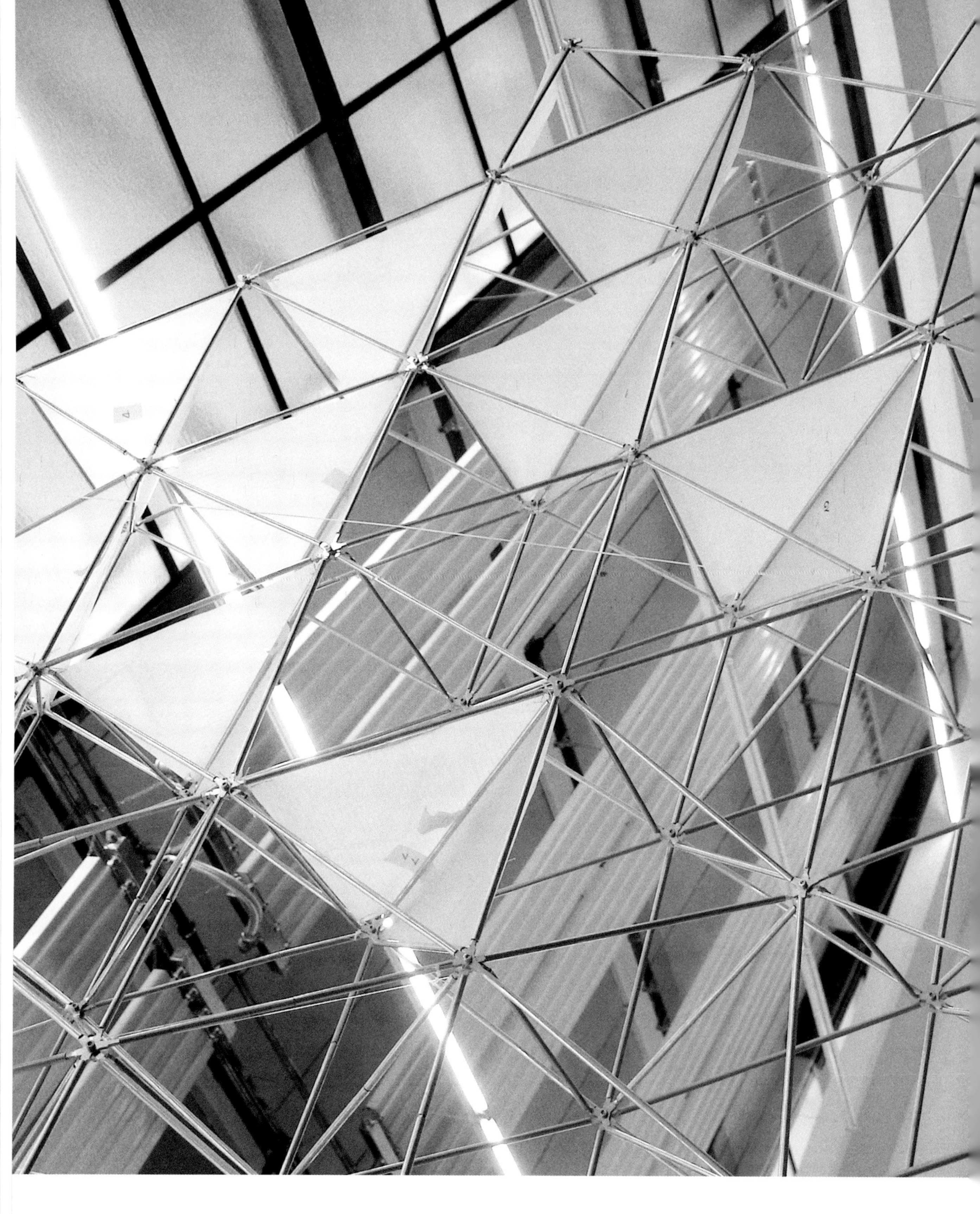

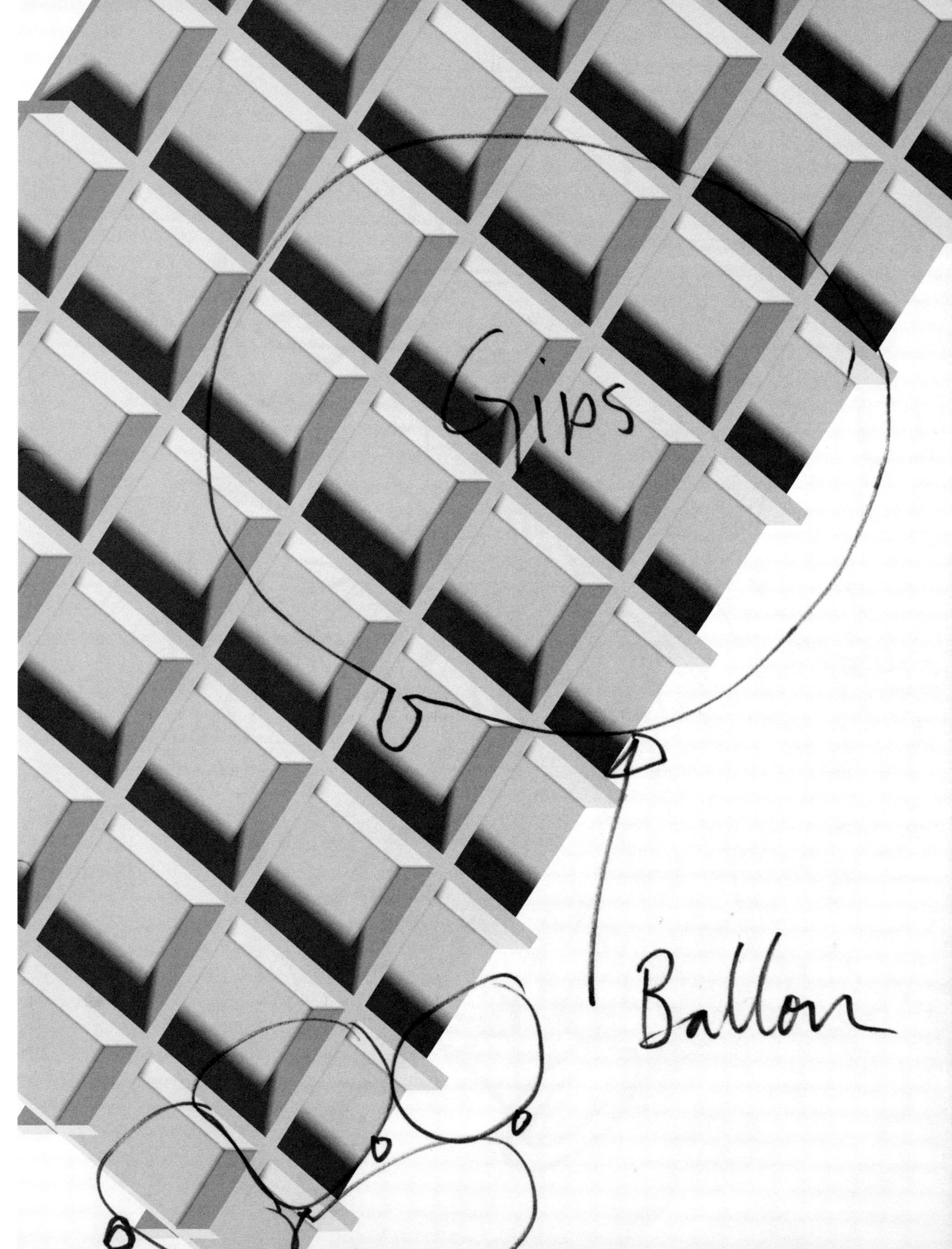
Gips
Ballon

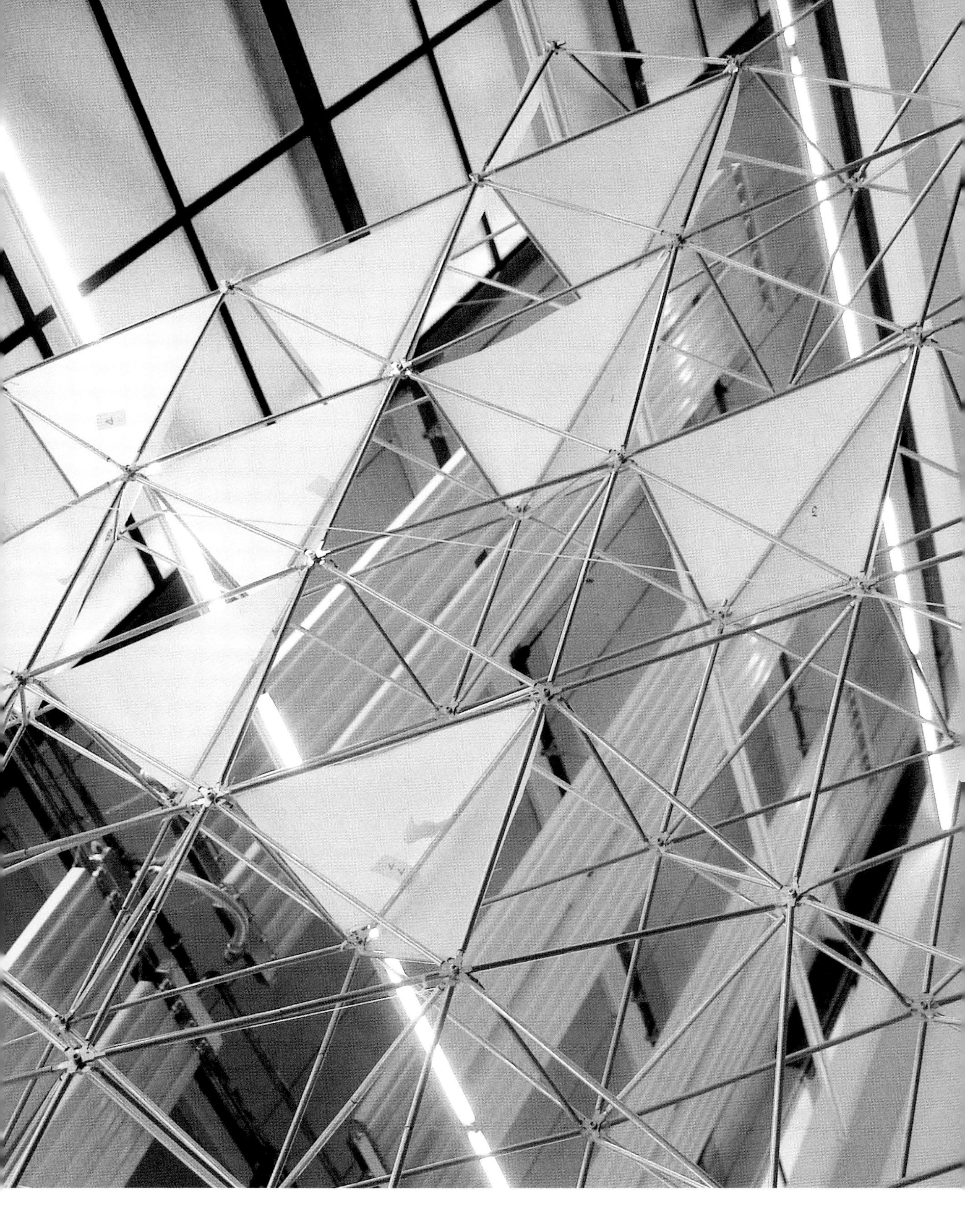

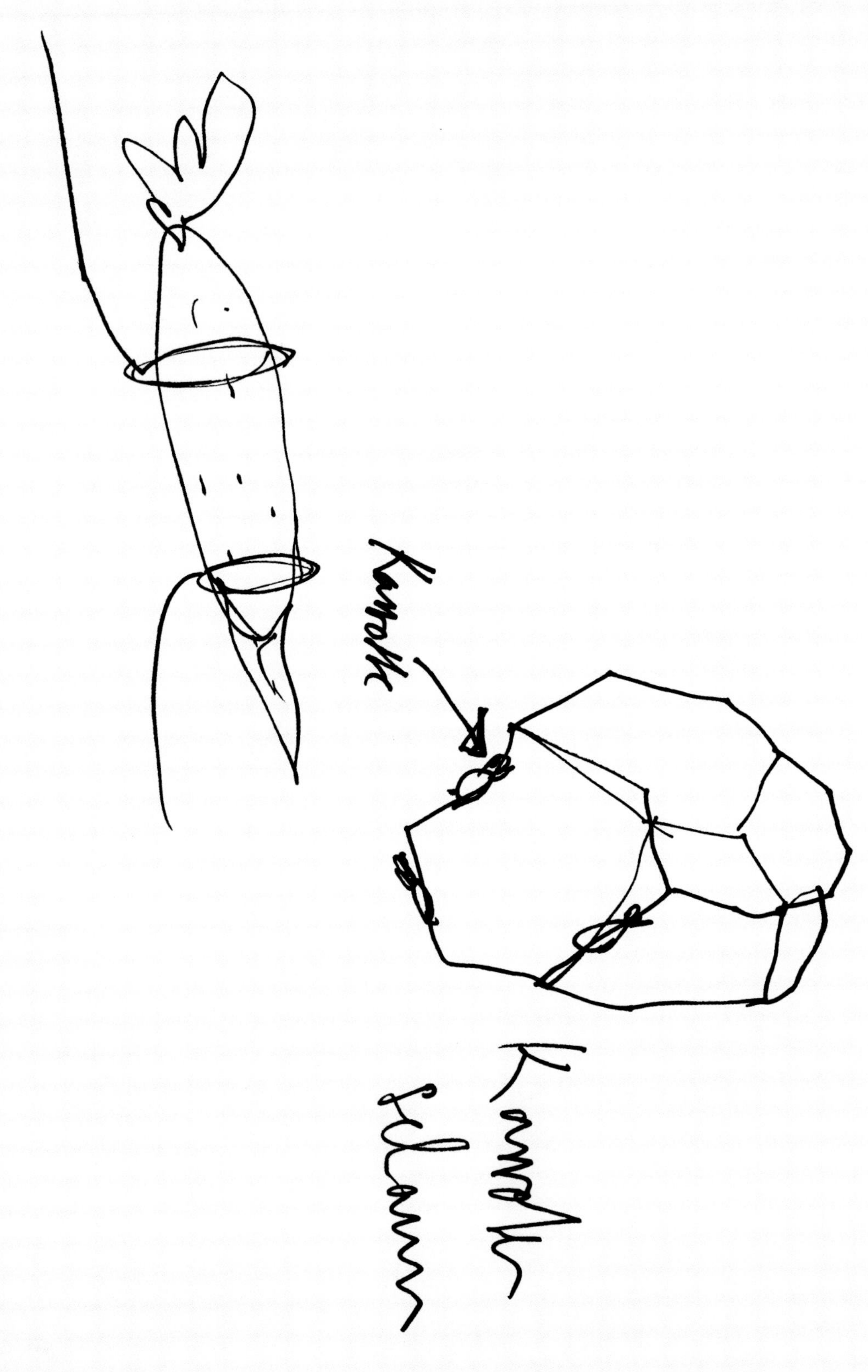

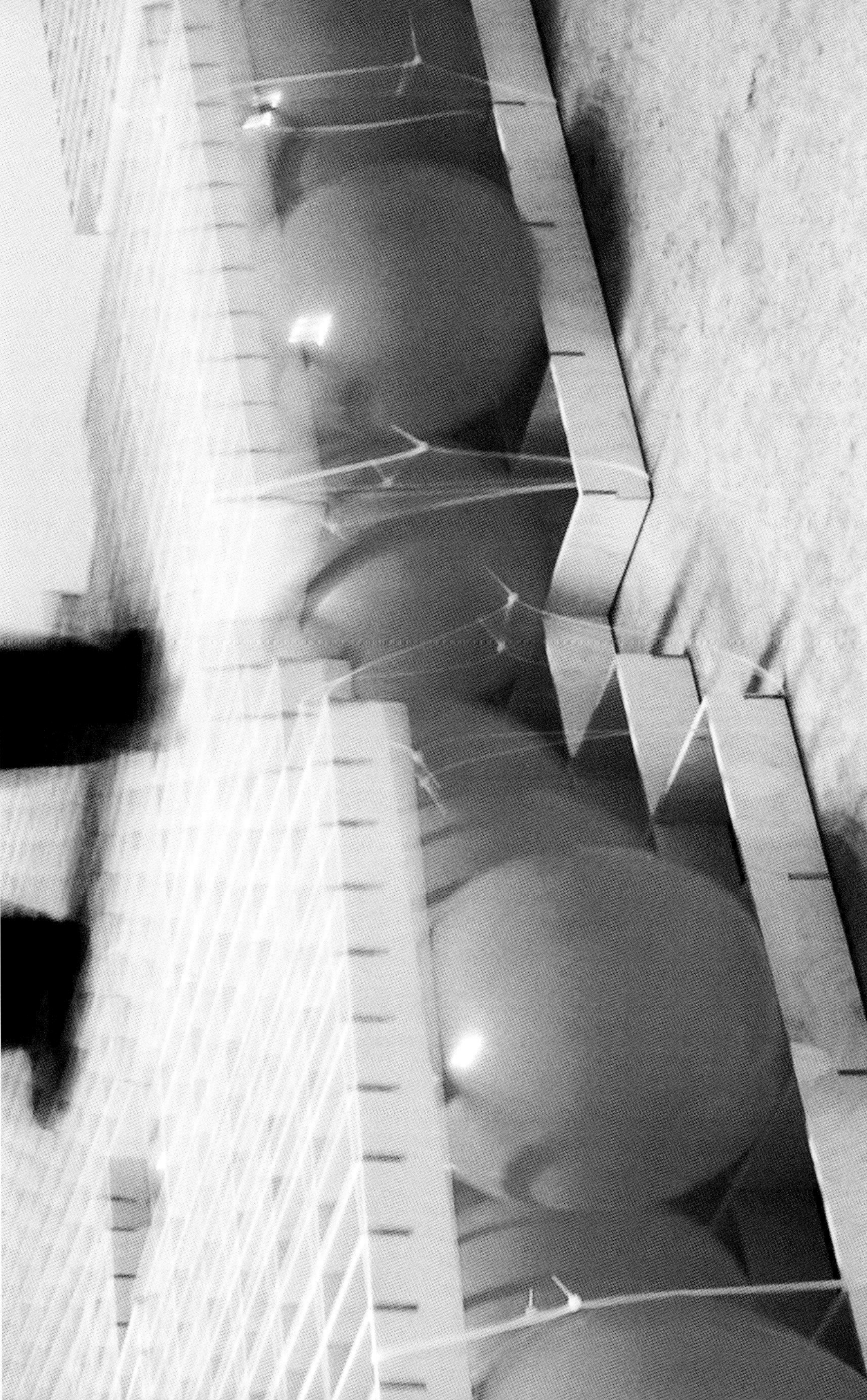

sachliche Anordnung

Karotte

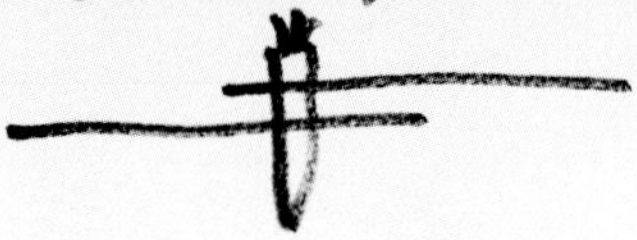

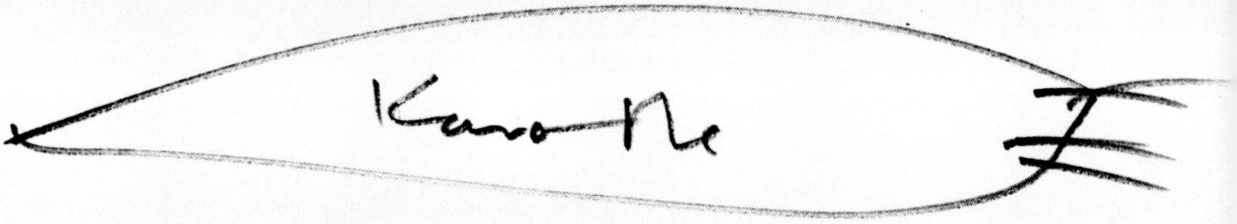

nach 24 Std ok
nach 48 Std rausgefallen
Karotte relativ
weich

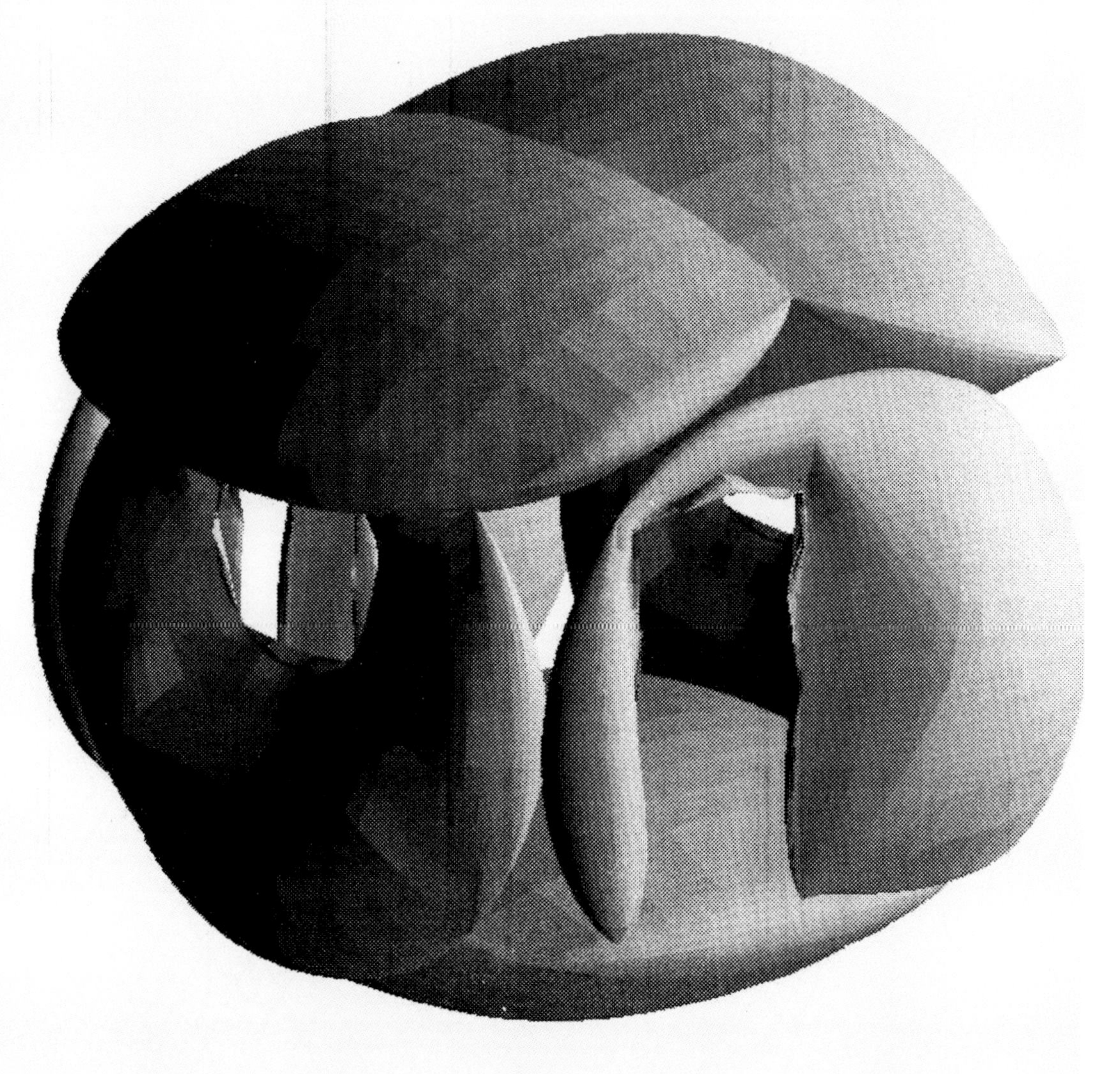

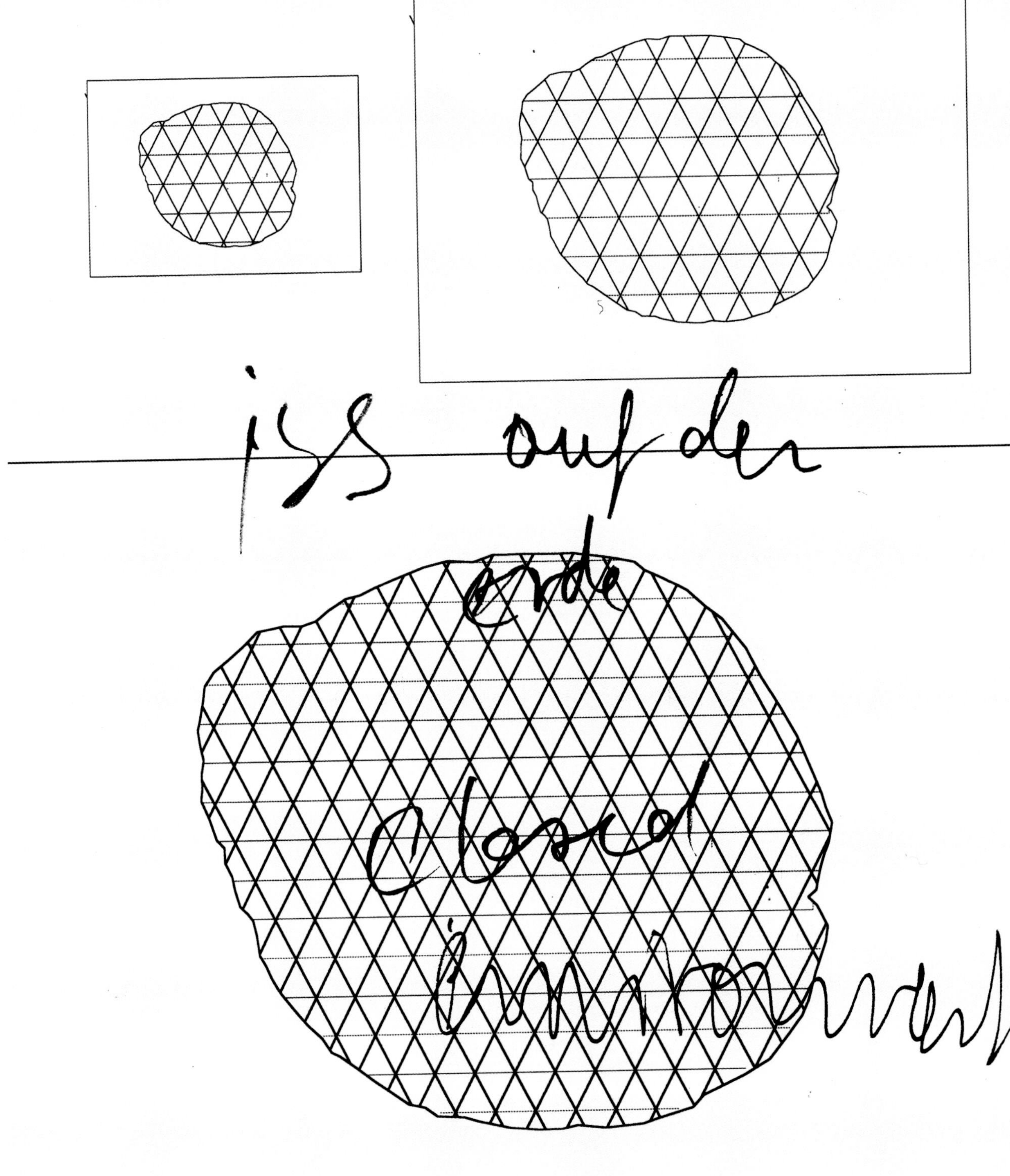
iss auf der
erde
Closed
environment

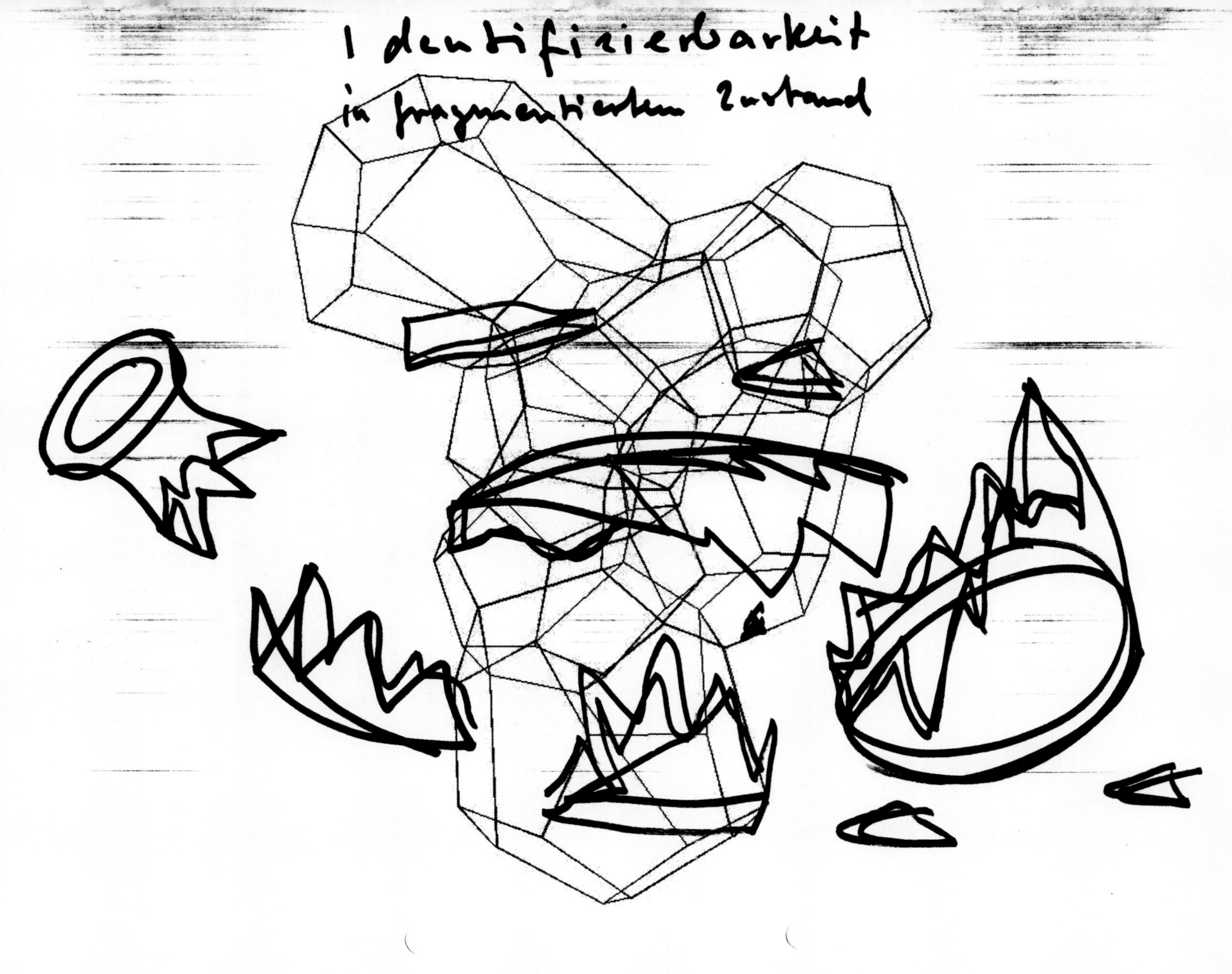
Identifizierbarkeit
in fragmentiertem Zustand

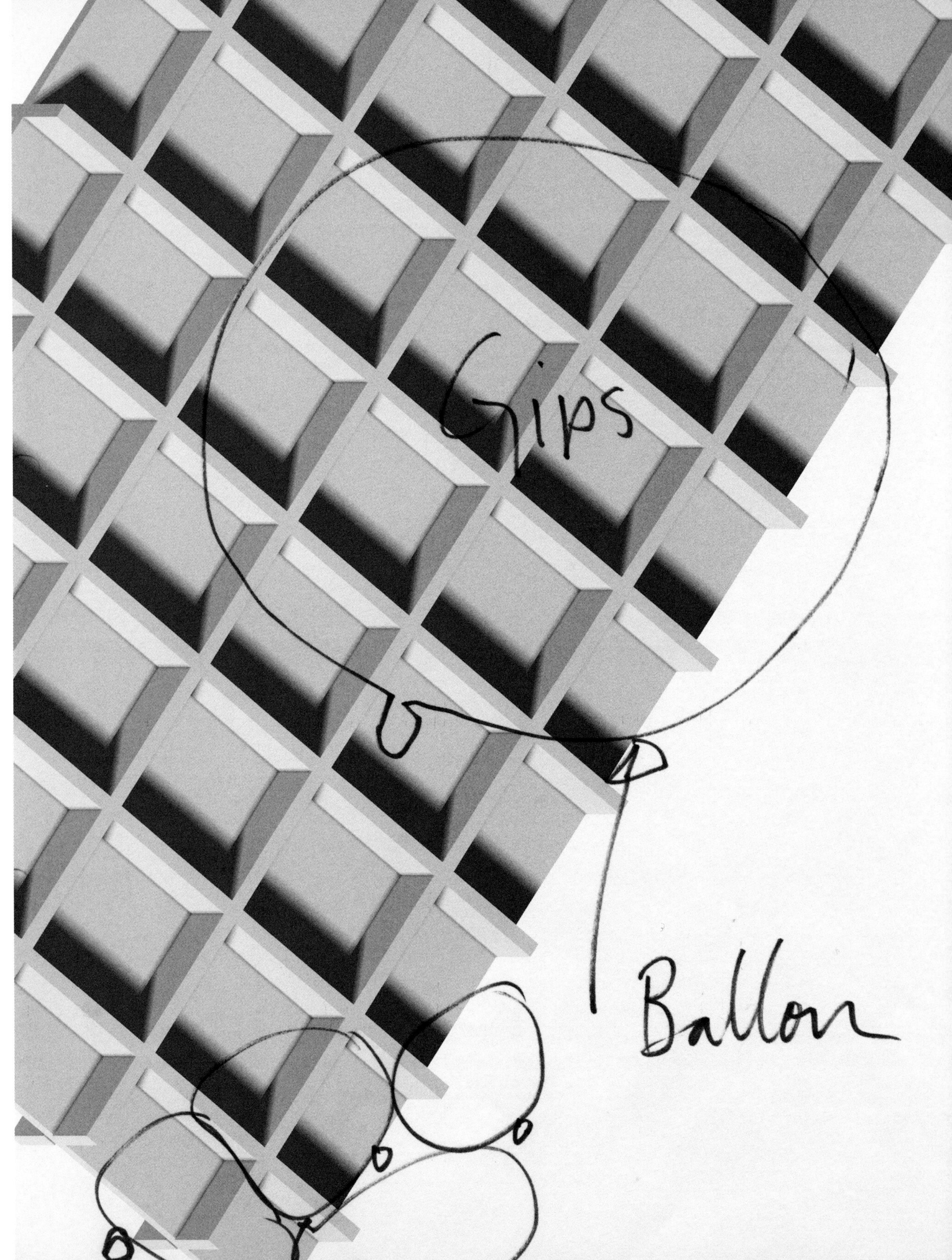

Gips
Ballon

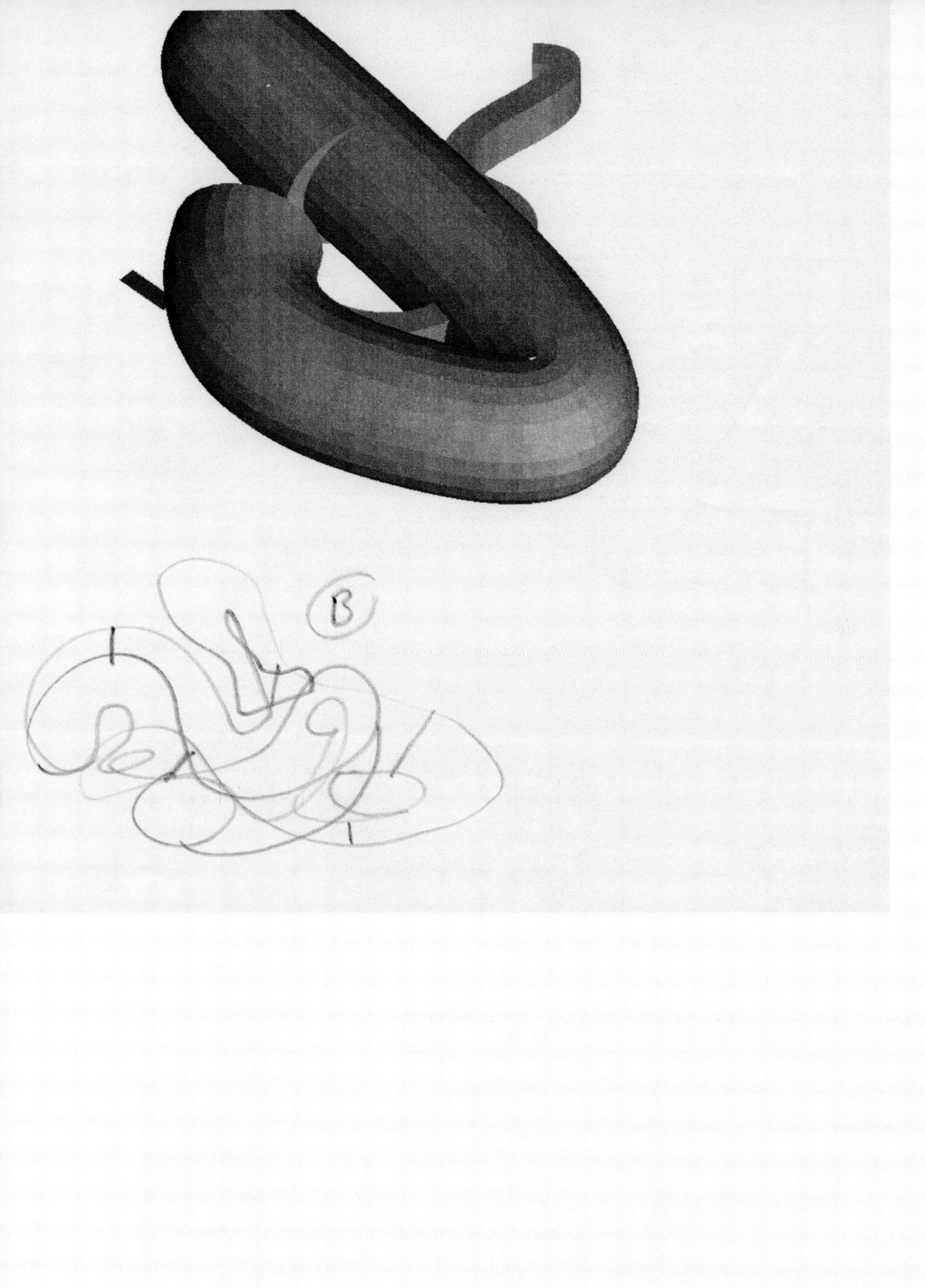
B

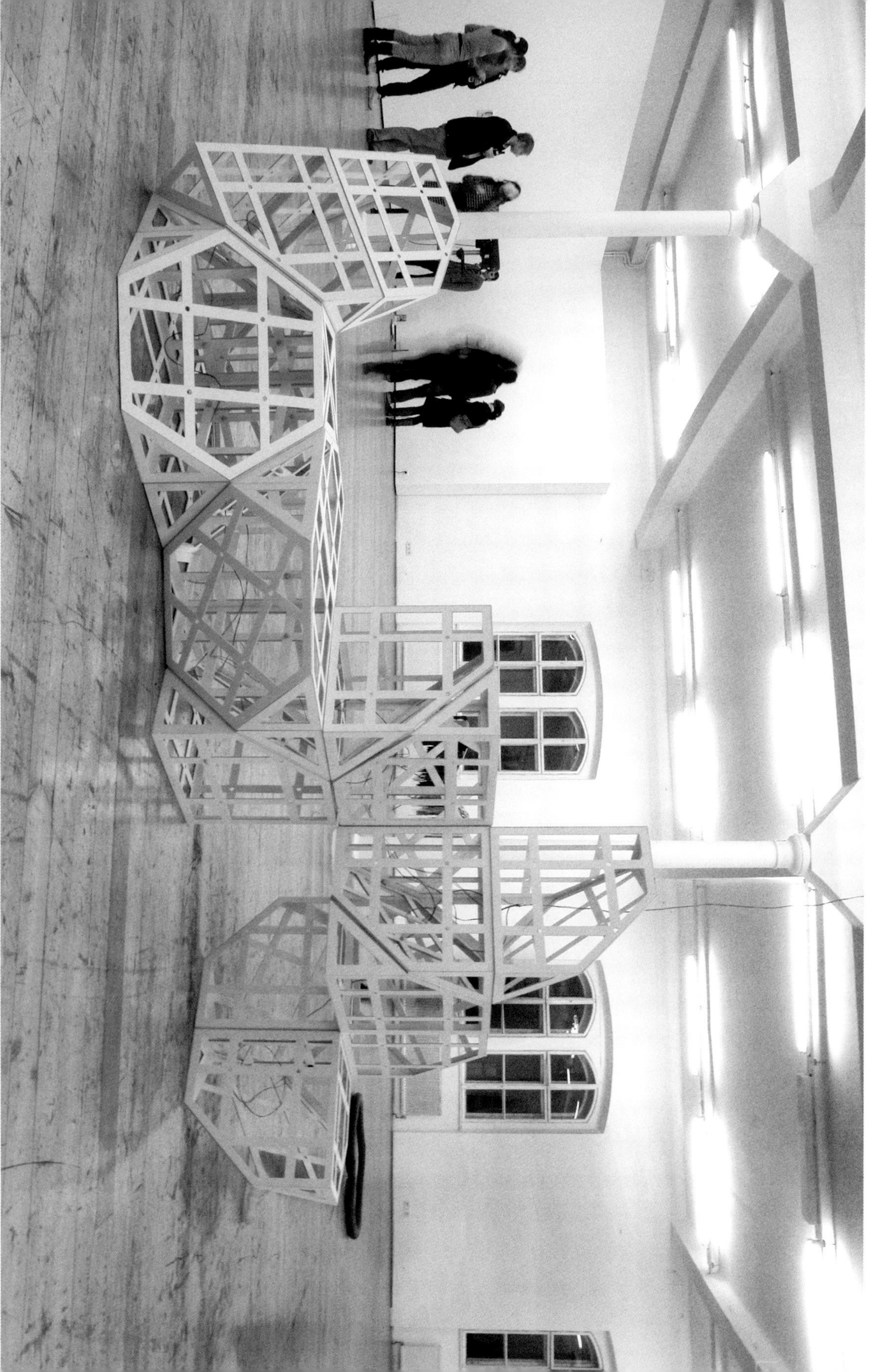

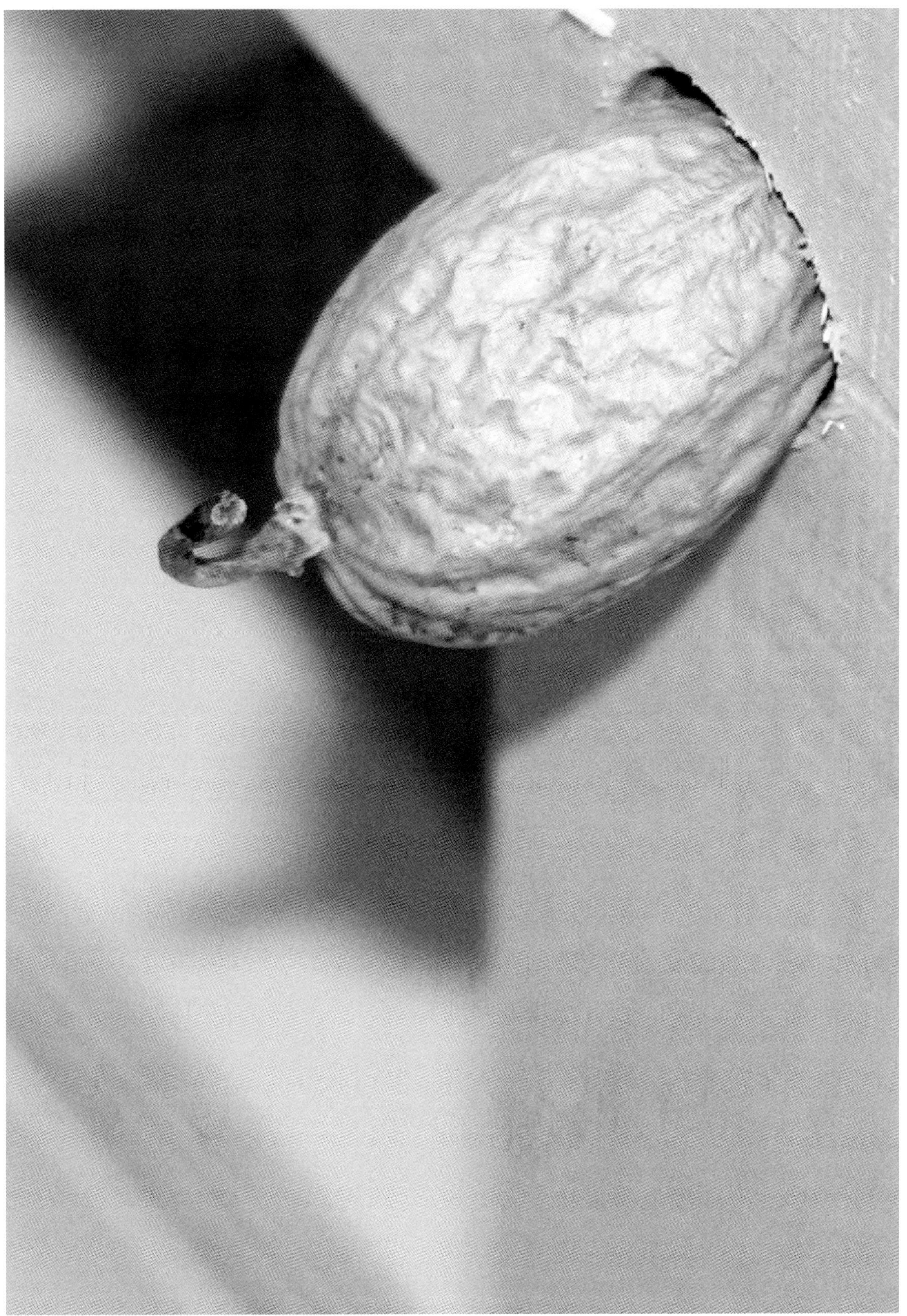

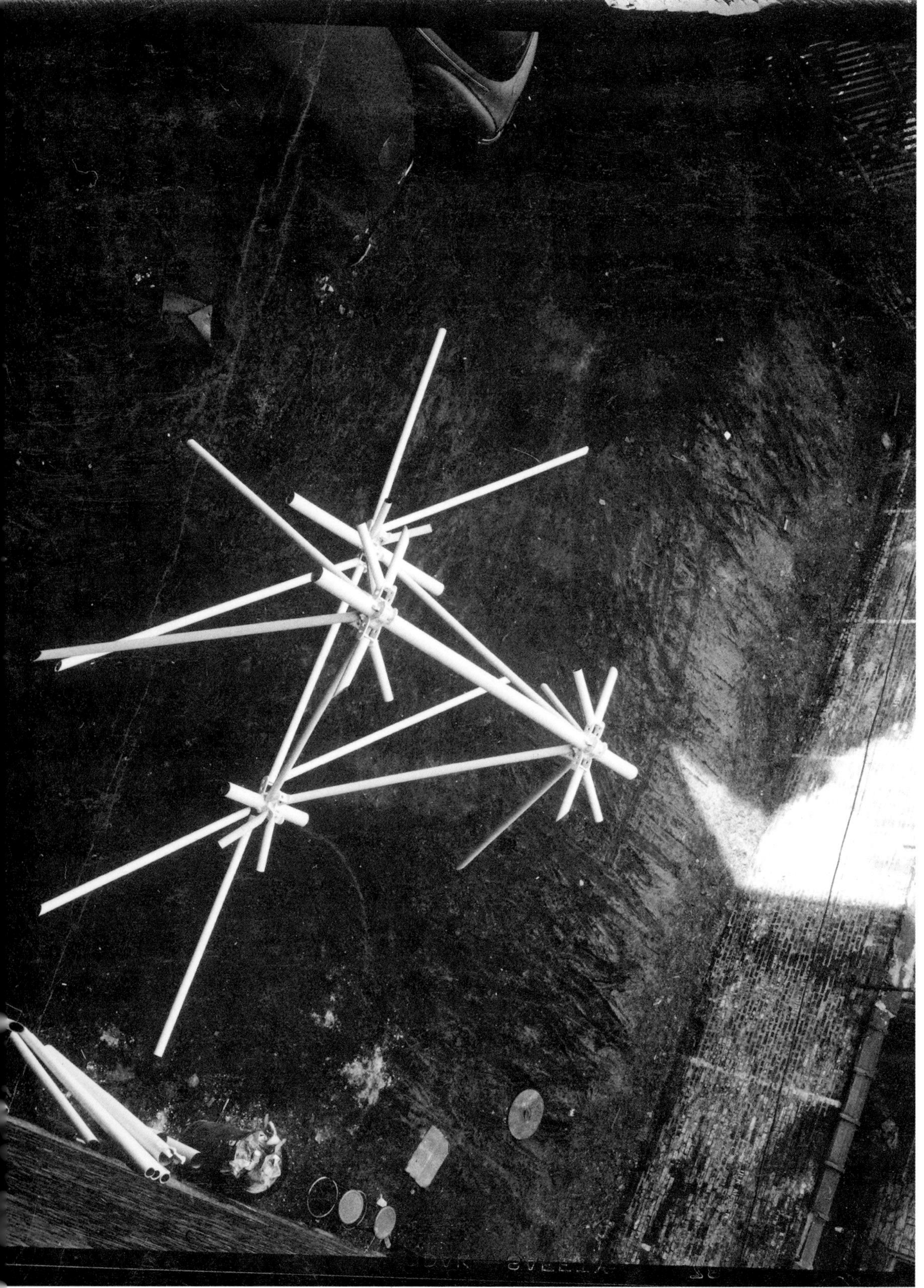

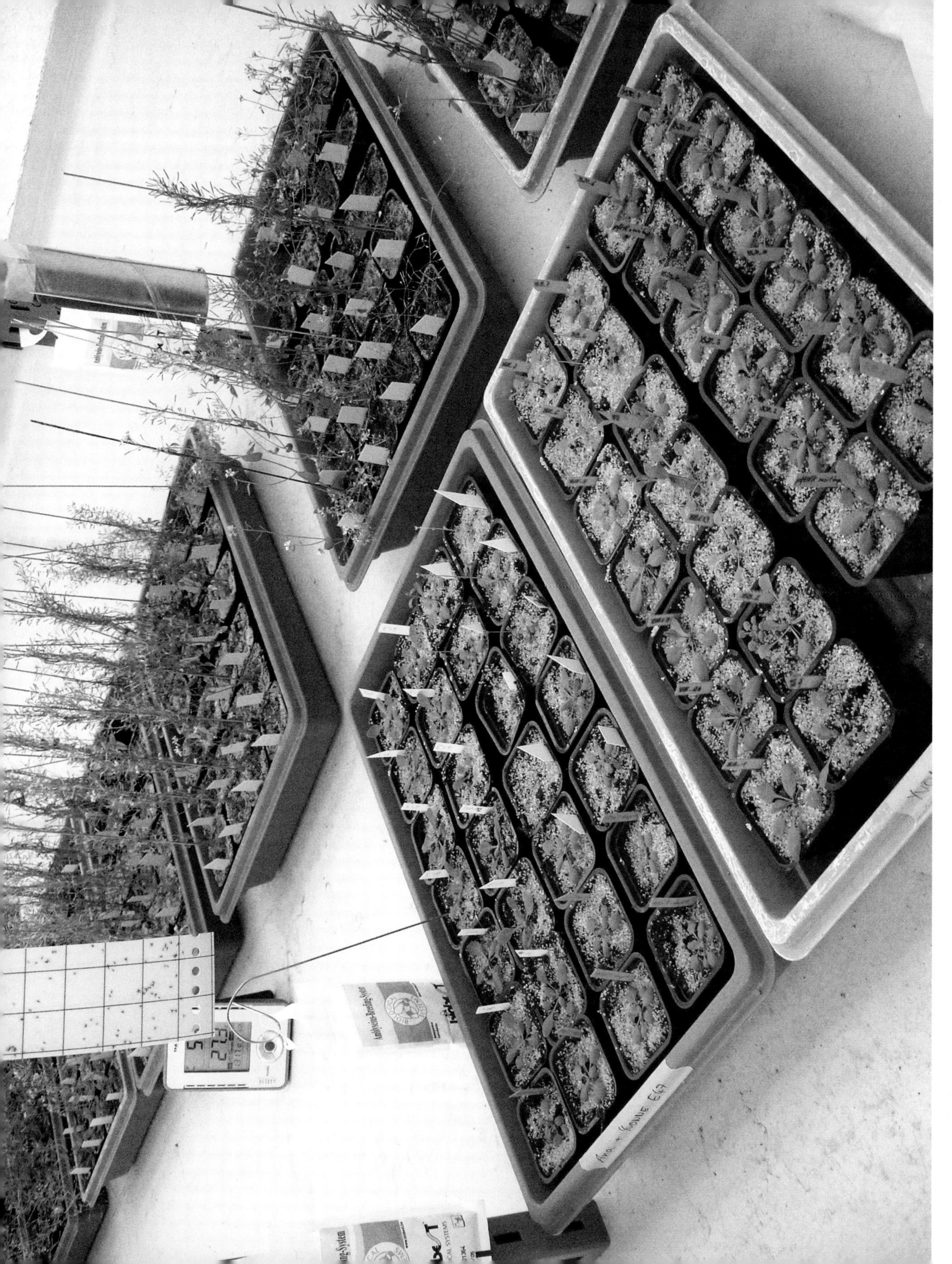

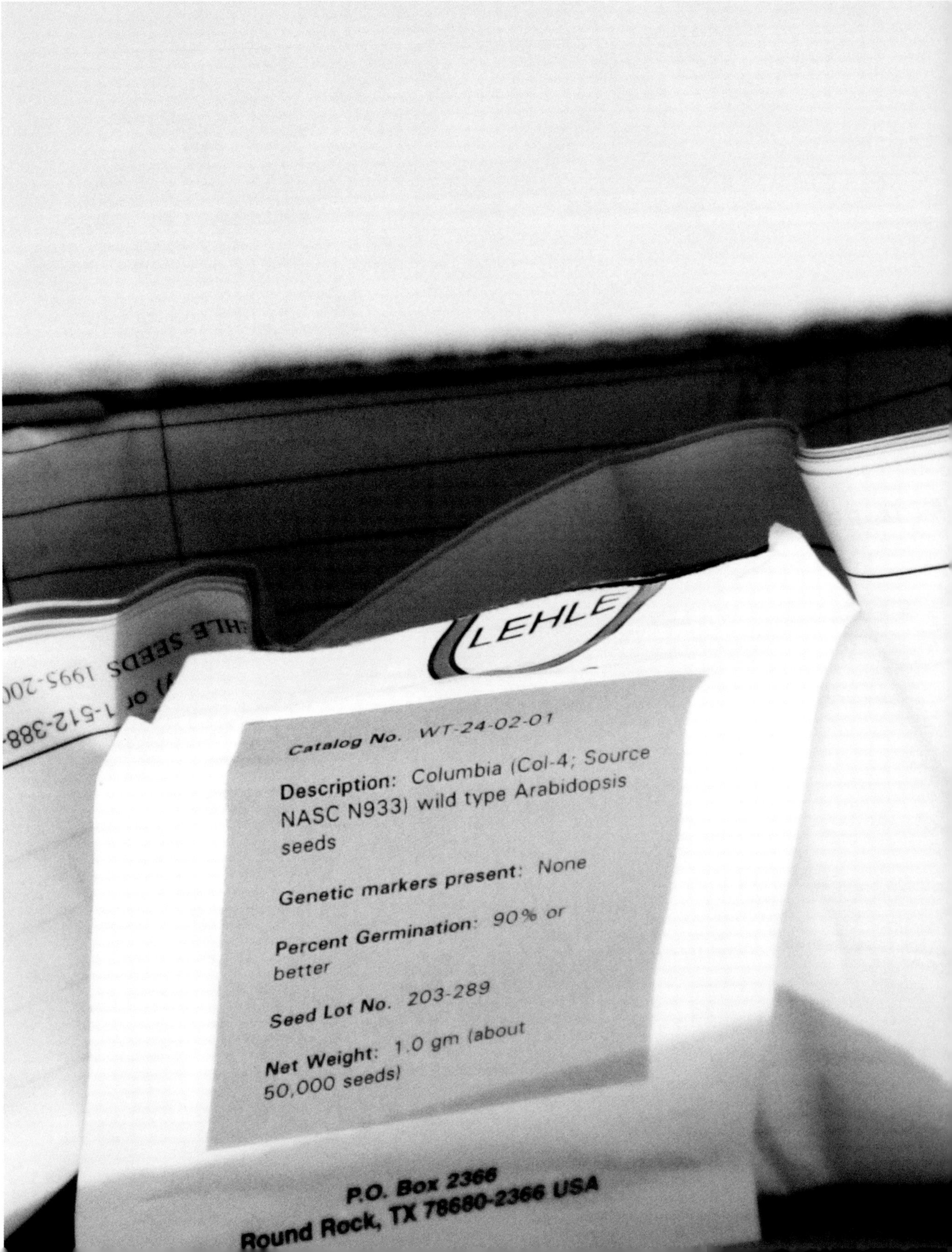

LEHLE

Catalog No. WT-24-02-01

Description: Columbia (Col-4; Source NASC N933) wild type Arabidopsis seeds

Genetic markers present: None

Percent Germination: 90% or better

Seed Lot No. 203-289

Net Weight: 1.0 gm (about 50,000 seeds)

P.O. Box 2366
Round Rock, TX 78680-2366 USA

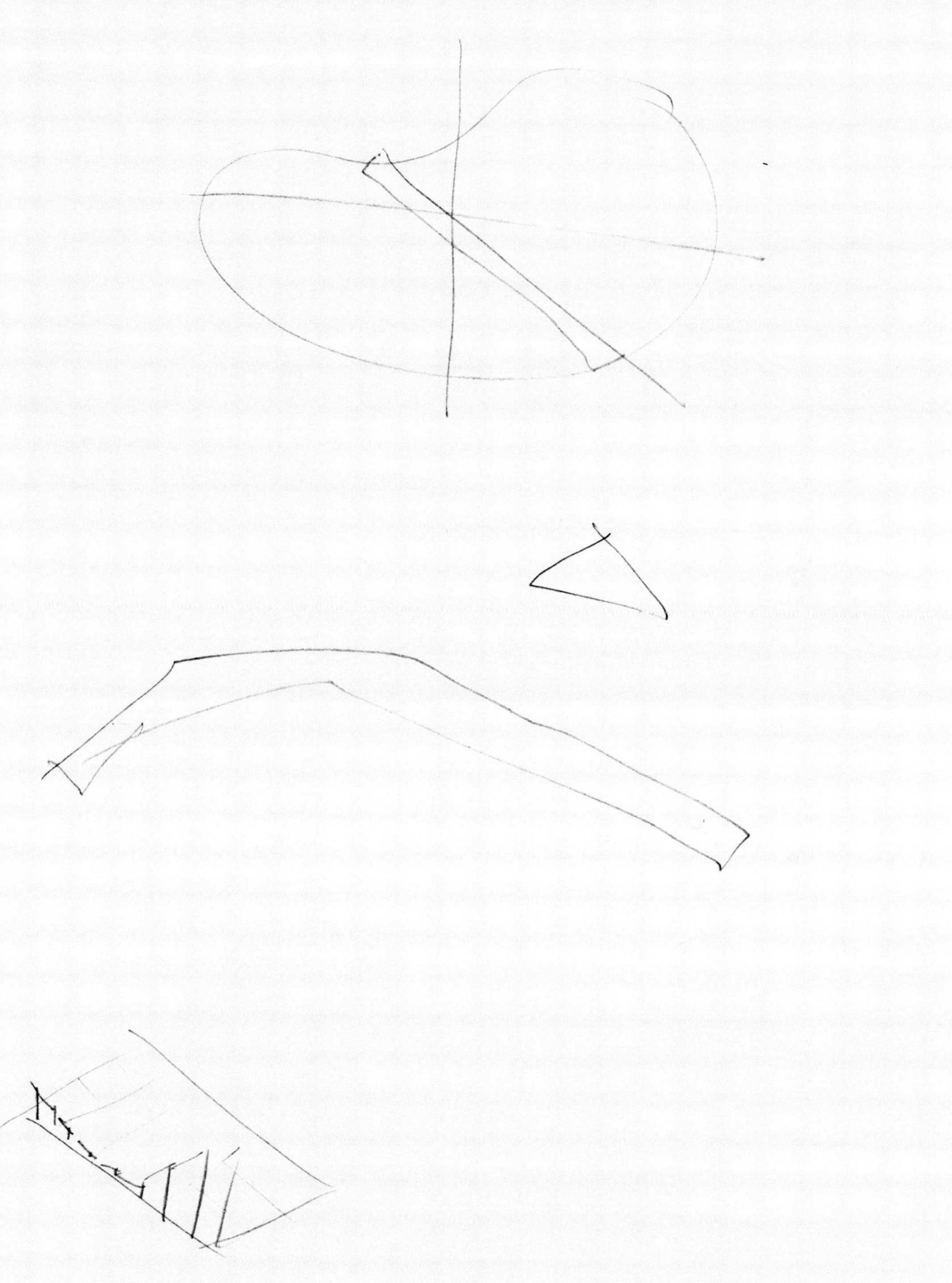

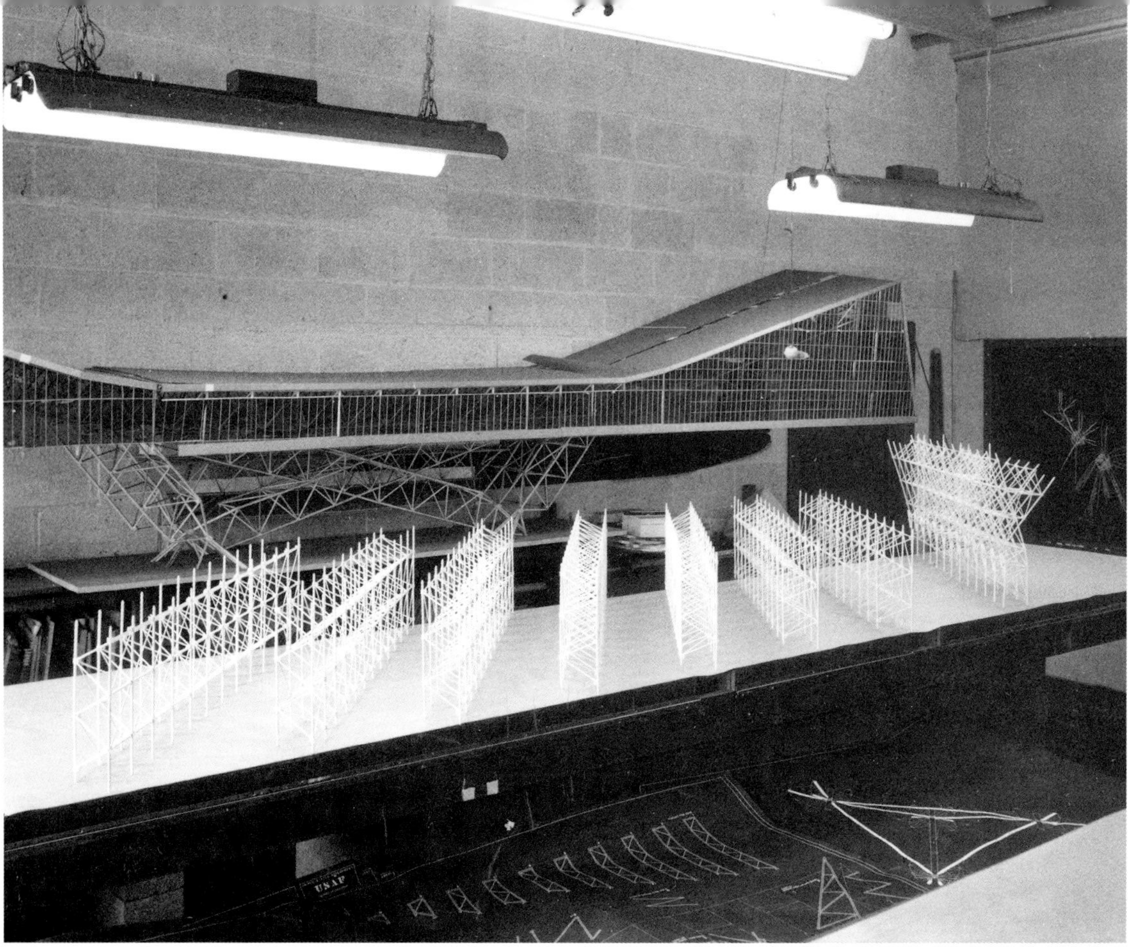

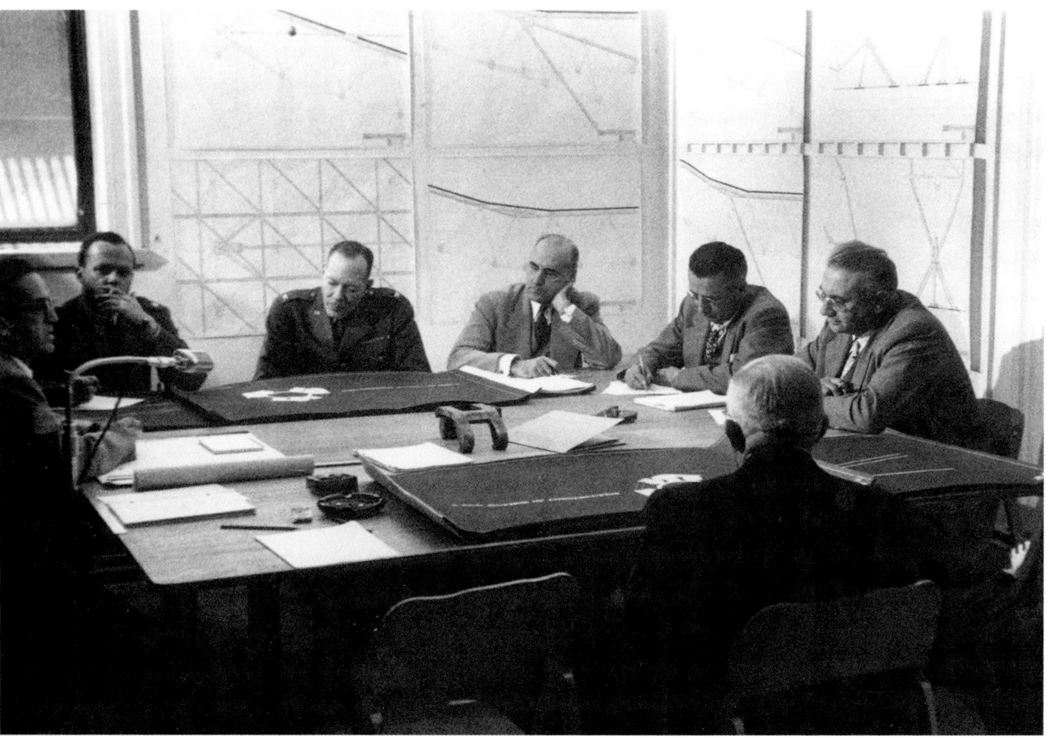

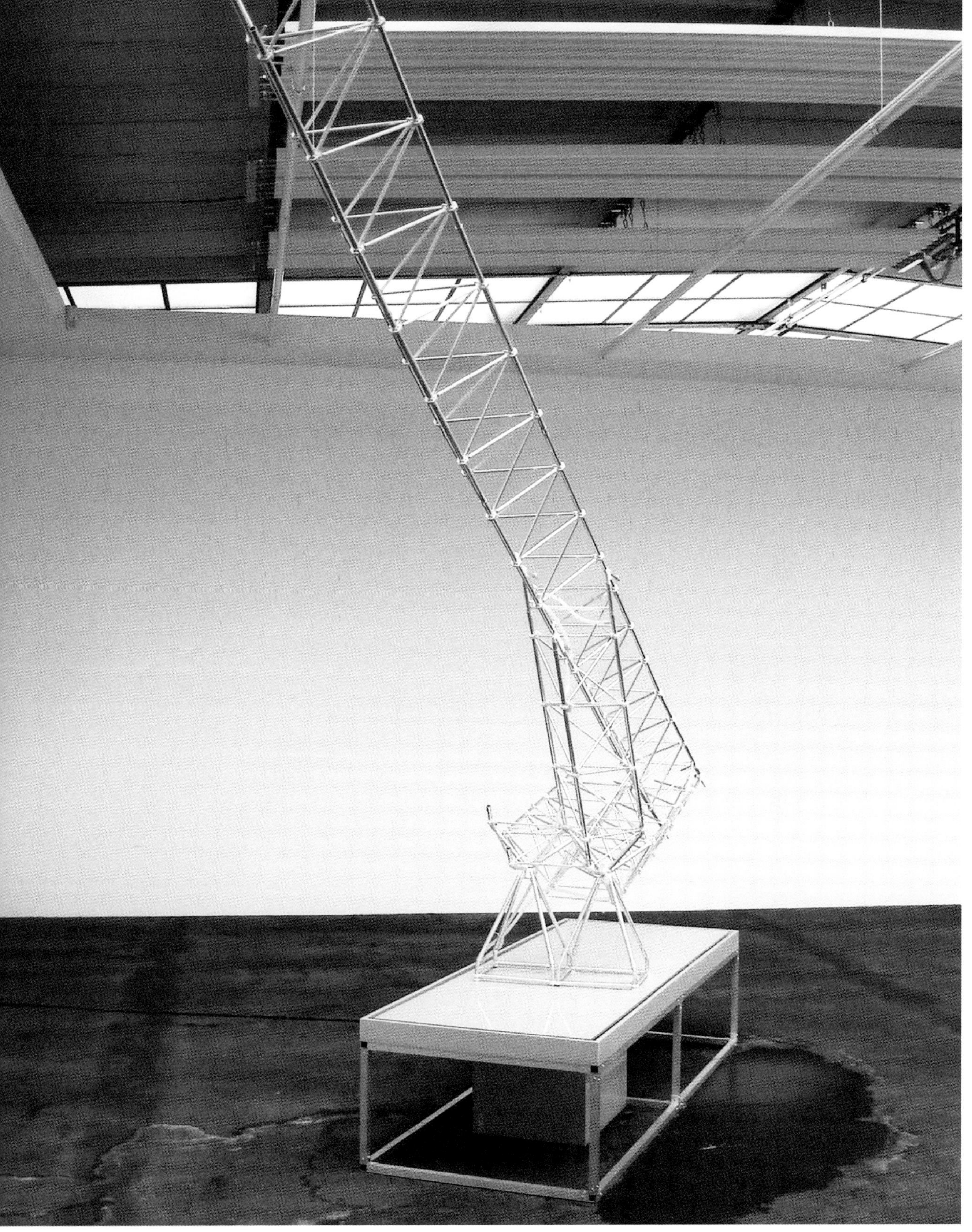

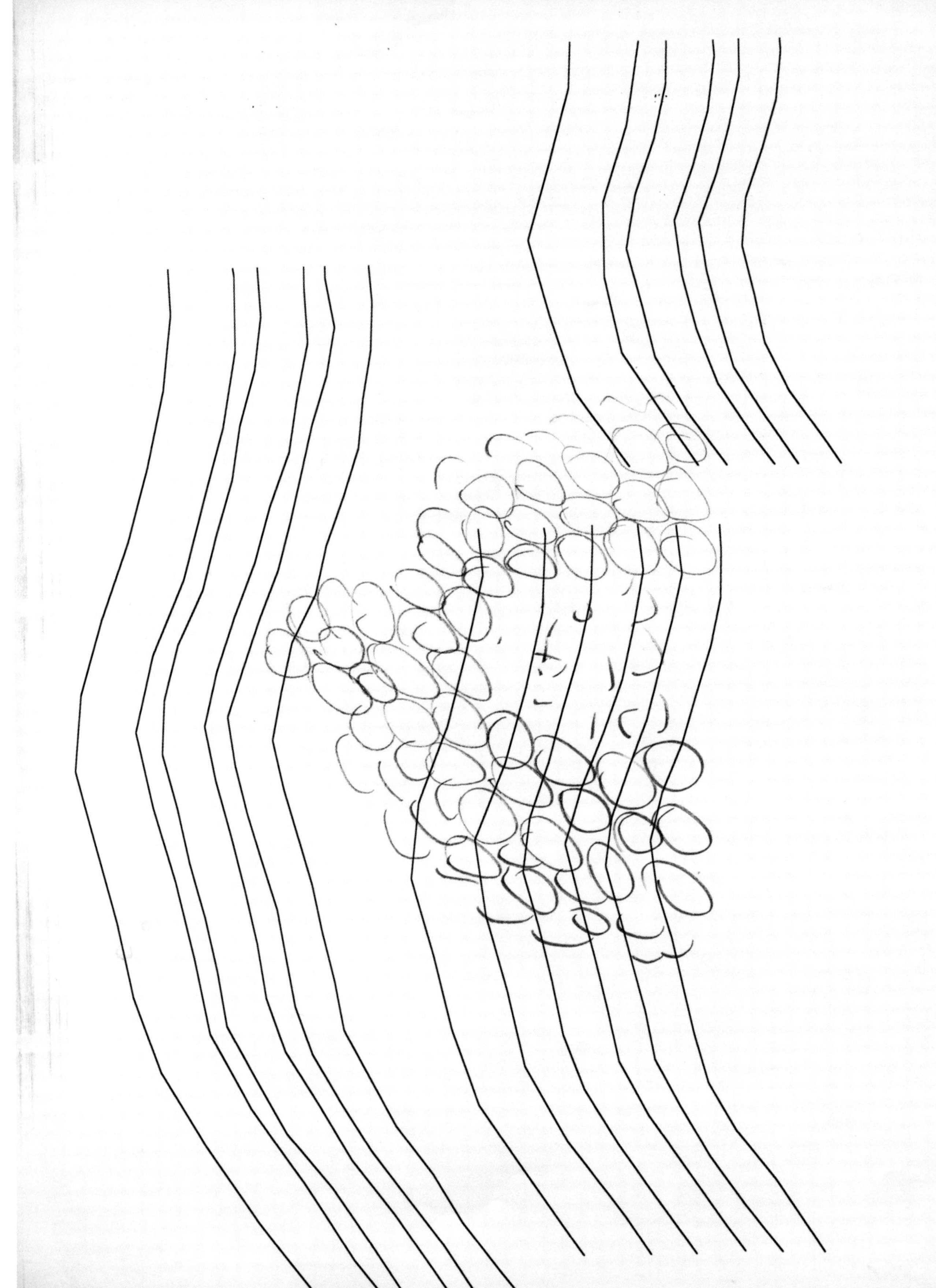

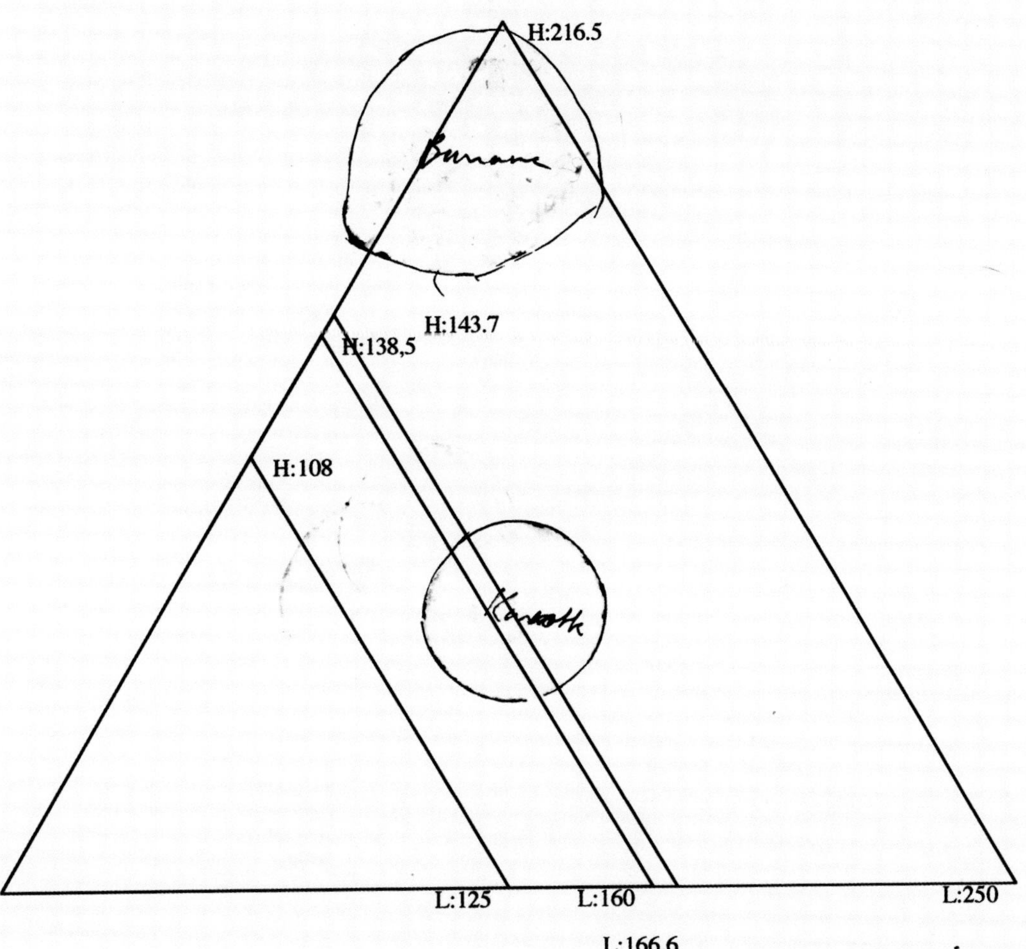

H:216.5
H:143.7
H:138,5
H:108
L:125
L:160
L:250
L:166,6

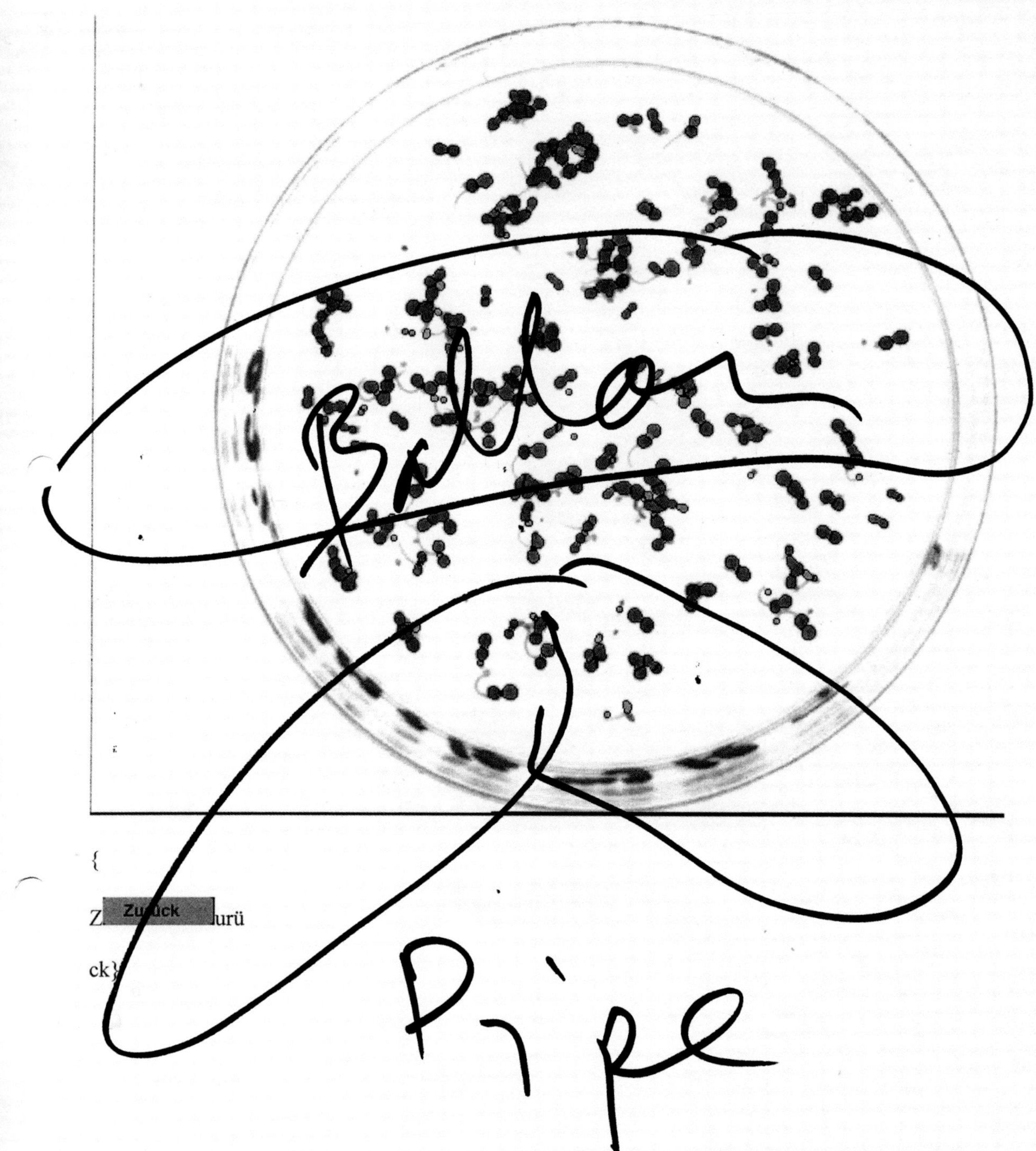

{

Z Zurück urü

ck}

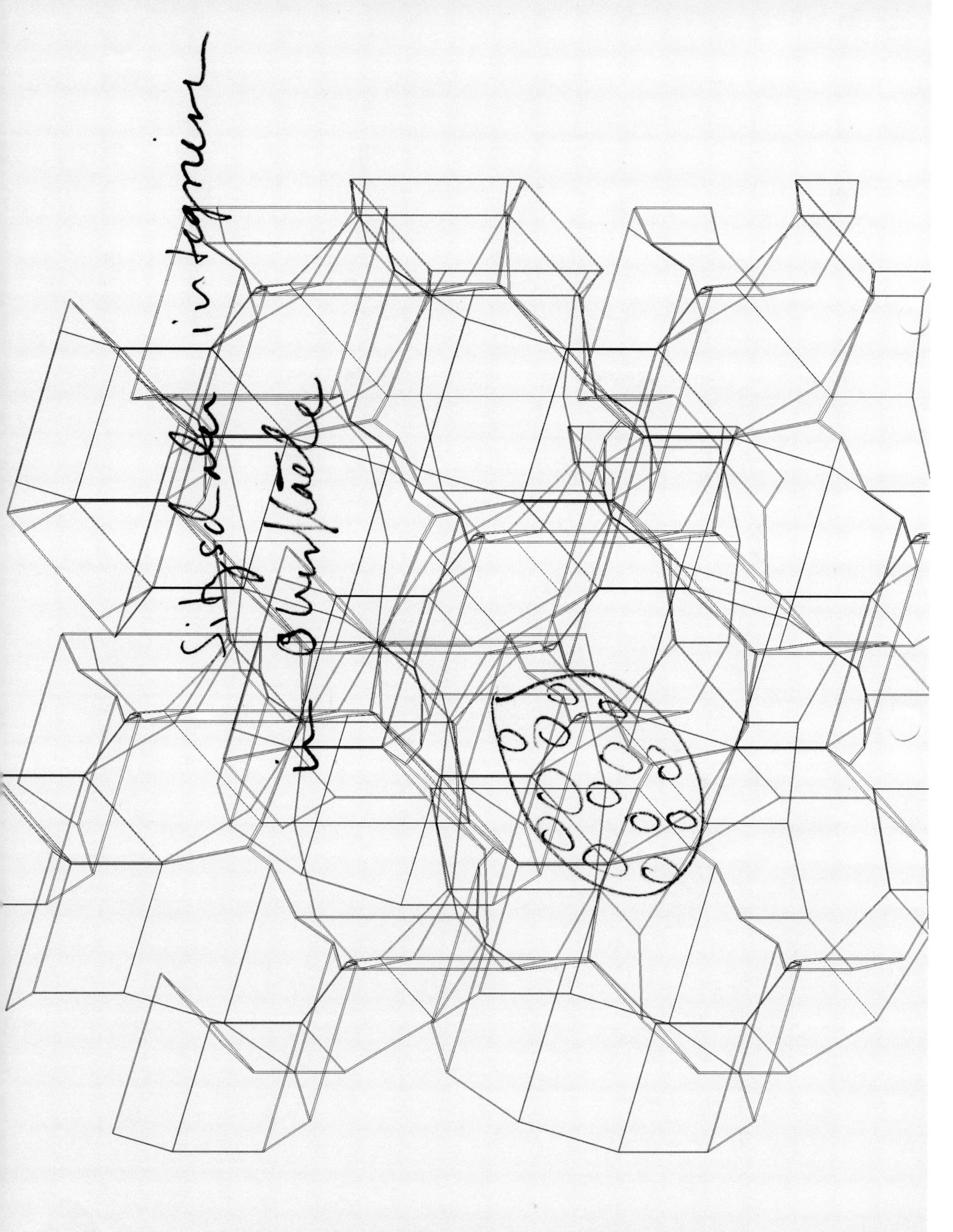

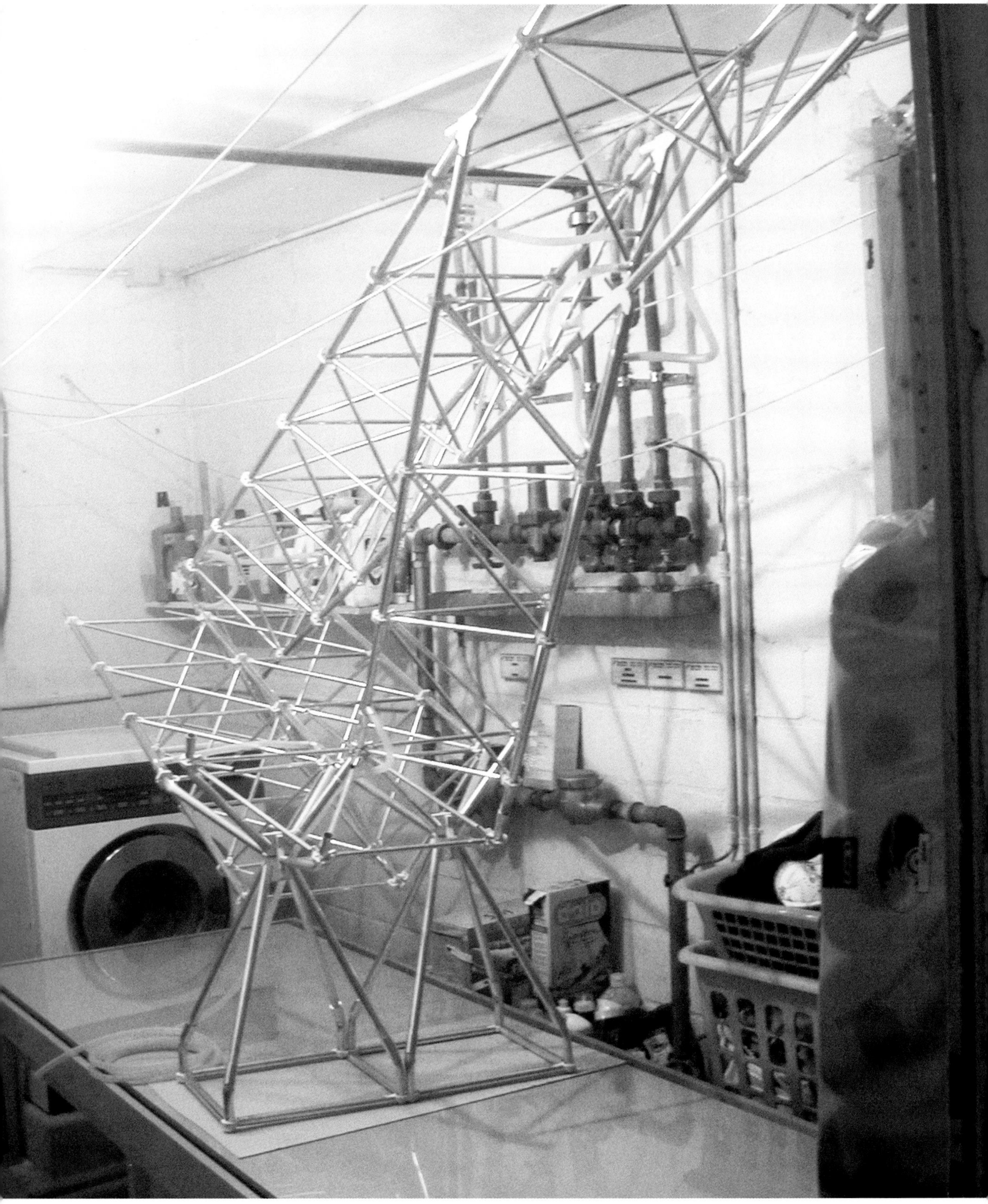

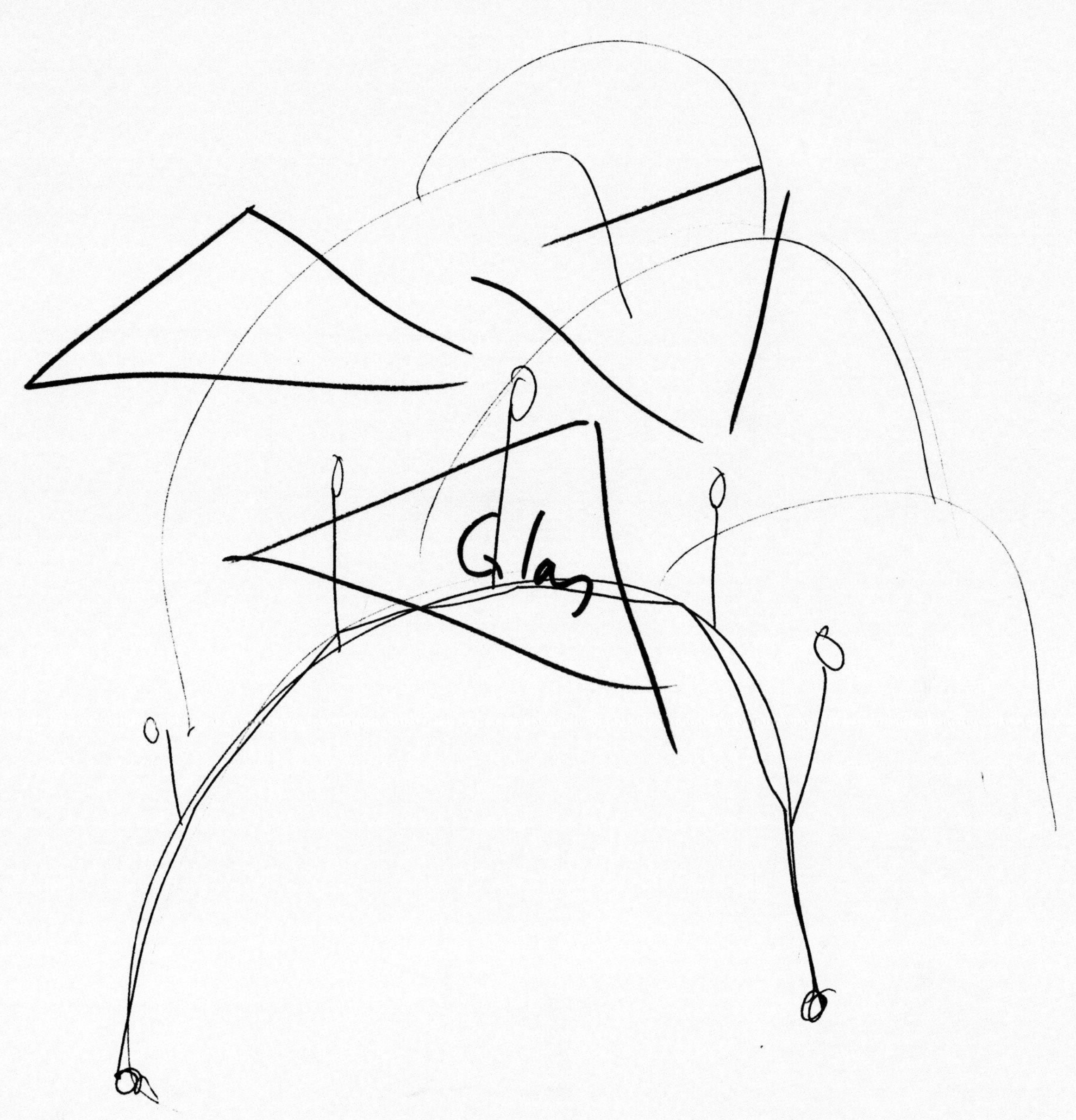

Glass

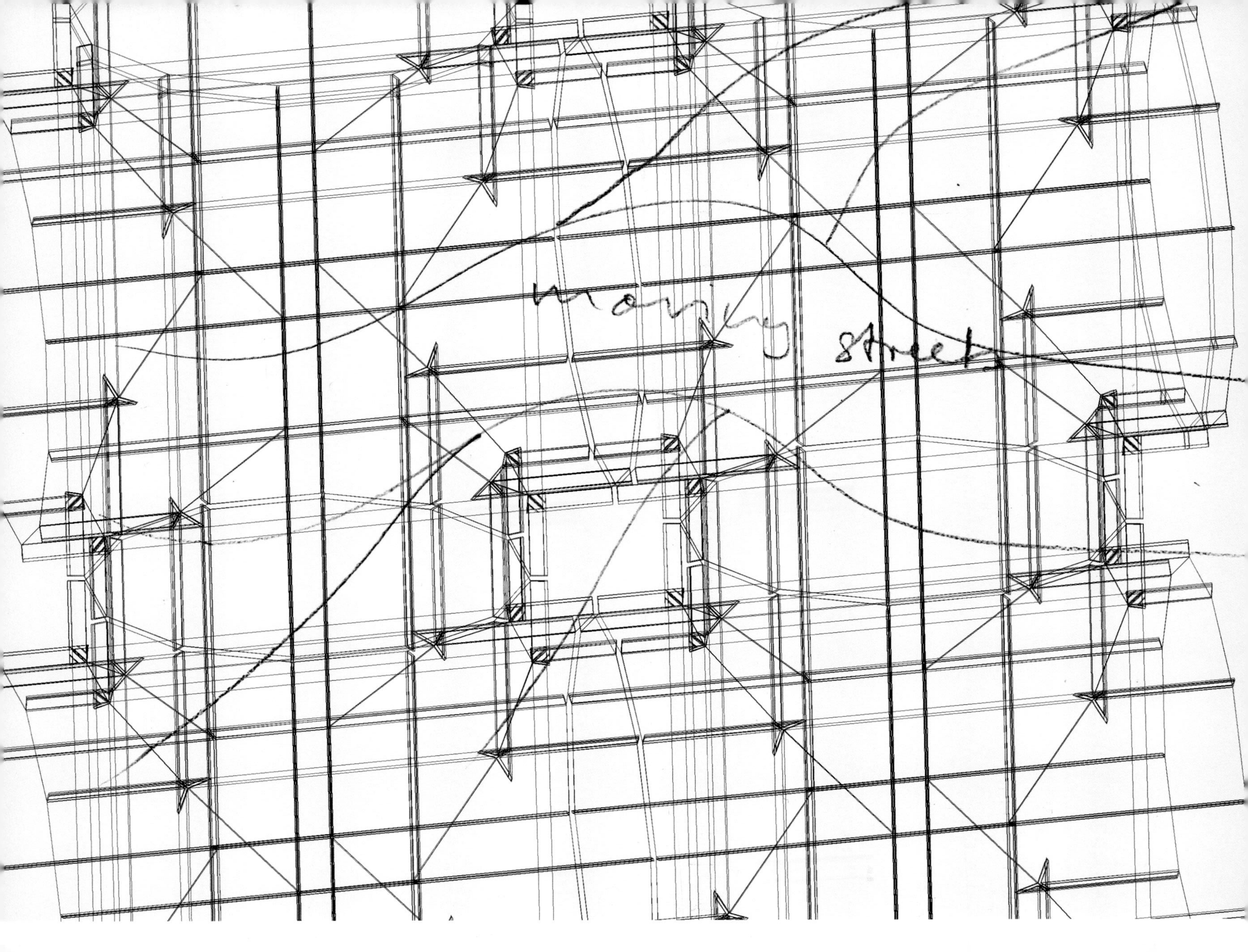
many street

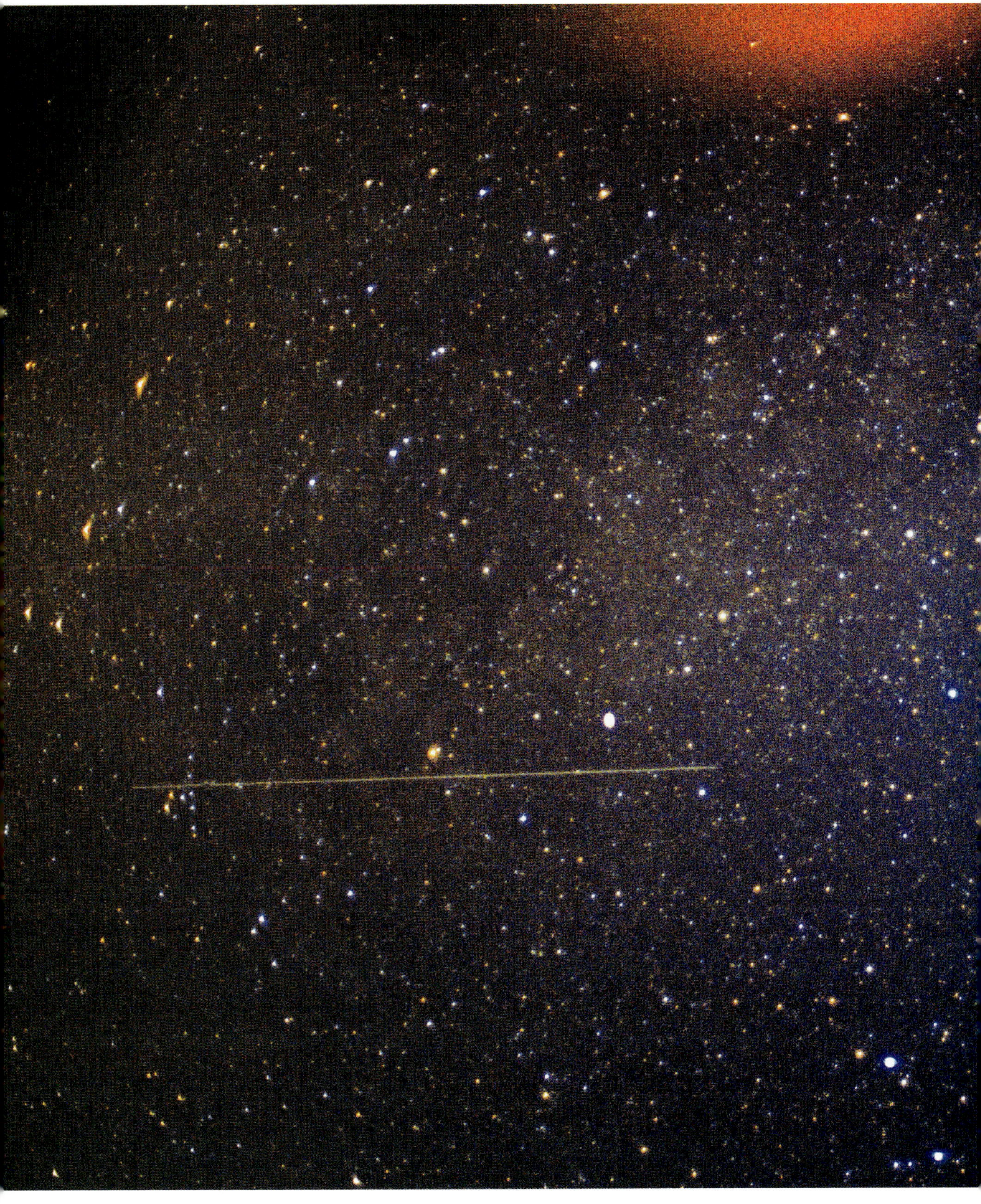

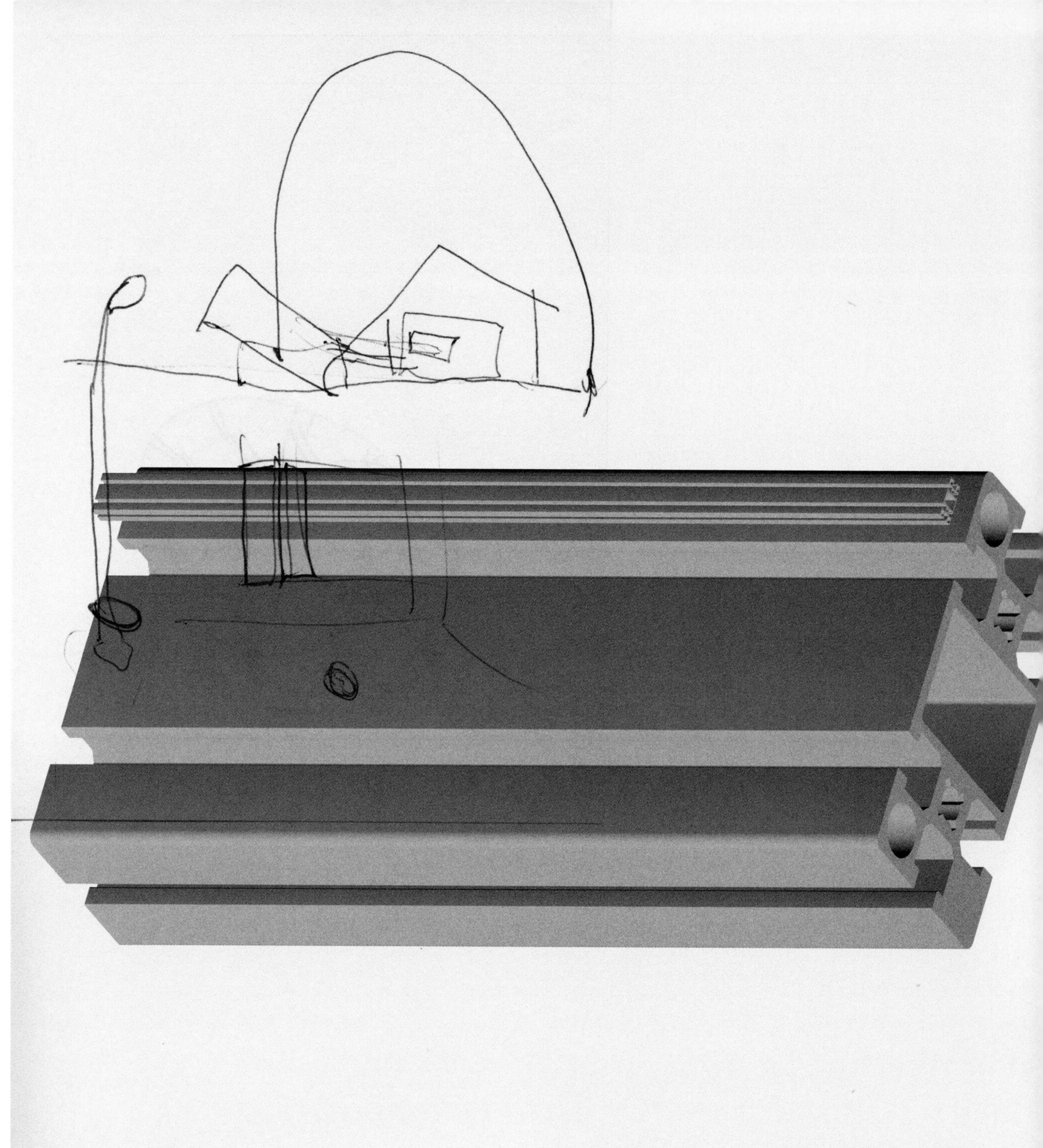

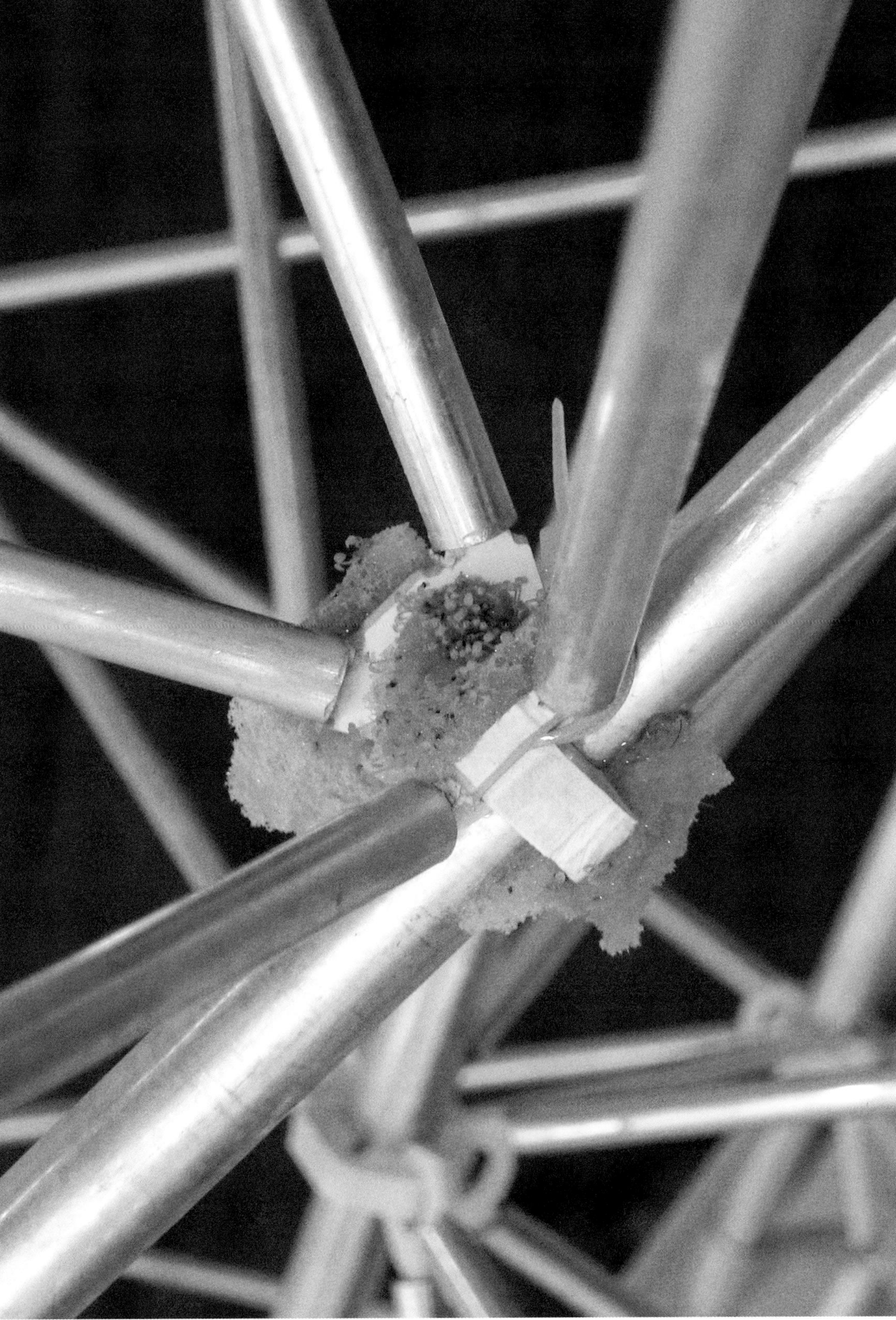

Öffnung durch mehrere Objekte durchgehend

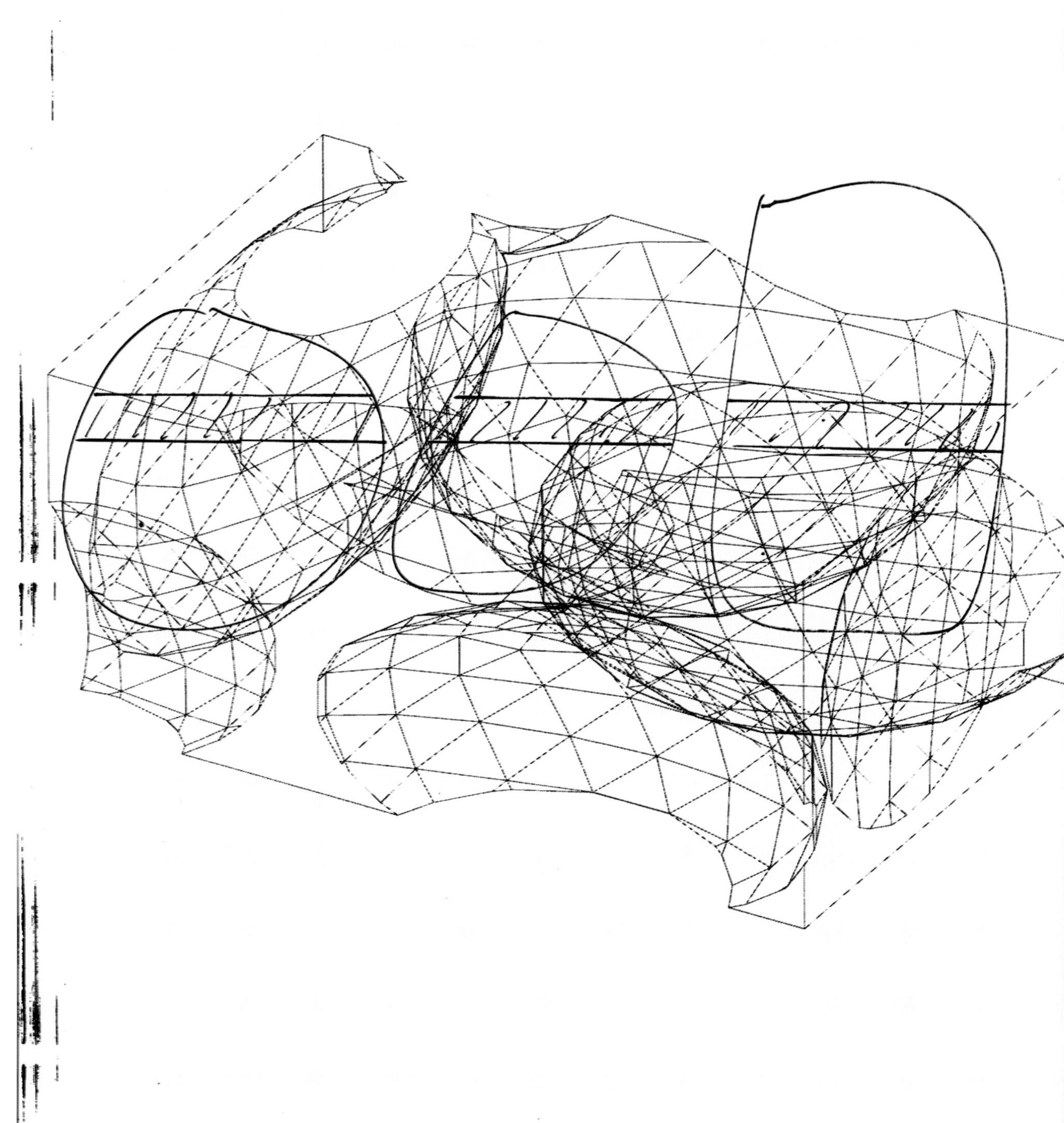

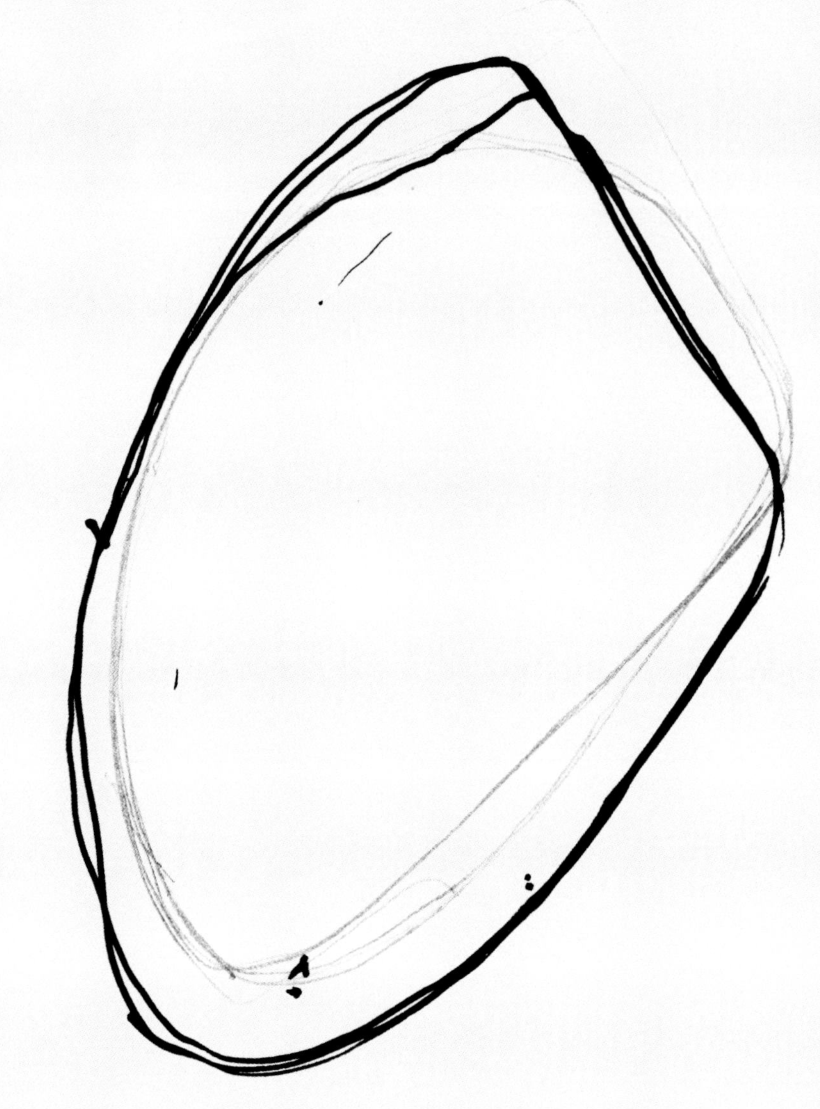

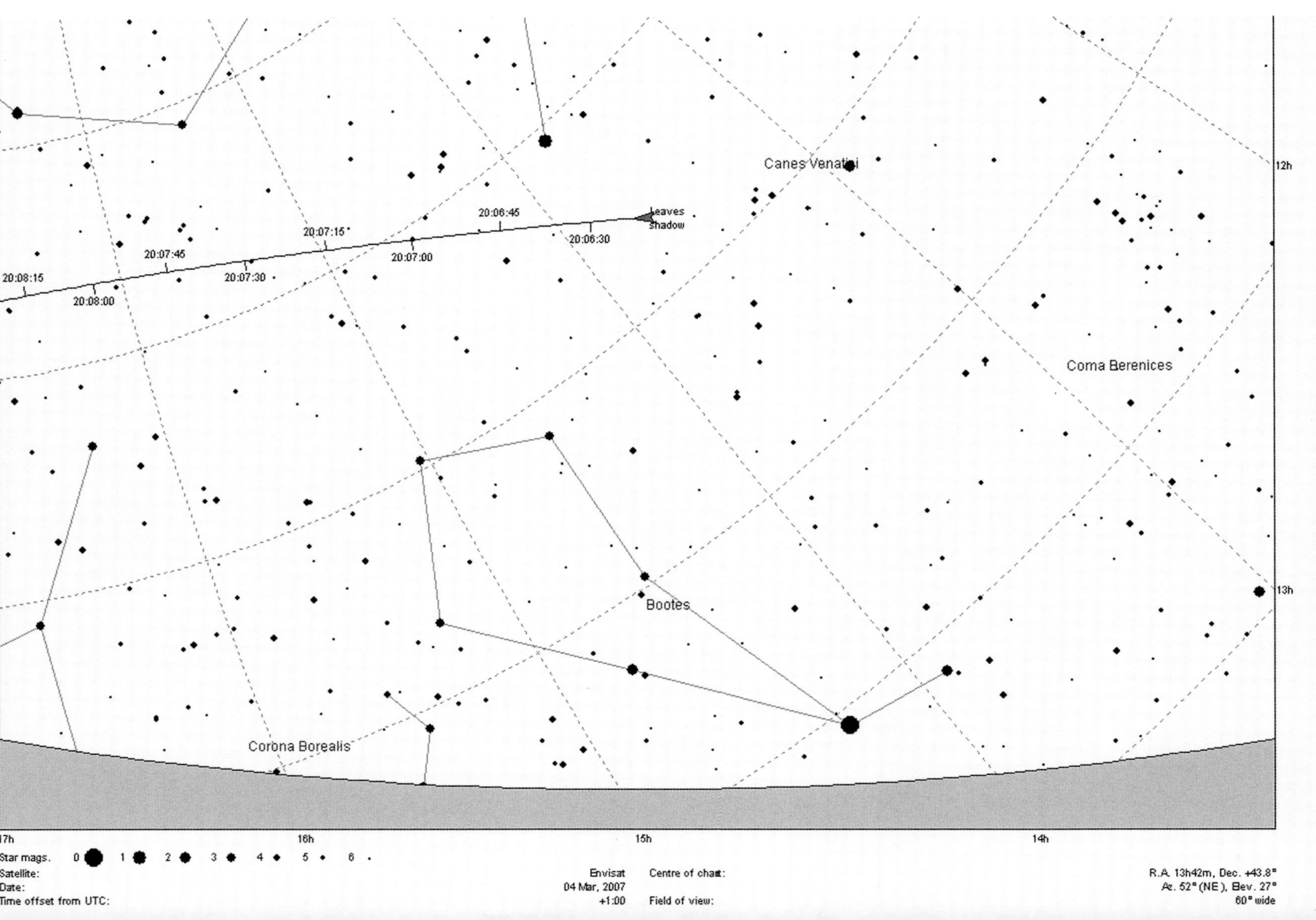

Canes Venatici
Coma Berenices
Bootes
Corona Borealis
Leaves Shadow
20:08:15
20:08:00
20:07:45
20:07:30
20:07:15
20:07:00
20:06:45
20:06:30
60°
50°
40°
12h
13h
14h
15h
16h
17h
Star mags.   0   1   2   3   4   5   6   .
Satellite: Envisat   Centre of chart:
Date: 04 Mar. 2007
Time offset from UTC: +1:00   Field of view:
R.A. 13h42m, Dec. +43.8°
Az. 52° (NE), Elev. 27°
60° wide

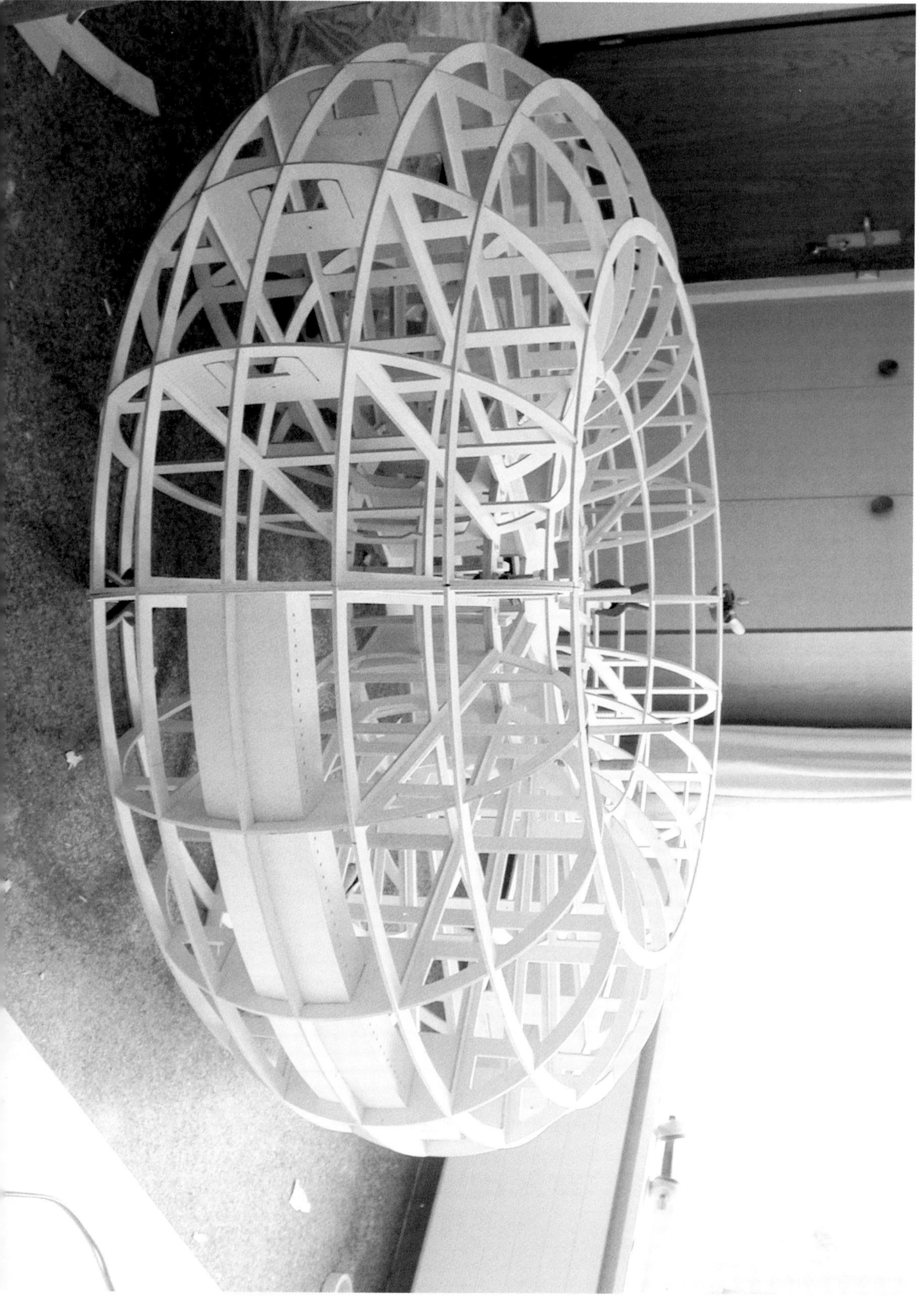

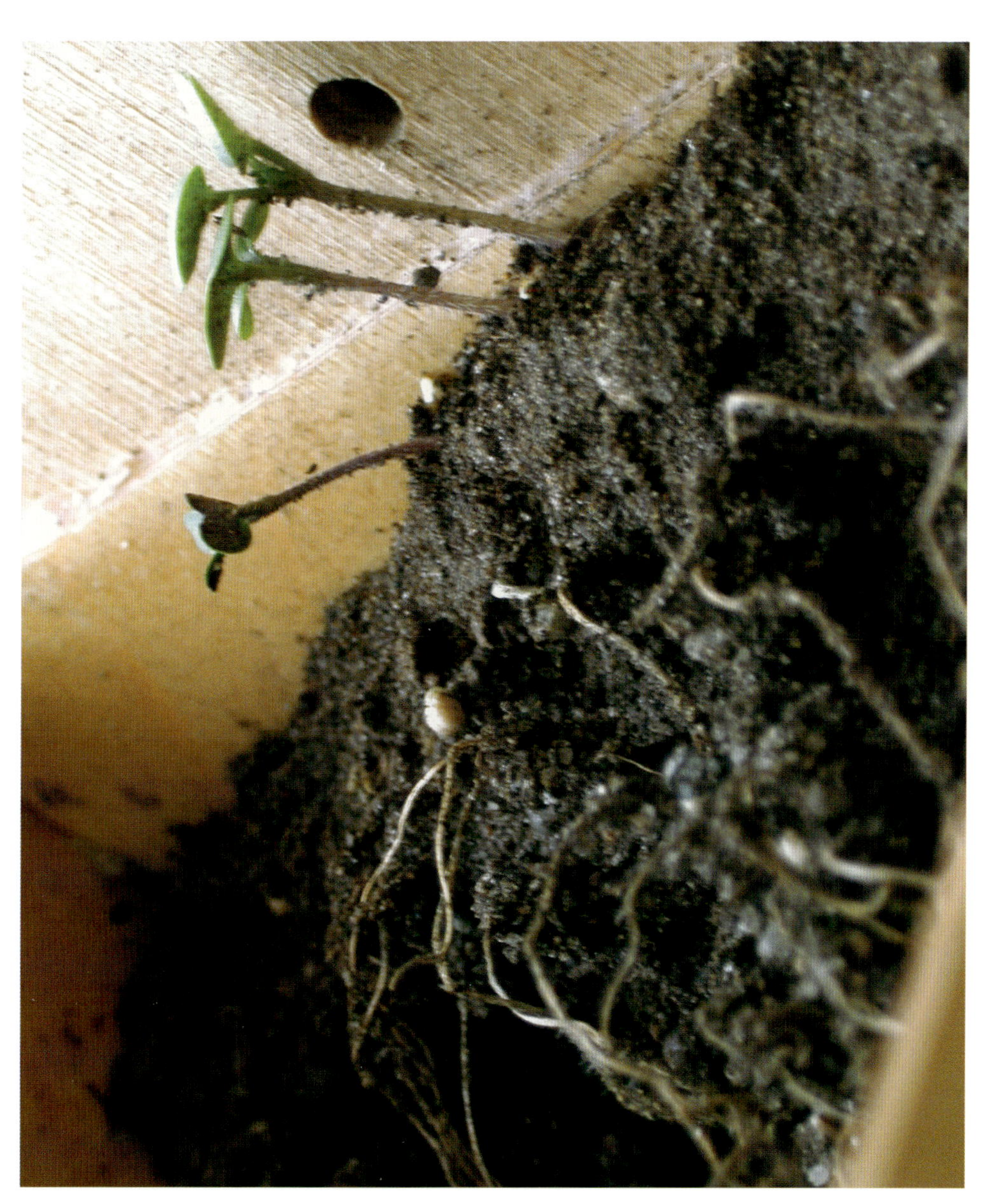

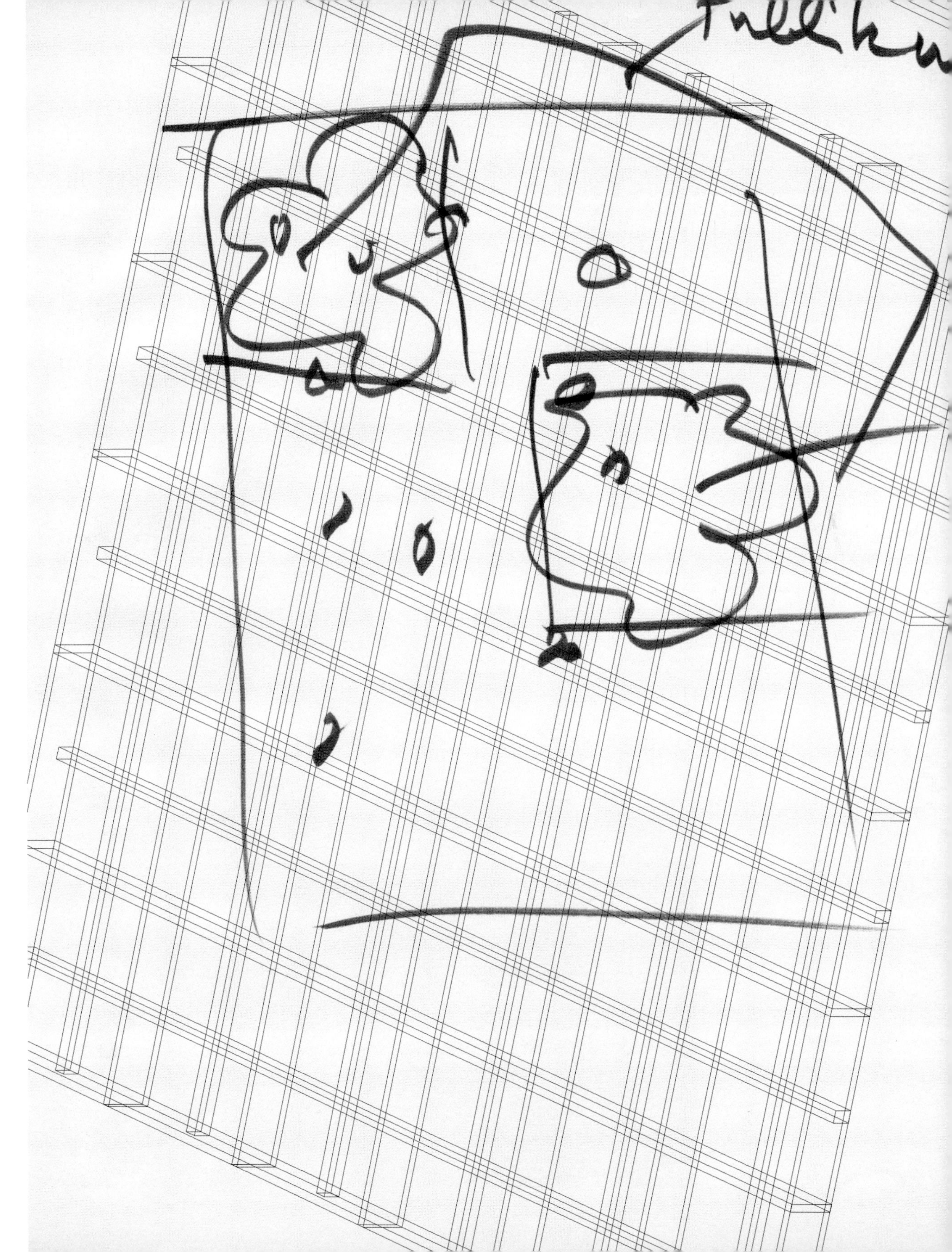

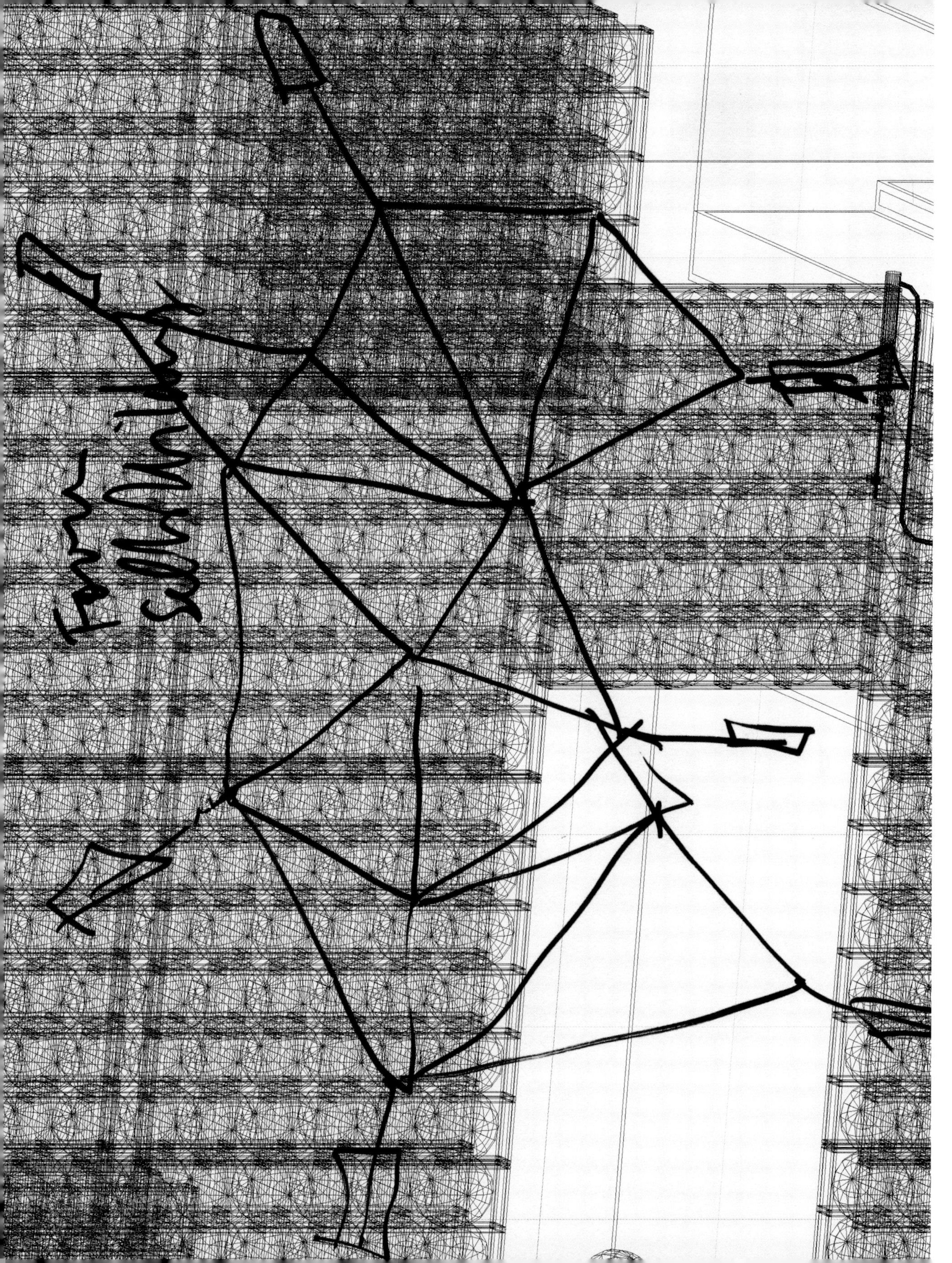

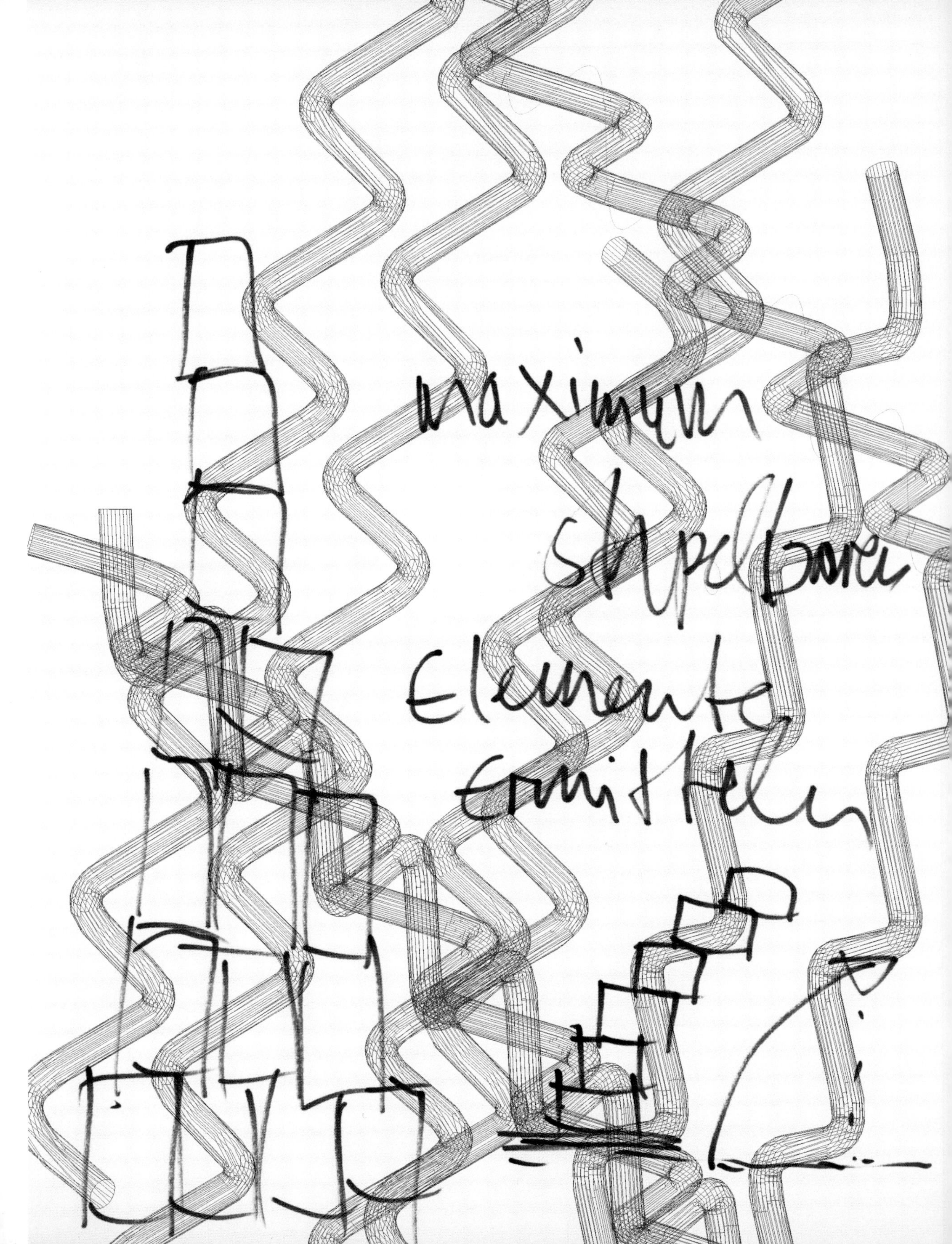

maximum
shapebarer
Elemente
ermitteln

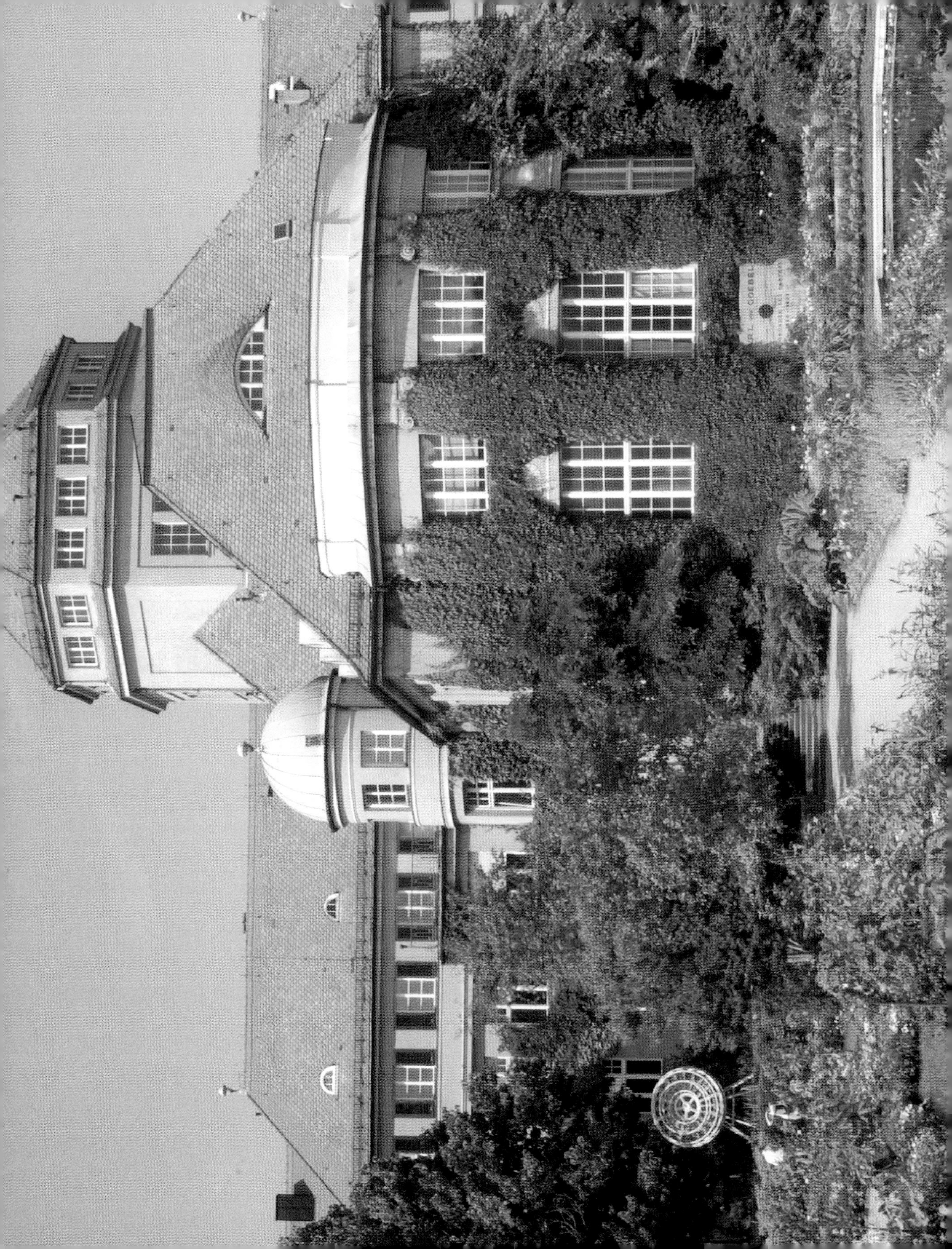

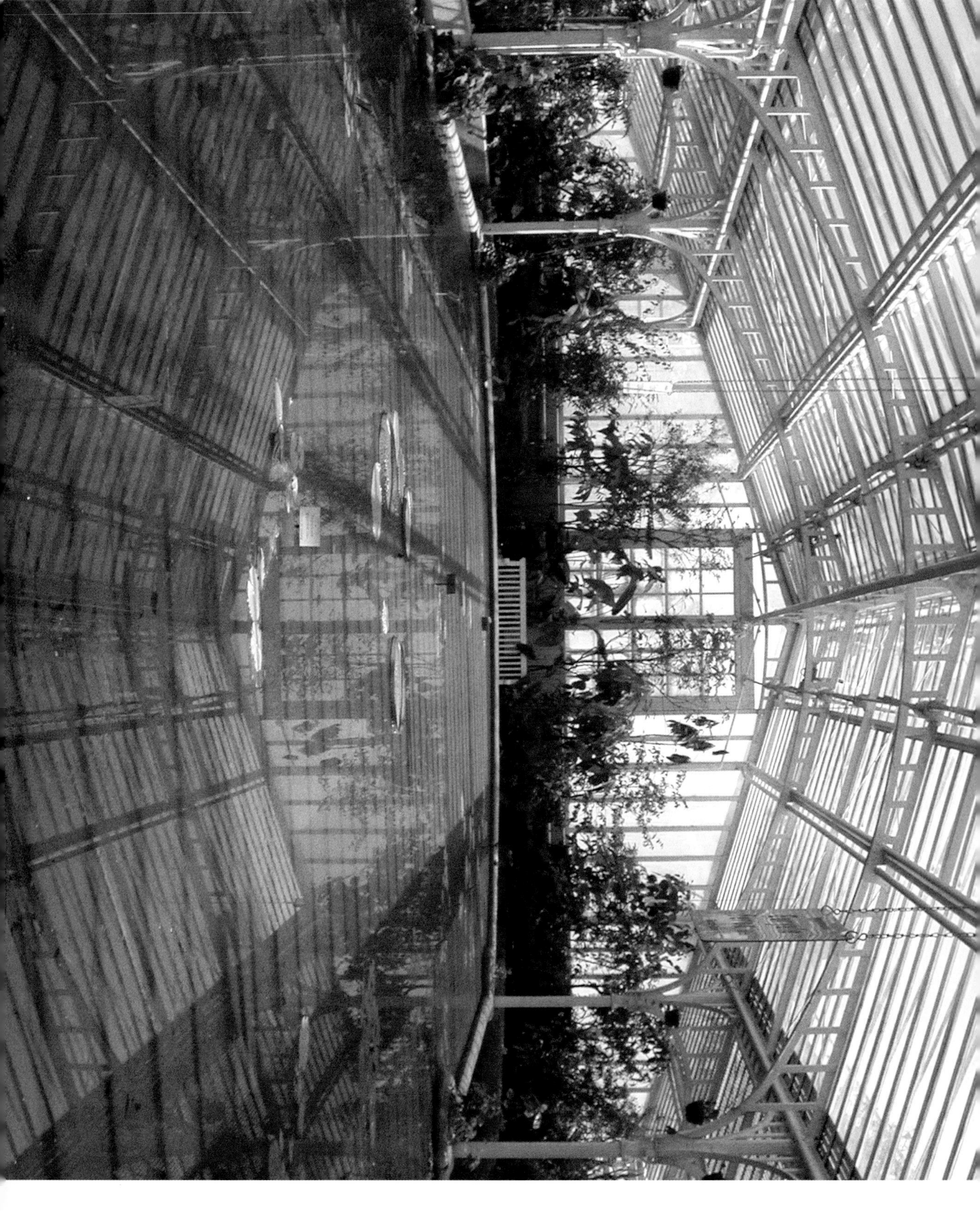

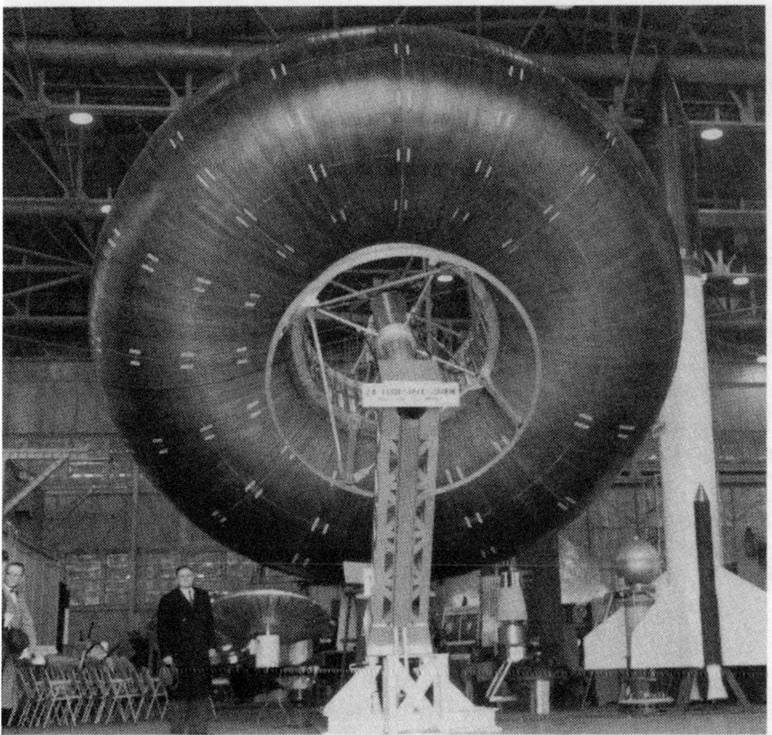

L-61-8693

e a huge pneumatic tire sitting on a giant car jack, Langley's full-size test
s 24-foot toroidal space station receives a visit from NASA Administrator

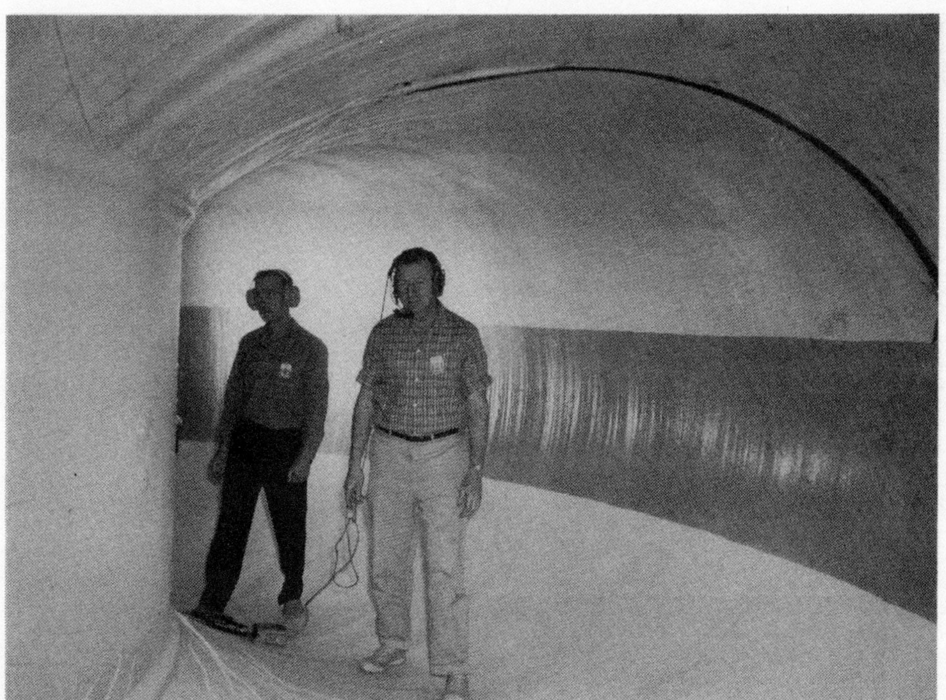

L-62-312

Langley engineers check out the interior of the inflatable 24-foot space station in
January 1962.

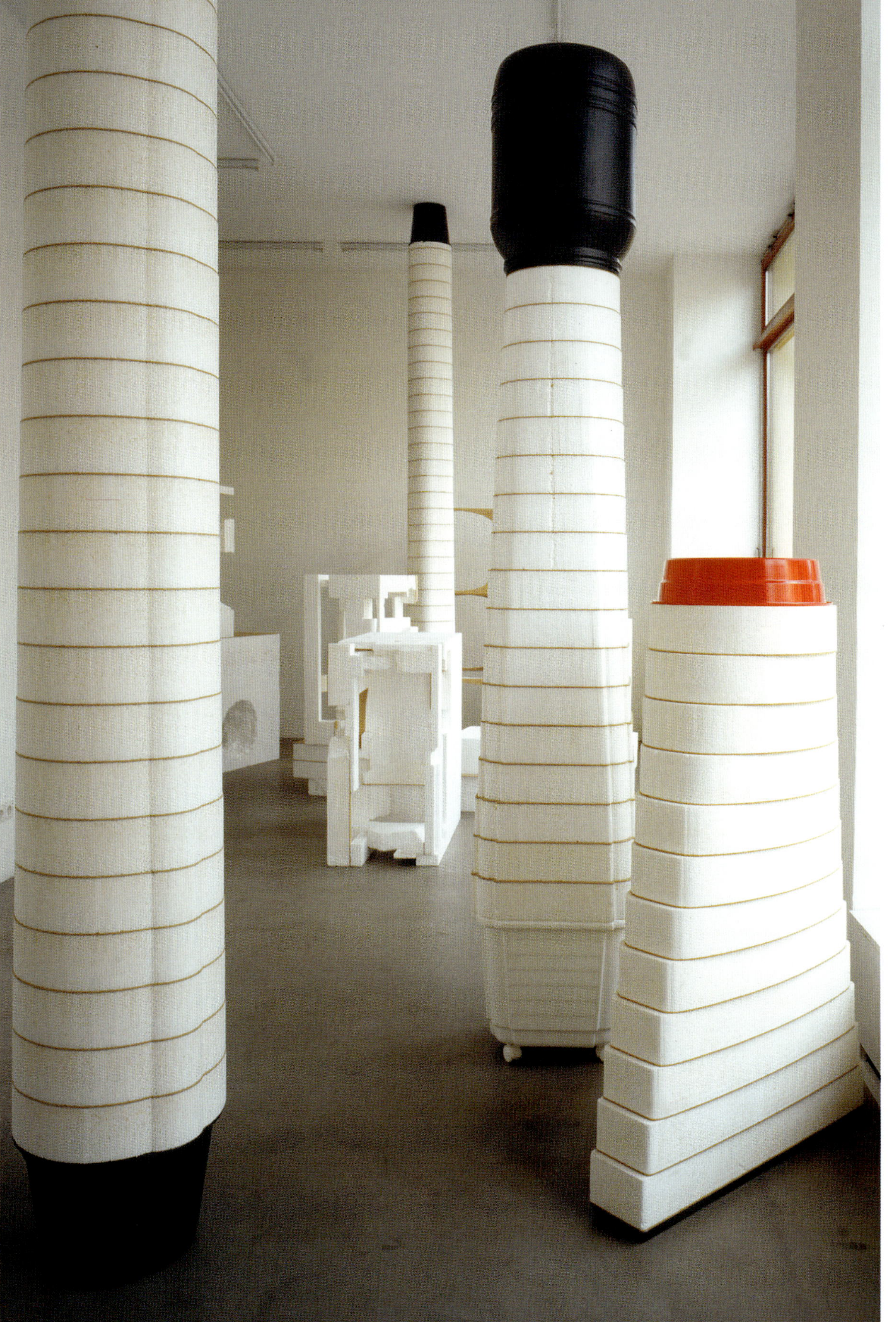

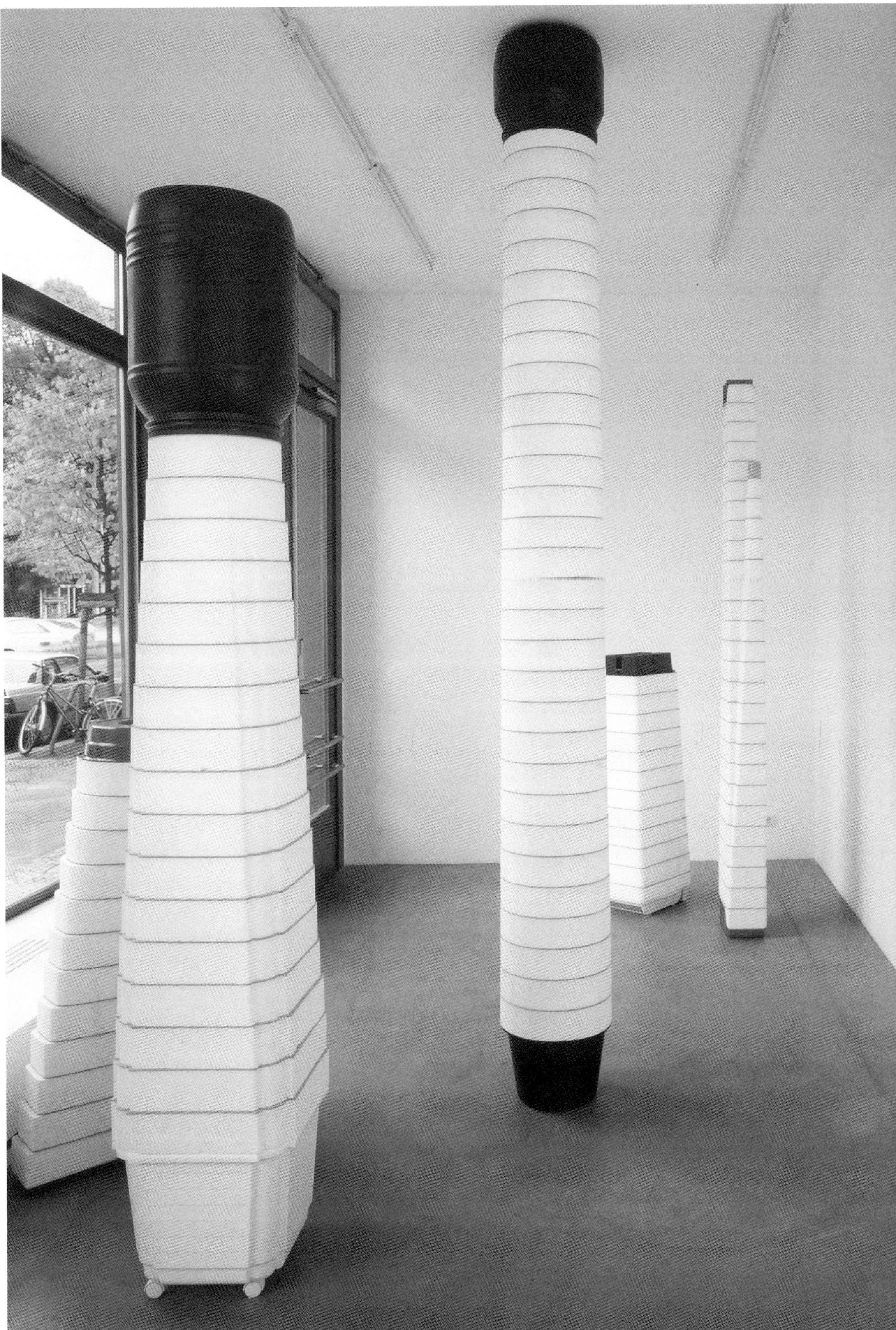

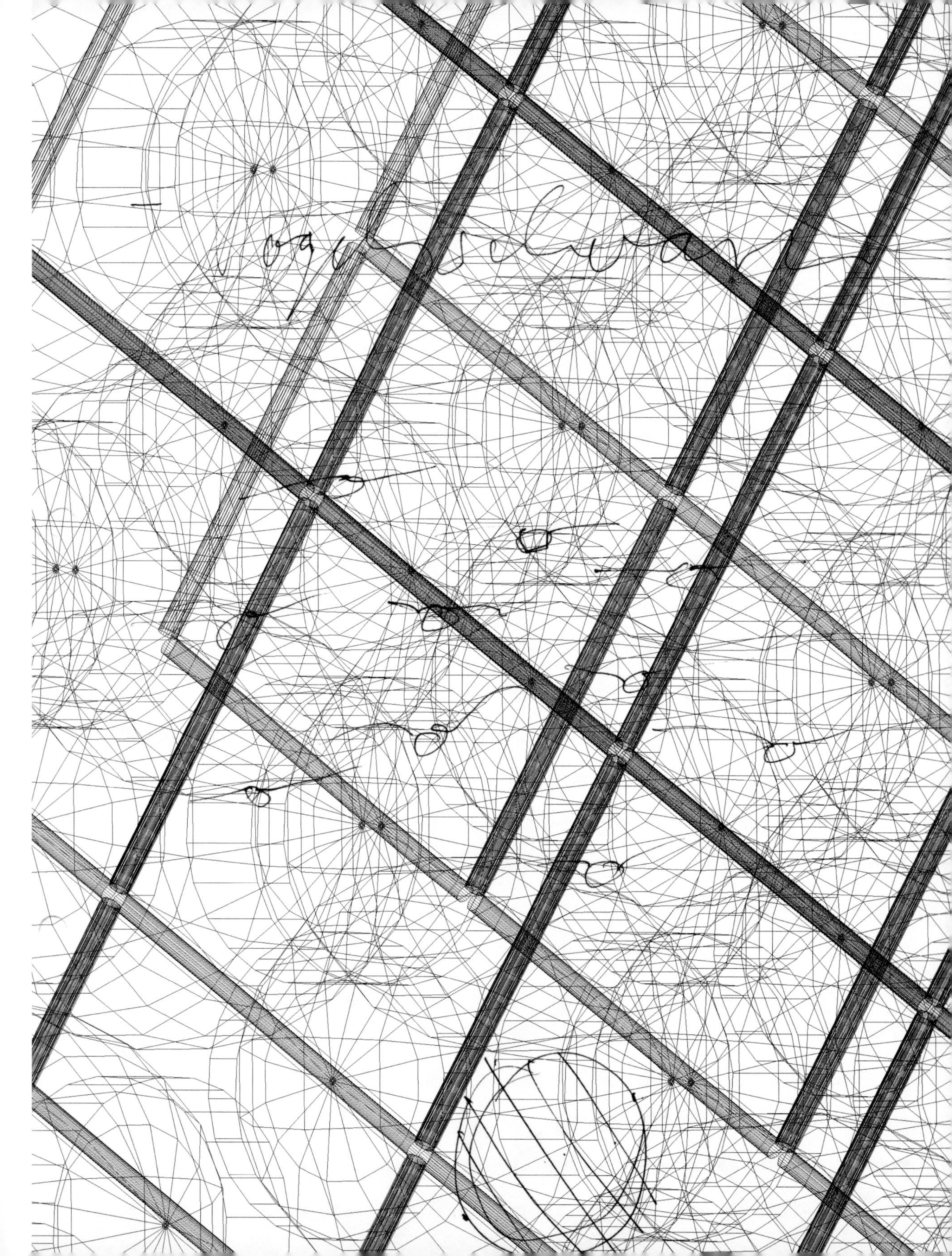

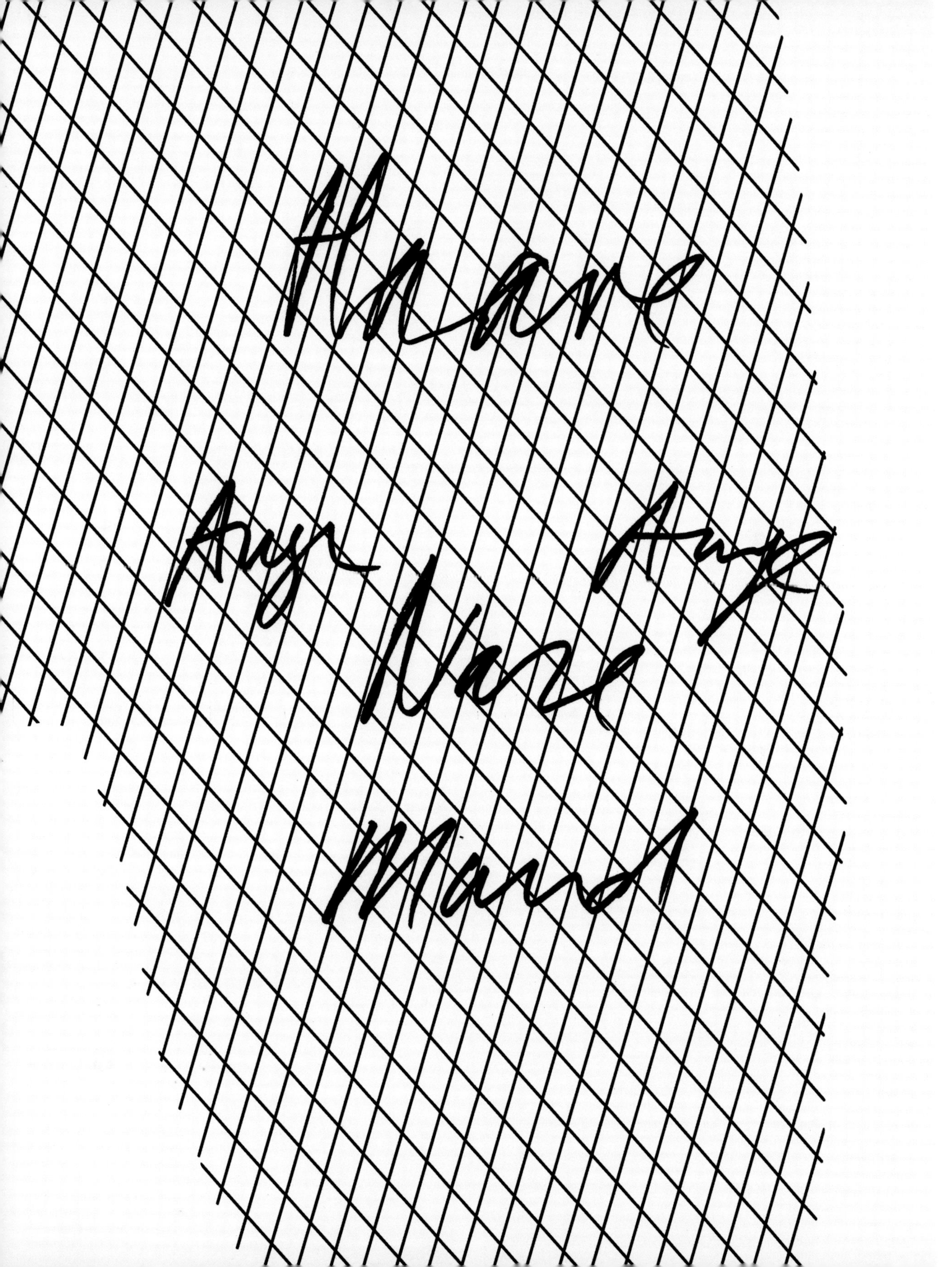

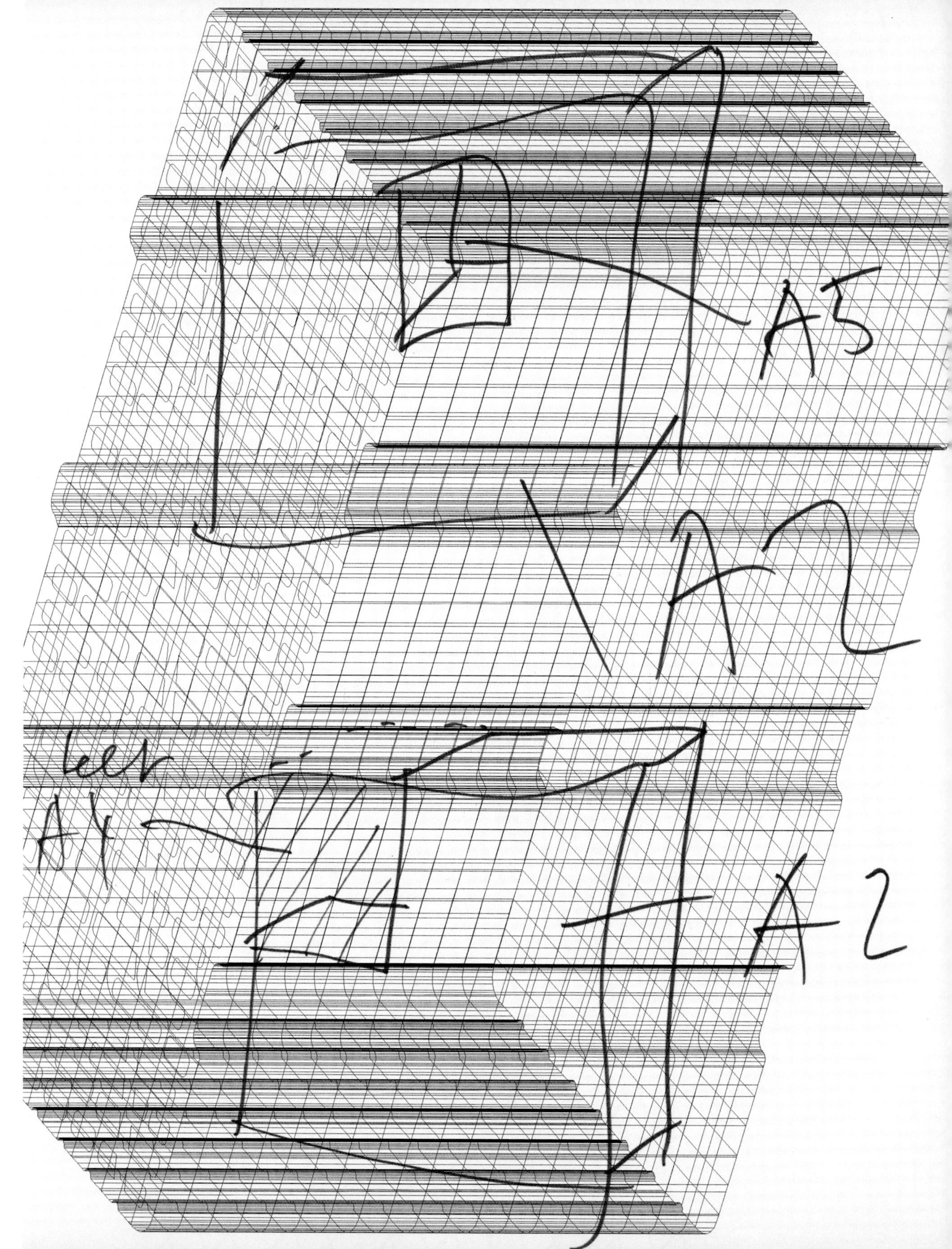
A3
A2
leer
A4
A2

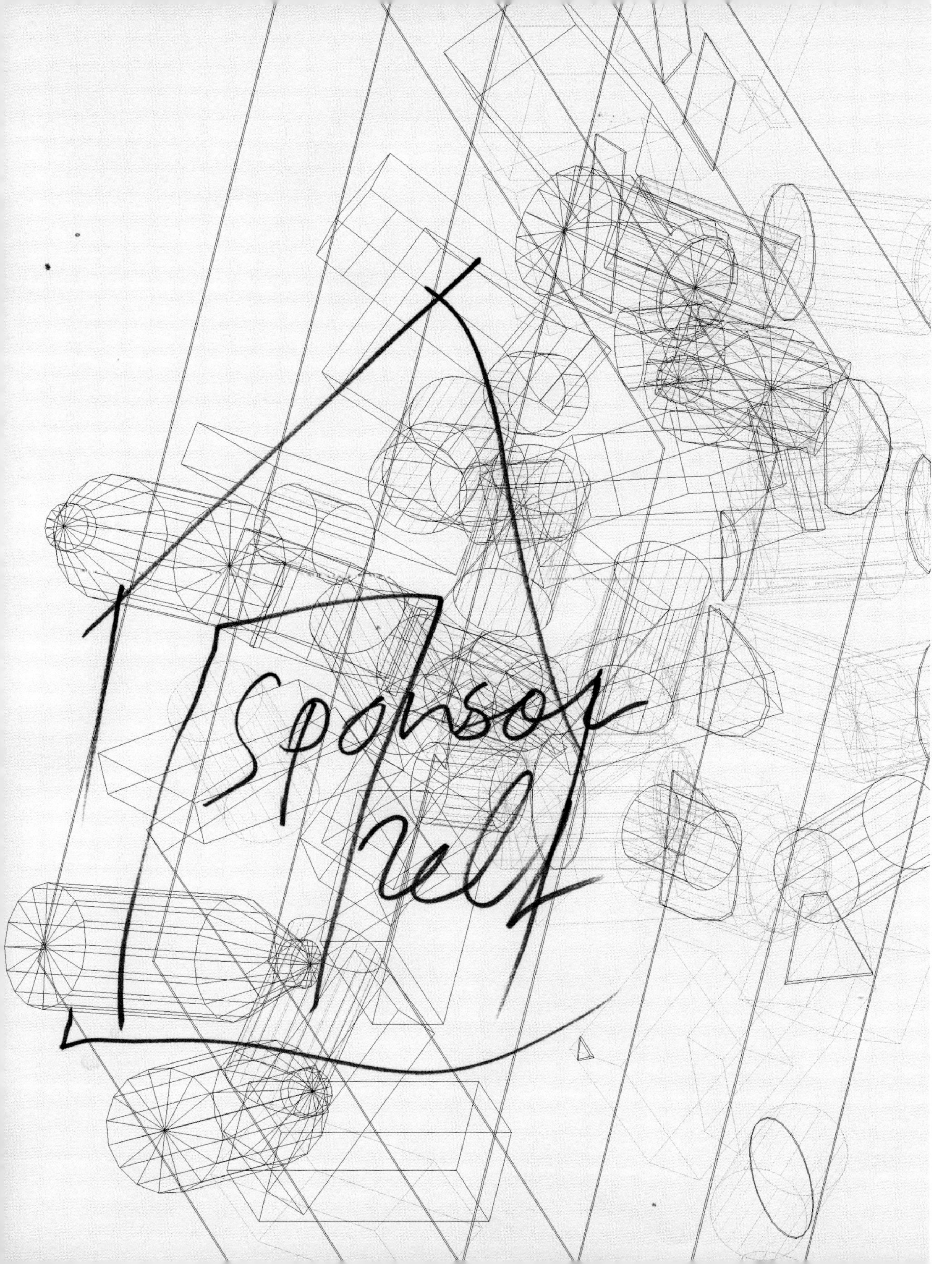
Sponsor

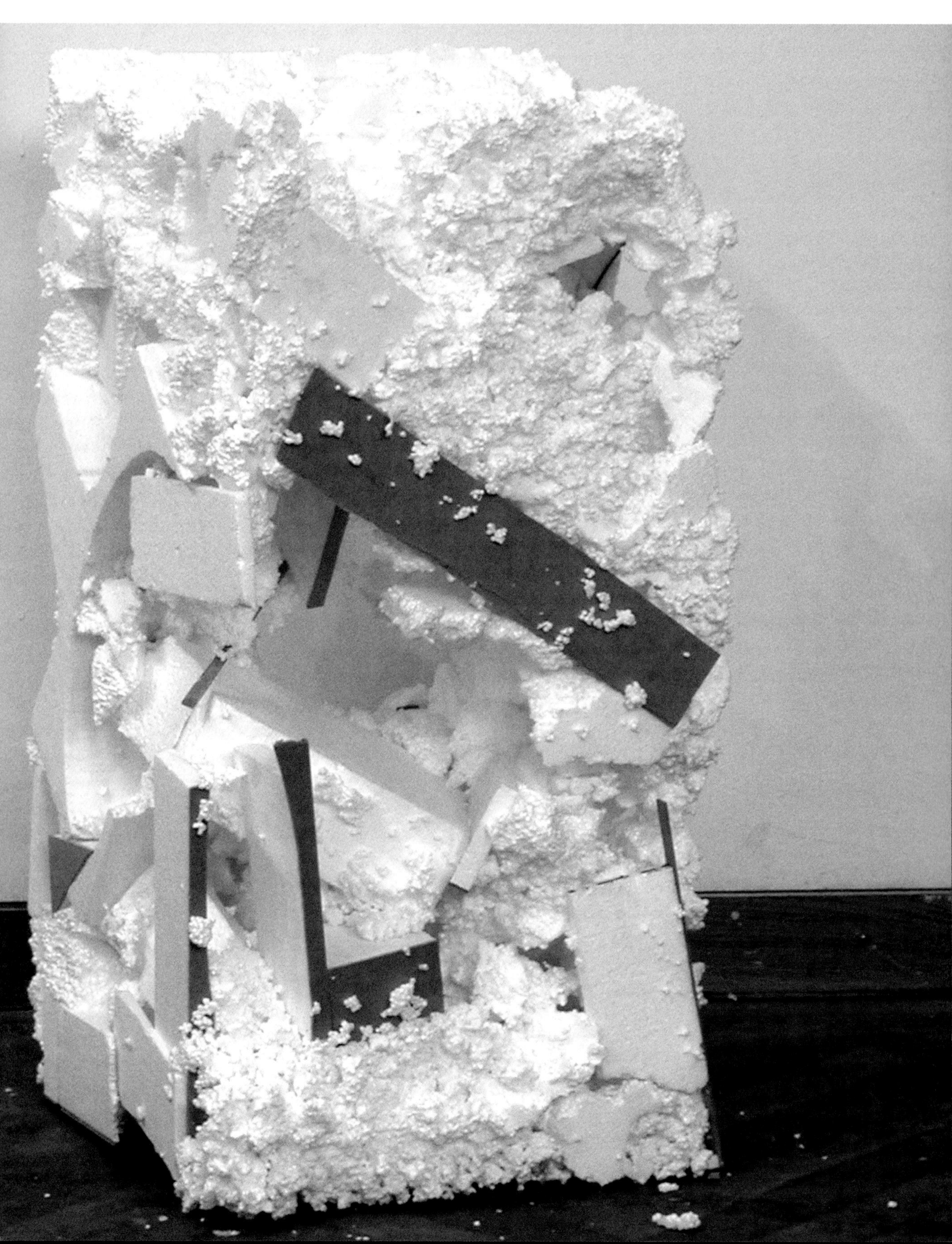

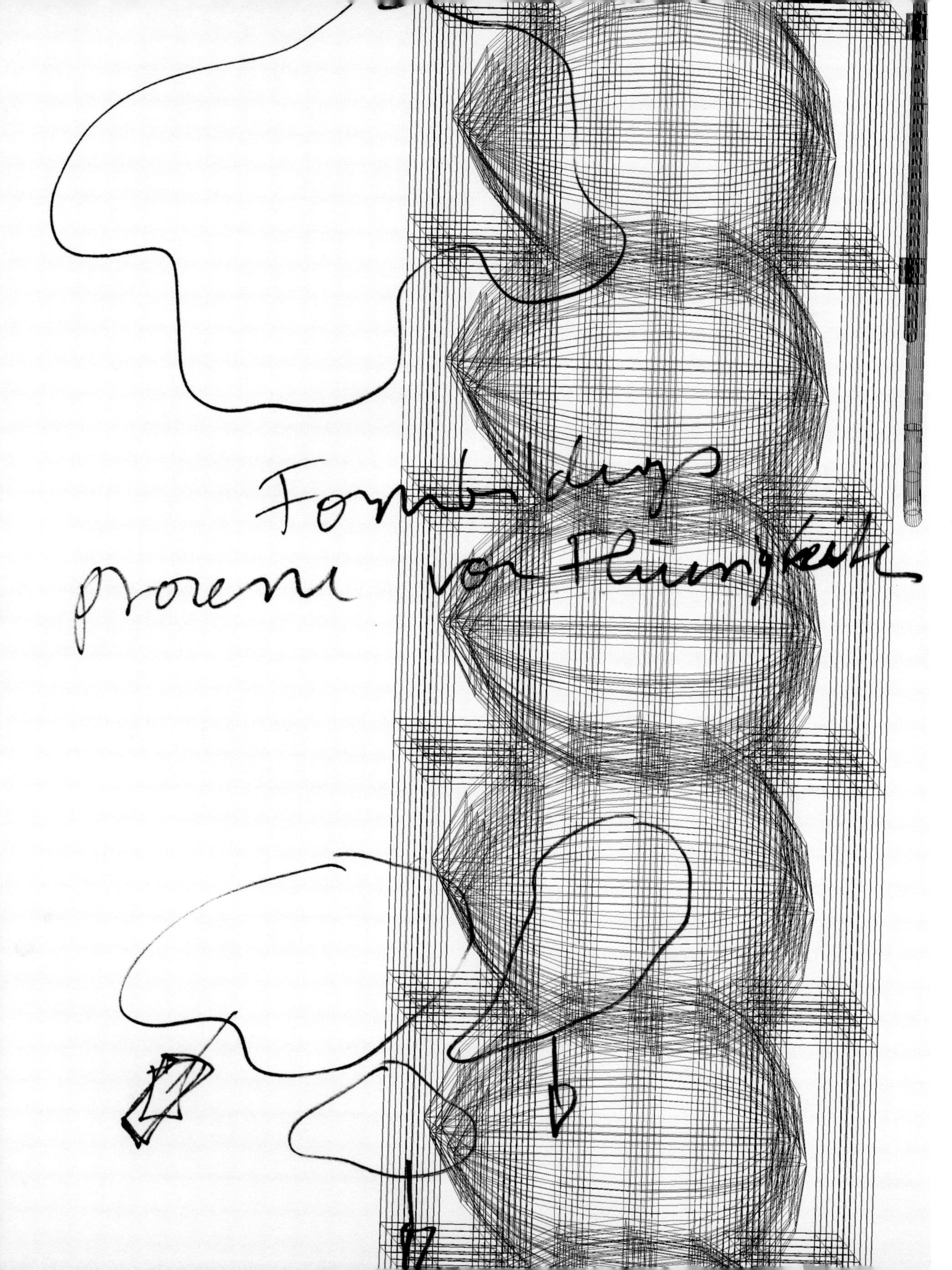

Formbildung
prozeß von Flüssigkeit

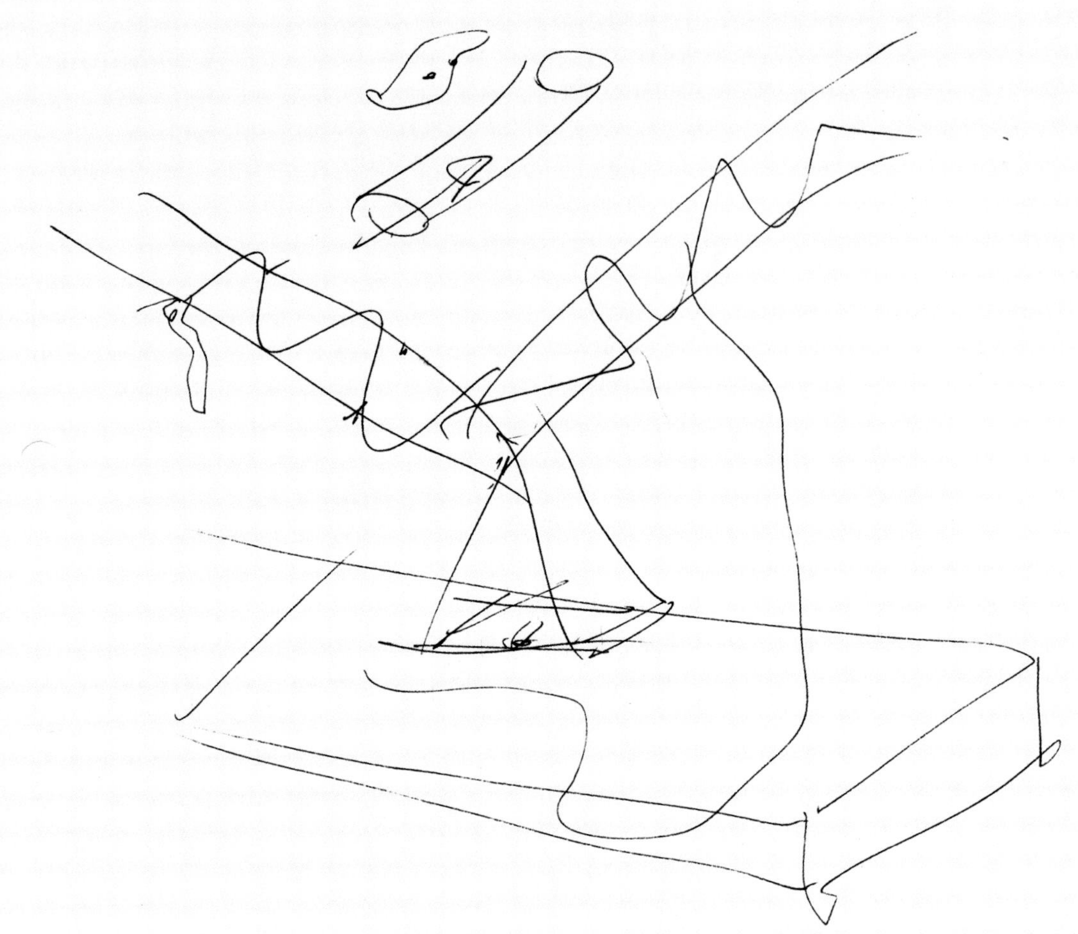

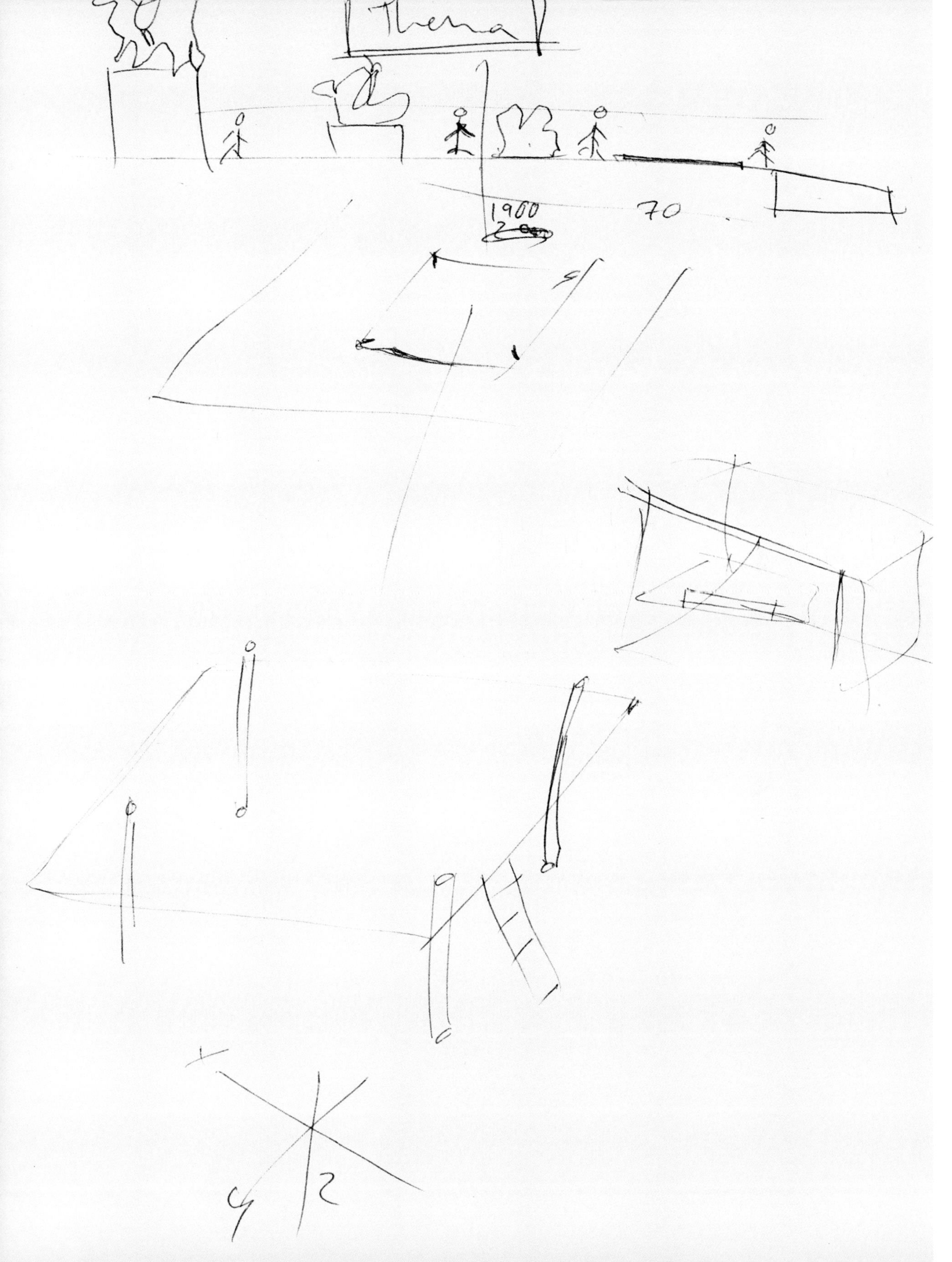

Thema
1900
70

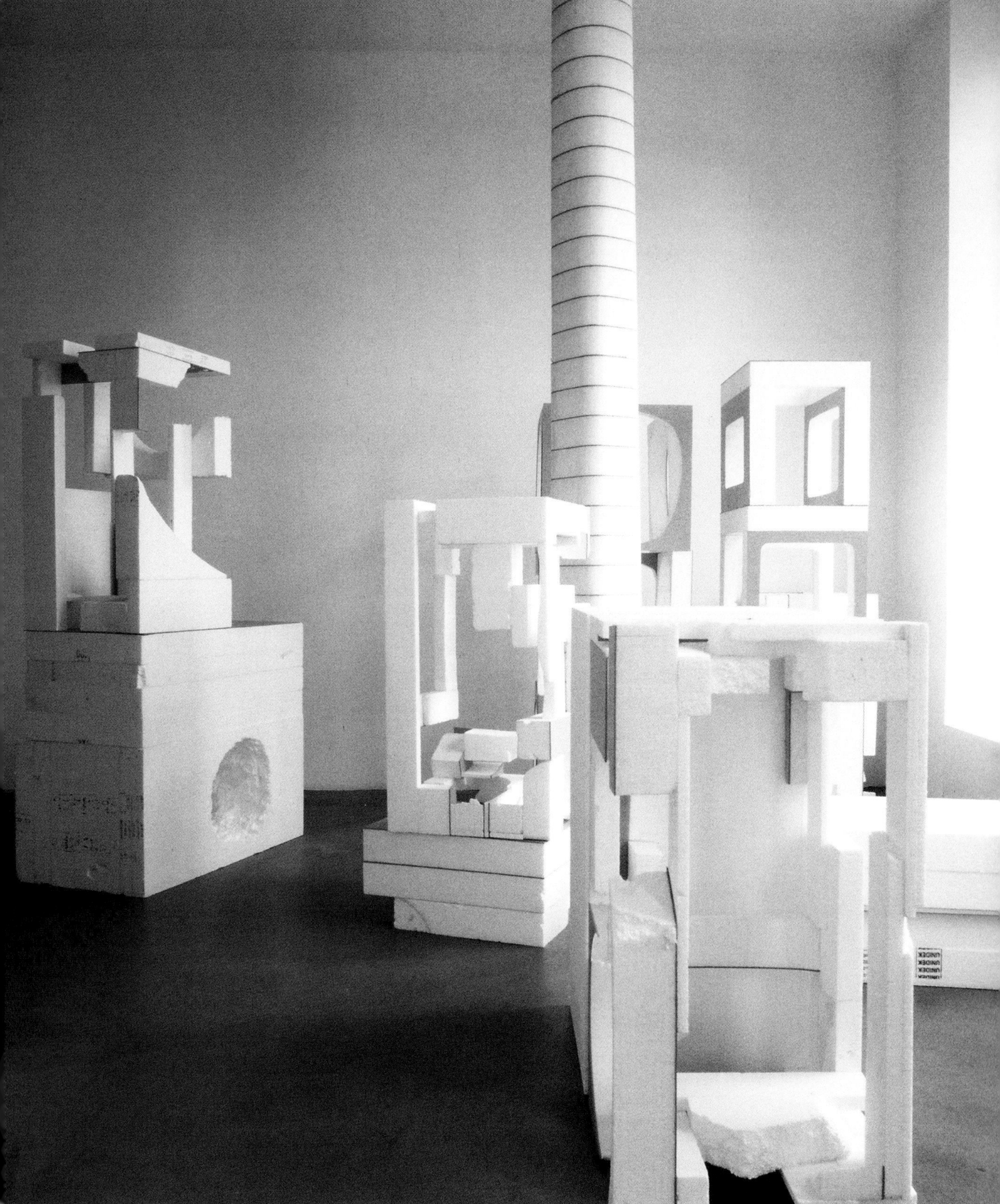

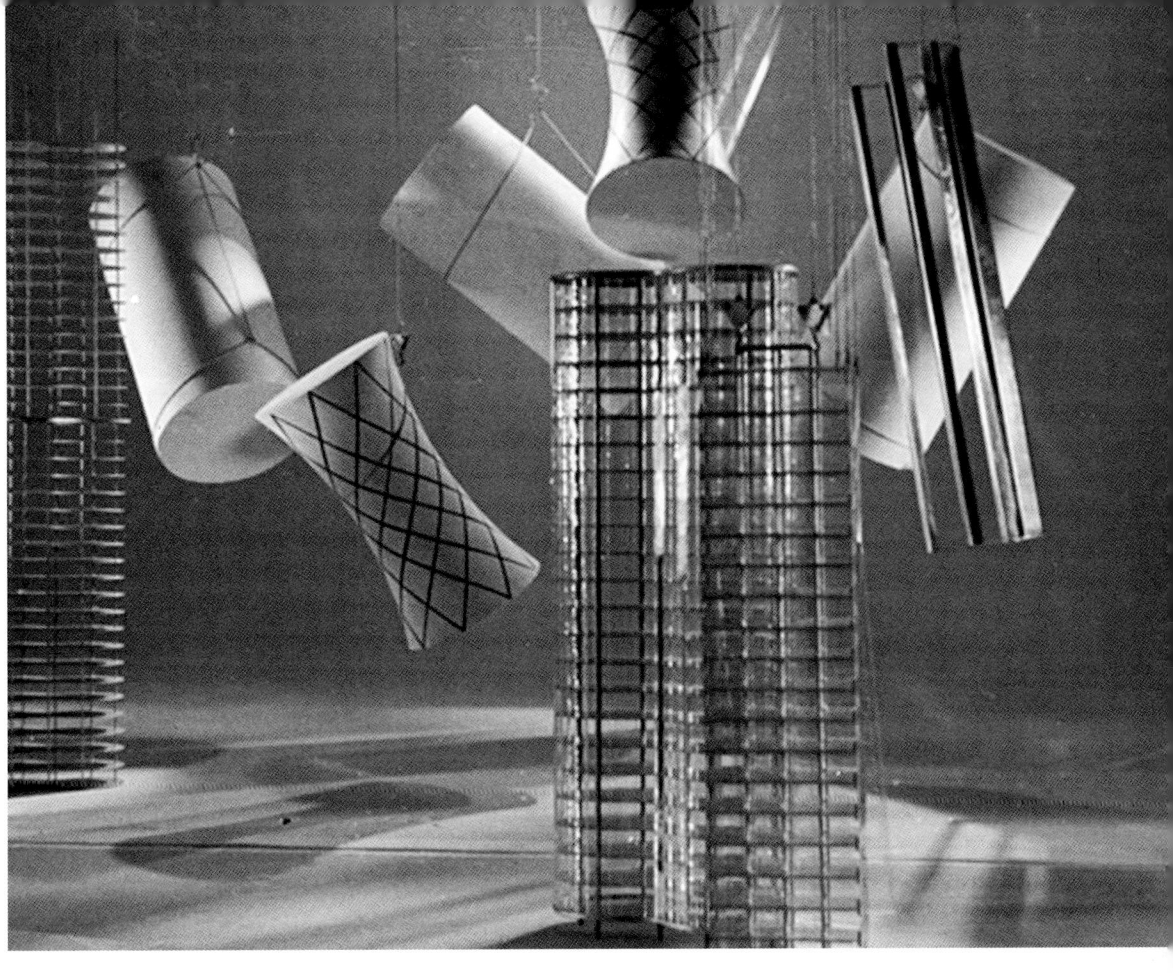

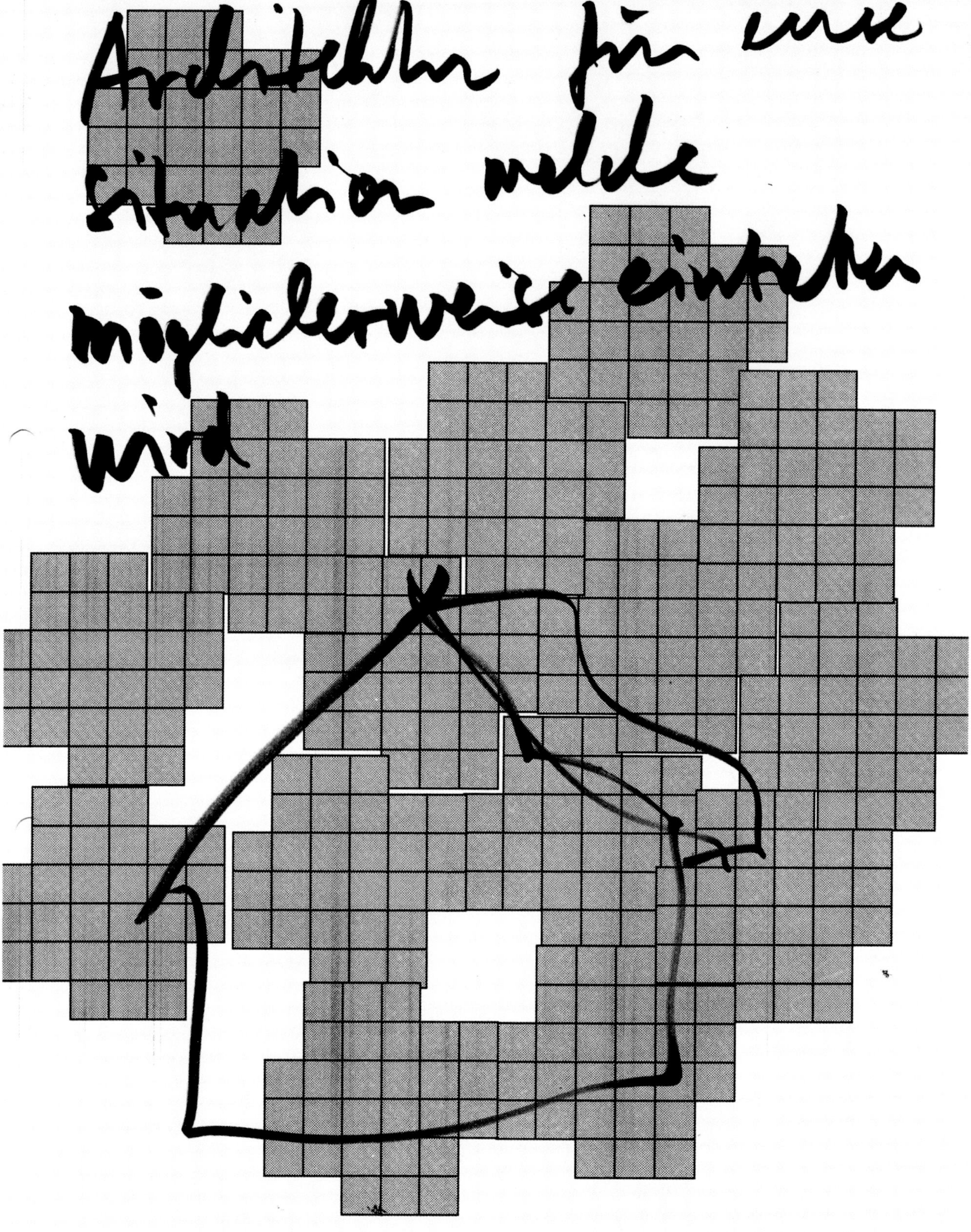

Architektur für eine
Situation welche
möglicherweise eintreten
wird

mini's

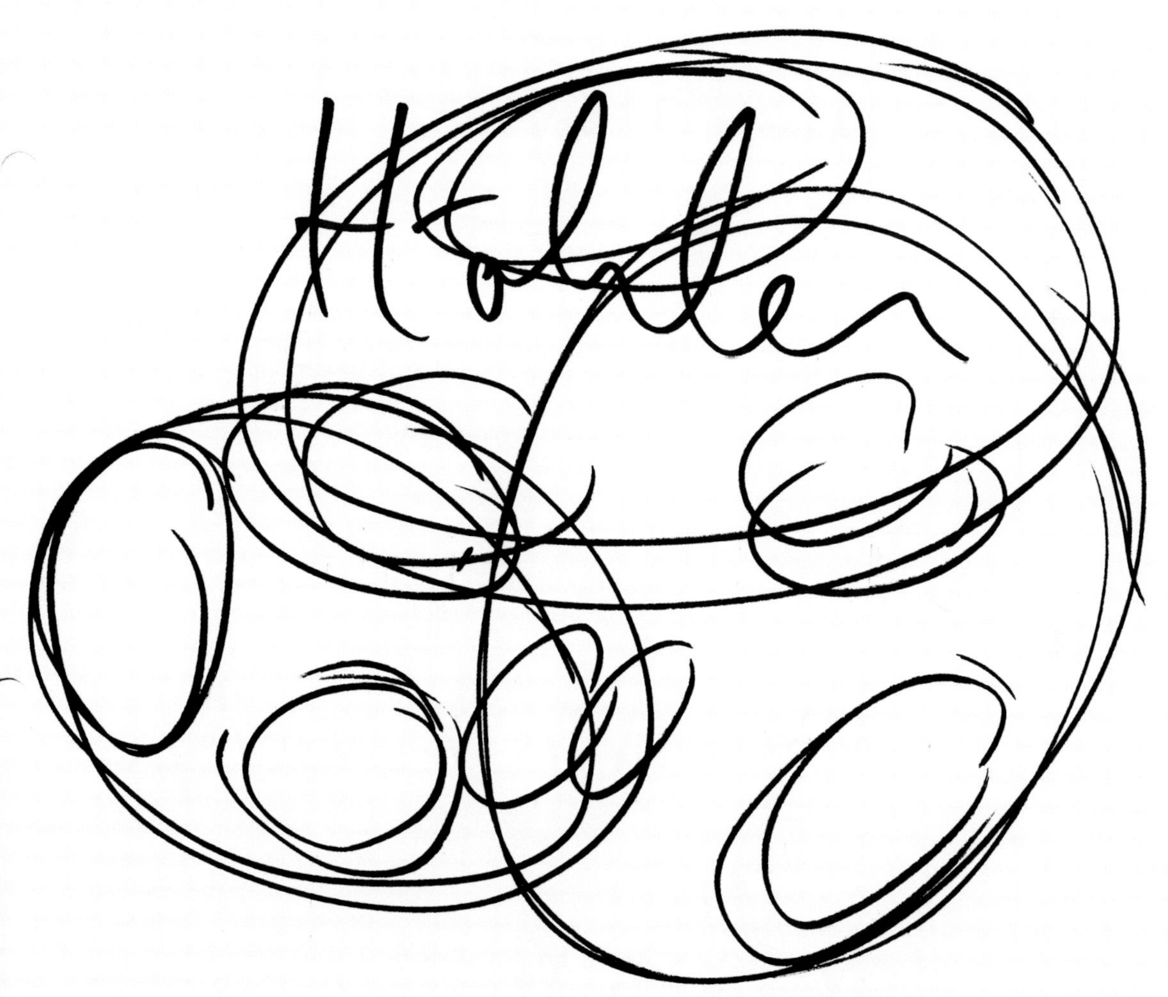

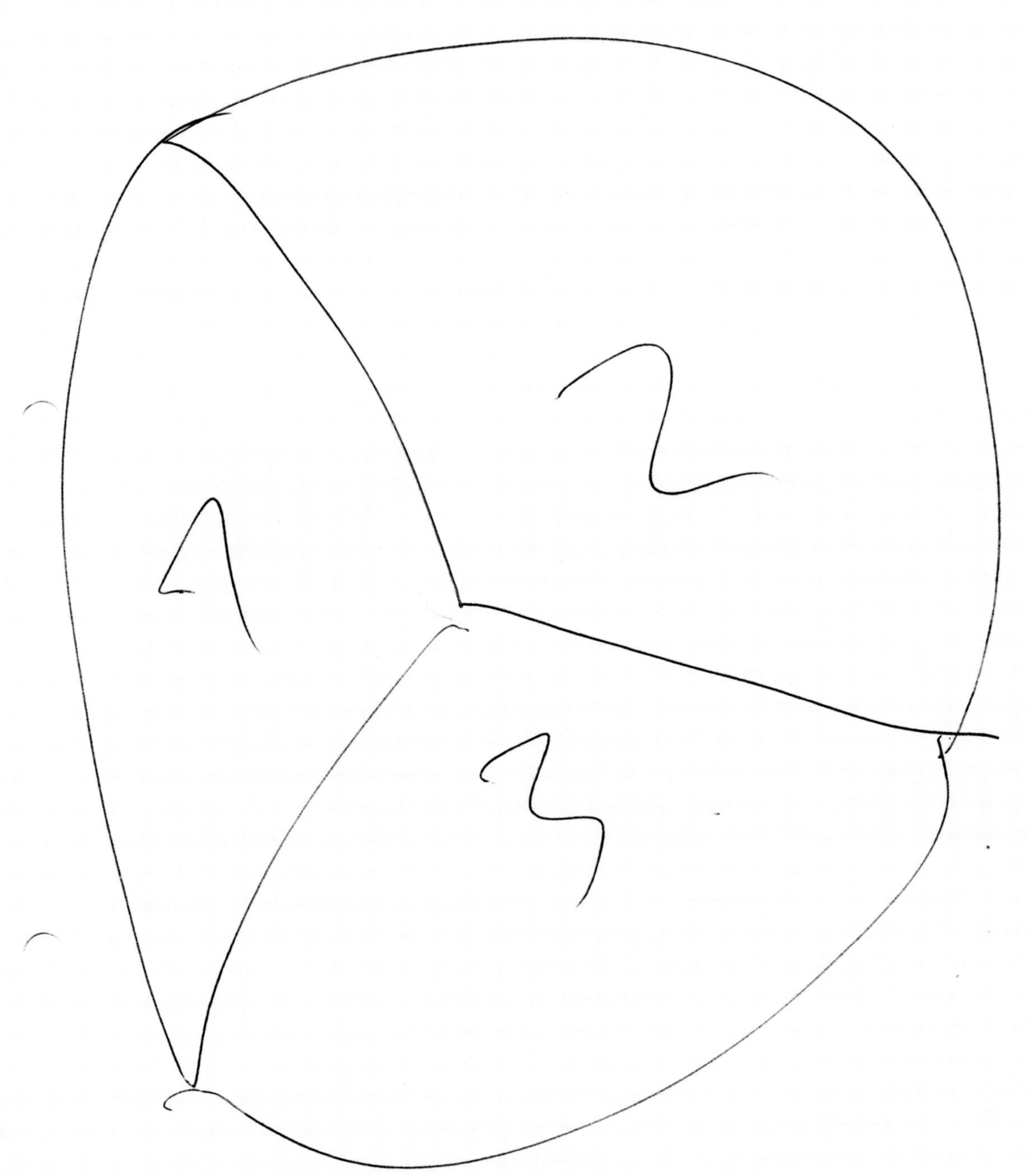

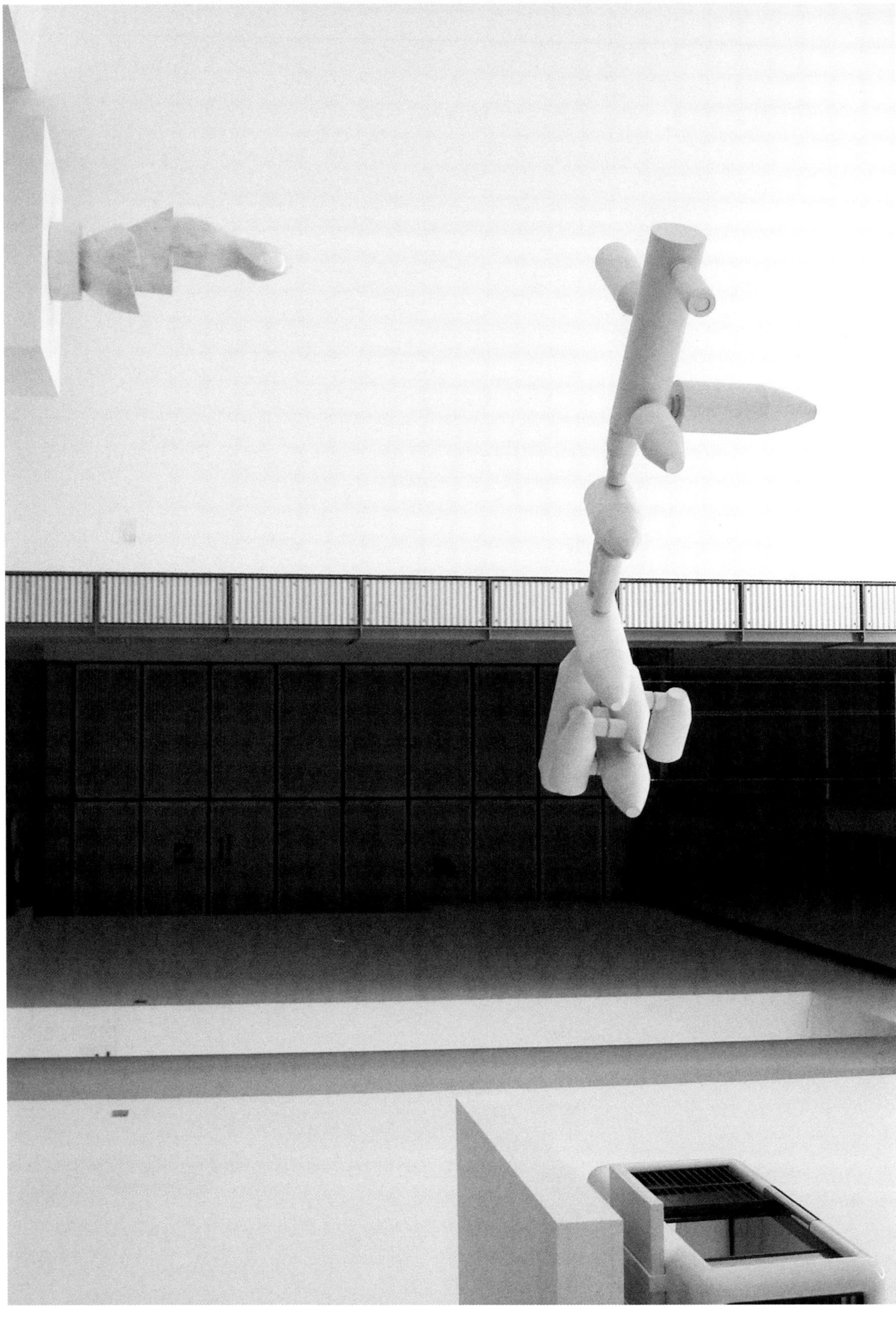

Andreas Zybach Die Arbeit „Ohne Titel" war in der Kunsthalle Exnergasse in Wien ausgestellt. Es handelt sich um eine Konstruktion aus halbierten Kuben, wobei die einzelnen Bauteile durch Erdnüsse und Elektromagnete zusammengehalten werden.

Daniel Baumann Also mechanische und elektrische Verbindungen.

AZ Es gibt im Maschinenbau die Tendenz oder den Versuch, mechanische durch elektrische Verbindungen zu ersetzen. Ziel ist es, eine Art Granulat herzustellen, woraus multifunktionale Maschinen zusammengesetzt werden können. Um das zu erreichen, müssen Elemente entwickelt werden, die koppelbar und wieder lösbar sind und im Verbund möglichst verschiedene Formen annehmen können. Dahinter steht letztendlich die Idee, eine Struktur zu produzieren, die autonom funktionieren würde, die sich selber umbauen und ihrer Aufgabe anpassen könnte.

DB Und warum nimmst du jetzt ausgerechnet eine Erdnuss als Dübel?

AZ Sie ist nur Platzhalter für eine beliebige mechanische Verbindung und verweist auf deren Austauschbarkeit. Mich interessiert die Vorstellung, dass sämtliche Nägel, Nieten, Schrauben usw. in Konstruktionen durch zeitlich begrenzte oder instabilere Formen von Verbindungen ersetzt würden...

DB Eine Erdnuss als Platzhalter ist schon auch absurd.

AZ Die Erdnuss speichert die zur Reproduktion der Pflanze notwendige Energie: Eine der größten Schwierigkeiten bei der Konstruktion dieser neuen Maschinen ist die Energieversorgung der Einzelteile.
Es geht mir darum, das bestehende Modell zu erweitern, das konkrete System zu öffnen, anstatt es nur zu beschreiben.

DB Diesen Sachverhalt, also die doch recht komplexe Frage nach dem Verhältnis von Konstruktion, Anpassung, Autonomie, Möglichkeiten und Grenzen könnte man auch im Rahmen eines Textes abhandeln. Warum soll es dreidimensional

Andreas Zybach The work "Untitled" was part of an exhibition at Kunsthalle Exnergasse in Vienna. It consists of a construction made of cubes that have been cut in half and then held together with peanuts and electromagnets.

Daniel Baumann Mechanical and electrical connections.

AZ In mechanical engineering, there is this tendency or effort to replace mechanical connections with electrical ones. The aim is to produce some kind of granulate that can be used to build multifunctional machines. To achieve this, elements have to be developed which can be interlinked and then opened again and which can take on as many different shapes as possible when being interconnected. Ultimately the idea behind it aims to produce a structure that would function autonomously, that could convert itself and adapt to its environment.

DB And why does it have to be peanuts instead of dowels?

AZ The peanut just functions as a fill-in for any optional mechanical connection and refers to the interchangeability of this connection. I am interested in the idea of all nails, rivets, screws etc. in a construction being replaced by temporally limited or rather unstable forms of connections...

DB A peanut as fill-in is quite absurd, too.

AZ The peanut stores all the energy that is necessary for the reproduction of the plant: One of the greatest difficulties in the construction of this new machine is the power supply of its component parts. I am concerned with expanding the model, with opening up the concrete system instead of just describing it.

DB These facts, meaning the quite complex question about the relationship between construction, adaption, autonomy, possibilities and limitations, could just as well be treated within the scope of a written text. Why should it be shown three-dimensionally? What is being gained by that?
There is this precarious area with accounted scientists and highly experienced specialists, and there is the exhibition space with an object that

dargestellt werden? Was gewinnt man da? Das ist ein prekärer Bereich, es gibt ausgewiesene Forscher und Spezialisten mit viel Erfahrung, und es gibt den Ausstellungsraum mit einem Objekt, das Kunst ist oder mindestens an diesem Ort als Kunst wahrgenommen wird.

AZ Indem ich in meiner Version einige Aspekte einer Vorlage ausschließe und andere hervorhebe, versuche ich die Aufmerksamkeit des Betrachters auf von mir ausgewählte Punkte zu lenken. Differenzen zwischen dem Ausstellungsobjekt und seiner Vorlage führen zu neuen Fragen. In manchen Projekten kombiniere ich auch Objekte oder Methoden, die historisch weit auseinanderliegen oder die thematisch nur geringe Schnittmengen aufweisen. An der Konstruktion aus Erdnüssen und Elektromagneten interessiert mich beispielsweise der undefinierte Maßstab meines Objekts im Verhältnis zur Realität. Die Manipulation des Maßstabs, in dem ein Objekt wiedergegeben wird, bildet ein eigenes Genre in der Kunst. In dem konkreten Fall interessiert mich einer der für die beteiligten Forscher kritischen Punkte besonders – die Miniaturisierung und damit das Aufrechterhalten der Behauptung, dass es irgendwann einmal möglich sein wird, kleinere und stabilere Elemente zu produzieren. Bis dahin wird ein Objekt als Reaktion auf äussere oder innere Belastungen meist vergrößert. Diesen Zwiespalt möchte mein Objekt befördern: Ist es ein Modell? Ist es größer oder kleiner gedacht?

DB Die meisten oder vielleicht alle deine Arbeiten interessieren sich für Konstruktionen, Systeme und die Denkweisen dahinter, beziehungsweise für die Frage der Übersetzung in die Sprache der Kunst, die du mit deinen Objekten vornimmst. Eine Übersetzung bringt immer Gewinn und Verlust, auf jeden Fall steht jedoch die Idee eines anderen Zugangs dahinter.

AZ Wer hat die Autorität zu bestimmen, wer sich wofür interessieren darf? Meist wird ja versucht, das bei Übersetzungen auftretende Rauschen zu unterdrücken. Ich sehe aber auch eine Qualität in seiner Verstärkung, oder in einem unvoreingenommeneren Zugang, wie ihn manchmal sogenannte Laien haben.
Im Projekt „Space frame potato chip" verwende ich eine Konstruktionsmethode zum Leichtbau von Flugobjekten, die von Alexander Graham Bell entwickelt wurde. Er versuchte, seine Forschungsziele so autonom wie möglich zu definieren.

DB Wie funktionierte die Arbeit „Two Loops" auf der Biennale von Venedig? Was war die Idee hin-

is art or is at least being perceived as art in that specific spatial context.

AZ In my versions of original models, I highlight some aspects inherent in the originals and exclude others. In doing so, I try to direct the viewer's attention to certain moments, which I chose. Differences between the exhibition object and its model lead to new questions. In some projects I also combine objects and methods that lay historically far apart of each other or thematically intersect at only a few points. What is interesting to me in the construction with peanuts and electromagnets is, among other things, the undefined scale of my object in relation to reality. The manipulation of the scale that is used for the reproduction of an object forms its own genre in art. In the concrete case of the construction with peanuts, I was interested specifically in the one moment that is usually critical for scientists: the issue of miniaturisation and the question of how to sustain the claim that it will once become possible to produce smaller and more stable elements. Until that point, enlargement of objects as a reaction to external and internal stress will remain a common practise. My object is there to raise this two-way conflict: Is it a model? Is it thought to be smaller or larger?

DB Most or maybe all of your works take an interest in constructions, systems, as well as the mindsets behind them. And by doing so, they raise the question of your objects' translation into the language of art. A translation always means profit and loss, but most importantly there is the idea of a different approach behind it.

AZ Who has the authority to decide who may be interested in what? In most of the cases, the effort will be to oppress any noise emerging from translations. However, I just as well see the worth in amplifying that noise, in making a rather unbiased approach that so-called laypeople might make. For the project "Space frame potato chip", I used a construction method that was developed by Alexander Graham Bell for the lightweight construction of flying objects. He tried to define his scientific goals as autonomously as possible.

DB How did the work "Two loops" at the Venice Biennale function? What was the idea behind the wooden stand and the sweater hung there that one could take away while leaving one's own sweater in exchange?

AZ The point of departure for that work was my interest in a Venetian letterpress printer from the 16th century named Aldus Manutius who was ac-

ter dem Stand aus Holzlatten und dem Pullover, der dort aufgehängt war und den man mitnehmen konnte, wenn man den eigenen im Tausch dort ließ?

AZ Ausgangspunkt war mein Interesse für einen venezianischen Buchdrucker namens Aldus Manutius aus dem 16. Jahrhundert, der zu Beginn des Buchdrucks tätig war. In dieser frühen Phase der Entwicklung der neuen Informationstechnik entstehen eine Vielzahl von Standards. Durch die erhöhte Produktivität bei der Generierung von Informationen wird der Schutz des Autors und seiner Arbeit immer mehr zu einem Problem. Es wird notwendig, neue von schon vorhandenen Informationen, das Original von der Kopie zu unterscheiden. In meinem Modell steht der Pullover für eine Informationseinheit, die im Marktstand temporär gespeichert wird. Indem ein Passant das Kleidungsstück mit seinem eigenen austauscht, ergibt sich eine fortwährend neue Skulptur bzw. eine Veränderung im Sinne des beschriebenen Kriteriums der Unterscheidung von neuer und bereits existierender Information. Der Marktstand verweist auch auf die Ökonomie, die bereits zu Beginn des Mediums Buchdruck seine Distribution mitbestimmte. Kurz gesagt handelt es sich um ein interaktives Experiment mit dem Besucher.

DB Es gab da ein gewisses Ungleichgewicht zwischen Resultat und Prozess und dementsprechend entwickelten sich die Missverständnisse.

AZ Die größte Konfusion hat sich dadurch eingestellt, dass es in Venedig plötzlich warm wurde und keiner mehr einen Pullover wollte.

DB Die Interaktion war ein Flop.

AZ Ja, aber es hat in gewisser Weise doch funktioniert. Es ergab sich ein ungleicher Tausch. Ich habe den Versuch trotz der Hitze dreimal initiiert, habe also dreimal einen Pullover hingehängt. Zweimal wurde er gegen Luft getauscht, das dritte Mal bin ich dann abgereist. Das Medium Luft hat mich danach auch in weiteren Projekten beschäftigt.

DB Das Projekt beschränkte sich aber nicht nur auf den Stand mit dem Pullover. Welche Rolle spielten die Zeitschriften, die du am gleichen Ort hinterlegt hast?

AZ Neben dem Stand befand sich eine Holzbank. Dort legte ich Zeitschriften hin, die ich zuvor an einem Zeitschriftenstand in der Nähe gekauft hatte und daraufhin auf ein von Aldus Manutius entwickeltes Format, in dem er seine Publikationen

tive at the beginning of letterpress printing. During this early phase of the development of this new information technique, a multitude of standards occured. Due to the increased productivity in the generation of information, the protection of the author and his work became more and more of a problem. It became necessary to distinguish new information from that which already existed in order to distinguish original from copy. In my model, the sweater stands for an information unit temporarily contained and stored by the market stand. New sculptures—a mutation in terms of the above mentioned criterion of the distinction between new and already existent information—will continuously arise each moment a passer-by exchanges the sweater with his or her own. In that sense, the stand also refers to an economy that codetermined the distribution of the medium letterpress from the moment that it had come into existence. In short: the work functions as an interactive experiment with the visitor.

DB There is a certain kind of imbalance between result and process, from which, accordingly, misunderstandings can develop.

AZ The biggest confusion arose from the fact that it suddenly became warm in Venice and nobody wanted a sweater anymore.

DB The interaction turned into a flop.

AZ Yes, but in a certain way it still worked. In the end an unequal exchange arose. Despite the heat, I had initiated the experiment three times—three times I hung a sweater on the stand. In two cases, it was exchanged for air, the third time I had already departed. The medium air then occupied my attention in subsequent projects.

DB But the project was not restricted to the stand with the sweater. What role did the magazines you had deposited at the same place play?

AZ There was a wooden bench next to the stand. I deposited magazines that I had bought before at a newsstand nearby and had tailored to a format developed by Aldus Manutius on the bench. The visitors sat down and looked at the magazines. Sometimes they realized only with some delay that parts of the information had fallen out. That way, the historical standard penetrated the standard of the contemporary magazine, creating new images and texts.

DB Why do you always start from other people's works and considerations?

herausgab, zugeschnitten habe. Die Besucher konnten sich hinsetzen und die Hefte anschauen, oft bemerkten sie erst mit einiger Verzögerung, dass Teile der Informationen weggefallen waren. So hat der historische Standard denjenigen des heutigen Magazins durchdrungen und es sind dadurch neue Bilder und Texte entstanden.

DB Warum gehst du immer von Arbeiten und Überlegungen Dritter aus?

AZ Es gibt für mich wenige Fragen, die nicht bereits gedacht worden sind.
Es besteht auch das Verdachtsmoment, dass sich Machtverhältnisse oft darüber definieren, inwieweit man in der Lage ist, Vergangenheit auszublenden und Neuheit vorzugeben, um Gegenwart und Zukunft zu behaupten, oder um Vergleichsmöglichkeiten zu verhindern.

DB Es interessiert dich also nicht nur, wie etwas funktioniert, sondern auch, zu welchen Formen von Standardisierung eine Methode führt und wie dadurch Umwelt und Denken geprägt und beherrscht werden. Wie beispielsweise die Formate A3 und A4 unseren Alltag durchdringen. Ich denke an das Projekt in Tbilissi, als du aus Boxen mit den Maßen dieser Papierformate eine begehbare Architektur gebaut hast. Ein Modul wird hergestellt, um Prozesse zu vereinfachen, Effizienz zu steigern, Zeit zu gewinnen und Gewinn zu generieren. Aber du behandelst das Thema im Kunstkontext, dem Ort, der davon lebt und sich darüber definiert, dass alles einmalig und nicht Standard ist, sondern Original und von der Funktion entbunden. Was interessiert dich am Standard?

AZ Verschiedenes. Modulare Elemente sind praktische Lösungen, um Produktionsprozesse in eine ökonomische Form zu bringen.
Betrachtet man den Prozess, geschieht Folgendes: Das potentiell offene Ende jedes Herstellungsprozesses wird im Voraus festgelegt, das Ende rutscht dadurch an den Anfang. Eine Vielzahl von Entscheidungen wird unter Ausschluss der Öffentlichkeit durch die Festlegung von Standards getroffen.
Schaffst du es, immer wieder in der gleichen Qualität den gleichen Apfelstrudel herzustellen, erkämpfst du dir einen Vorteil im Vergleich zu denen, die mit dieser Qualität ringen. Die Herstellung von Dingen wird durch Standardisierungen auf eine Vielzahl von Autoren, Arbeiter oder Firmen aufteilbar. Aus dieser Situation ergibt sich ein starker Druck auf Hersteller von Apfelstrudel wie auch auf Künstler, weiterverwertbare „Zwischenstücke" zu produzieren.

AZ To me, there are very few questions which have not been thought through yet. There is also the suspicious fact that power relations are often defined by the capability to blind out the past and pretend newness in order to stress presence and future, or to avoid the possibility of a comparison.

DB Besides being interested in how something functions, you are also concerned with the forms that certain standardizations of methods can take and the way these can not only effect but also control the environment and human thinking. For example, how the standard formats A3 and A4 penetrate our daily life. I am thinking of the project in Tbilissi where you built an accessible architecture out of boxes with measurements of these paper formats. In general, a module is produced in order to simplify processes, to increase efficiency, to gain time and generate profit. But you treat that theme inside the art context which lives on and takes its definition from the idea that despite being a standard, everything is unique, original and released from function. What is it that makes you interested in the standard?

AZ Various things. On a functional level, modular elements present practical solutions to give an economic shape to the production process. If you take a look at the production process, this is what happens: The potentially open end of each production process is already established at the very beginning, causing the end to slip at the beginning.
A number of significant decisions are taken by the determination of standards without ever reaching a significant public. If you manage to produce the same apple strudel of the same quality all over again you eke out an advantage in comparison to those who struggle with that quality. As a result of standardizations, the production of things can be divided up amongst a multitude of authors, workers or firms. A strong pressure to produce ‚intermediate pieces' that can further be utilized results from this situation—for manufacturers of apple strudel as well as for artists.

DB That is an issue that has always provoked modern art: on the one hand to be part of and connect with a certain history, on the other hand to claim seclusion, singularity and autonomy. Because the art object cannot be ‚constructed' any further, it cannot be further exploited, which makes it lose power and meaning, dislocating it to the aesthetic realm. There, a symbolic value is attributed to it, which, however, remains unstable. Your work deals with the conditions, possibilities and paradoxes of production today, it focuses on certain processes and their functioning. At the same time,

DB Daran hat sich die moderne Kunst gerieben, sich einerseits in die Geschichte einzuschreiben, andererseits Abgeschlossenheit, Einzigartigkeit und Autonomie zu behaupten. Da sich das Kunstobjekt nicht weiter „bauen" lässt, ist es nicht weiter verwertbar, womit es Macht und Bedeutung verliert, beziehungsweise in die ästhetische Zone verlagert. Dort erhält es symbolischen Wert, der aber instabil bleibt.

In deinen Arbeiten geht es um Bedingungen, Möglichkeiten und Paradoxien von Herstellung heute, sie interessieren sich für bestimmte Prozesse und ihr Funktionieren, gleichzeitig forcierst du den skulpturalen und formalen Aspekt des Objektes, das sich dann im Ausstellungsraum als minimale Skulptur präsentiert. Die Verbindung von reduzierter Formensprache, das Interesse für Kontext, Geschichte und Politik und der Einsatz erzählerischer Mittel werden heute nicht mehr als gegensätzlich empfunden. Das verbindet deine Werke mit den Arbeiten und dem Vorgehen von Künstlern deiner Generation. Aber nochmals, warum sollen solche Fragen, wie du sie untersuchst, über die Kunst angegangen werden?

AZ Ich denke an eine kunstgeschichtliche Konstante, dass in der Kunst die herrschenden Machtverhältnisse reproduziert, dass letztlich die Mächtigen porträtiert werden. Im 20. Jahrhundert ergibt sich dazu ein scheinbarer Widerspruch, der Autor wird im Verhältnis zum Auftraggeber immer deutlicher sichtbar. Er hat offenbar mehr Möglichkeiten, sich seine Themen auszusuchen. Darin sehe ich aber keine Abkehr vom beschriebenen Prinzip, es bedeutet lediglich eine Verschiebung hin zu einem Subjekt, welches nun einen Anteil an Mitbestimmung hat. Dieser Anteil ist jedoch so klein, dass seine Entscheidungen erst durch die Organisation in einer Masse von Gleichgesinnten ihre Wirkungen entwickeln. Mich interessiert nun die Frage, was diese Massen entstehen lässt.

DB Was ist deine Vermutung?

AZ Ein Teil der Antwort hat wahrscheinlich mit dem Aufenthaltsort zu tun an dem unser Gespräch stattfindet.

DB Deine Arbeiten sind als Porträts von Machtverhältnissen zu lesen, wie beispielsweise Standardisierungen Macht hervorbringen, nur dass dies getarnt verläuft und nicht im gleichen Maß sichtbar wird, wie früher beispielsweise durch Landbesitz. Deine Arbeiten orientieren sich am Modell des Historienbildes und streben die gleiche formale Vollendung an, wie ein Maler, der die Mächtigen möglichst vollendet repräsentieren wollte. Könnte

you push the sculptural and formal aspects of the object which then presents itself as a minimal sculpture in the exhibition space. The connection between a reduced formal language, the interest in context, history and politics and the use of narrative means is no longer conceived as contradictory today. This connects your works with the approach other artists from your generation take. But once again, why shall such questions as the ones you investigate in be approached by art?

AZ I think of an art historical constant: that art reproduces ruling power structures, that art in the end portraits the ones who are in power. During the 20th century, a seeming contradiction occured: The author gradually became more visible in relation to the client. He obviously had more possibilities to choose his subjects. However, I don't see any renunciation of the described principle in this; it rather points to a displacement towards the subject who now gained a certain portion of codetermination. This portion, however, is so small that the decisions taken by the subject can only display their effect by their organisation in a mass of like-minded people. I am interested in the question what it is that allows for these masses to evolve.

DB What do you assume?

AZ: Part of the answer probably has something to do with the location of this discussion.

DB So your works should be read as portraits of power relations, of the way—to give an example—how standardizations generate power, only that this happens in a camouflaged way which will never allow for the same visibility as landed property used to do. Your works are orientated along the model of the historical painting and aspire to the same degree of formal completion. Just like a painter who tried to represent the ones in power with complete perfection. If one wants to make the point, would it make sense to say that you set up monuments that are analogue to statues of figures of power?

AZ In some way. In the case of the monument; however, the mediation mostly happens in relation to gravitational laws. My position could therefore be compared to the state of zero gravity...

My focus lies in the search for images or objects in which balances of power are displayed as forms. In the project "90 minutes", I merged the maximum useable size of interior spaces of the fifteen biggest cargo systems for space transportation and created one single object out of them. This allowed a comparison between the capacities of the differ-

man zugespitzt sagen, dass du analog zu einer Herrscherstatue Denkmäler aufstellst?

AZ In gewisser Weise. Bei einem Denkmal verläuft die Vermittlung jedoch meist entsprechend den Gesetzen der Schwerkraft. Meine Position wäre daher mit einem Zustand der Schwerelosigkeit vergleichbar...
Mein Fokus basiert auf der Suche nach Bildern oder Objekten, in denen sich Kräfteverhältnisse als Formen abbilden. Im Projekt „90 Minuten" führte ich die maximal nutzbaren Innenräume der fünfzehn größten Frachtsysteme für den Transport von Material ins Weltall zu einem Objekt zusammen. Dadurch wird ein Vergleich der Kapazität der verschiedenen Firmen möglich. Ein identisches Problem, das Transportieren von Fracht, führt zu unterschiedlichen formalen Lösungen.

DB Du untersuchst Machtverhältnisse und gibst ihnen präzise Form. Deine Arbeiten lassen sich als Porträts verstehen, die auf lakonische Art und Weise wichtige Tatsachen erkenntlich machen. Ist das ein Alleingang oder siehst du dich als Teil einer Gruppe? Hast du den Eindruck, Teil eines breiteren zeitgenössischen Diskurses zu sein?

AZ Momentan arbeite ich an einem Projekt, das sich um eine Person dreht, die unter einer Stadt ein Stollensystem angelegt hat. Das darin gesammelte Regenwasser diente der Erzeugung von Energie durch Wasserkraft. Die dadurch gewonnene Energie wurde zur Produktion von Stoffen genutzt. Die unterirdischen Bauarbeiten fanden ohne Kenntnis der Allgemeinheit statt. Bis heute sind die exakten Dimensionen des Bauwerks unbekannt. Ich versuche nun, das Prinzip, mit einem Tunnel Wasser zu sammeln, auf den Kopf zu stellen und mit den Besuchern zusammen eine Art Regen zu produzieren.

ent firms. An identical problem leads to different formal solutions.

DB You examine power structures and give them a precise shape. Your works can be understood as portraits that render important facts perceptible in a laconic way. Does this happen single-handedly or do you see yourself as part of a group? Do you have the impression that you are a part of a broad contemporary discourse?

AZ At the moment, I am working on a project that is about a person who has built a gallery underneath a city. The rain water that was collected in there was used to generate energy through waterpower. This energy was in turn used to produce textiles. All the necessary construction work was carried out without the public's knowledge. Until today, the exact dimensions are unknown. I am now trying to turn the principle of producing water with the help of a tunnel upside-down and to produce a kind of rain together with the visitors.

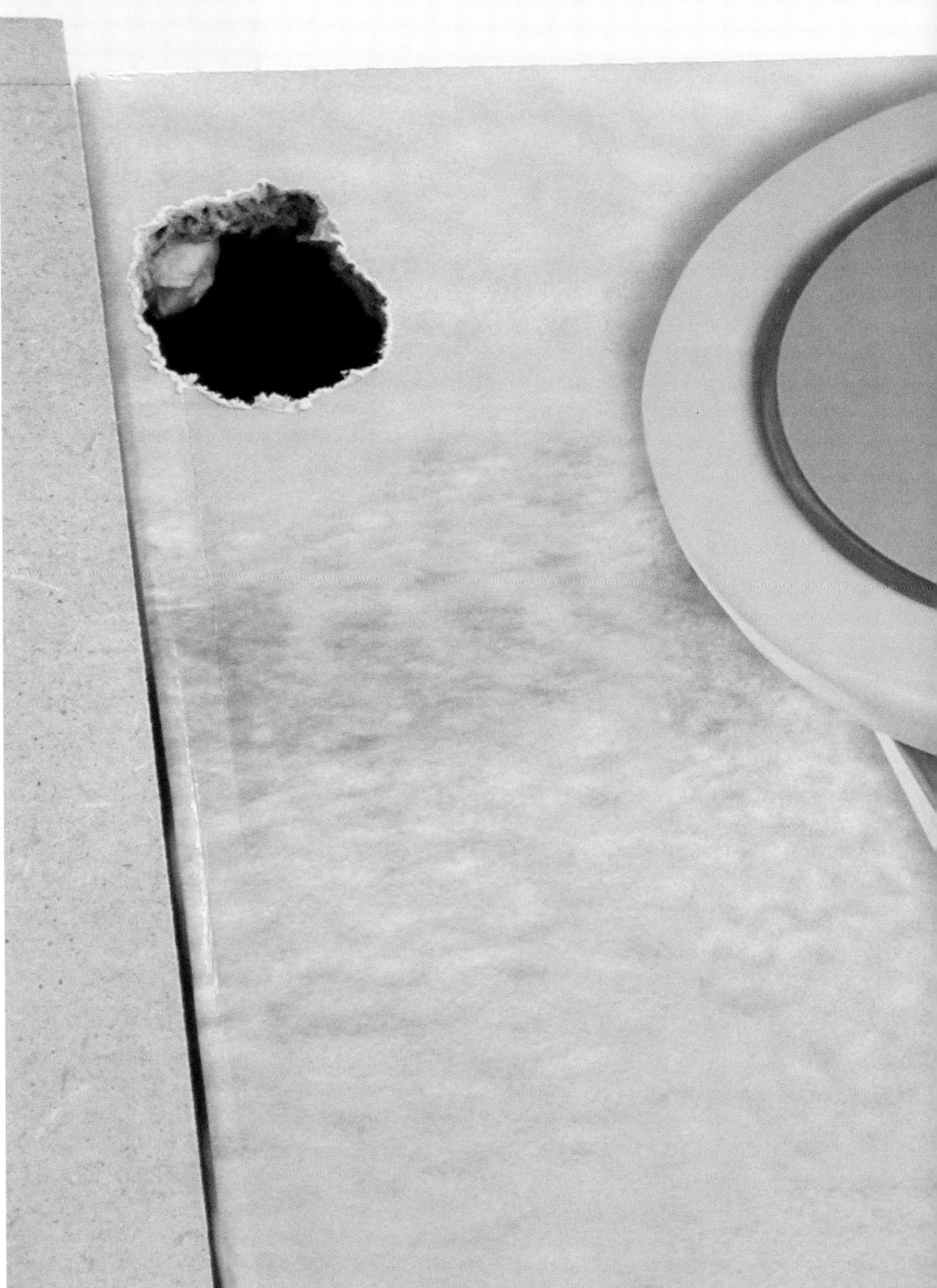

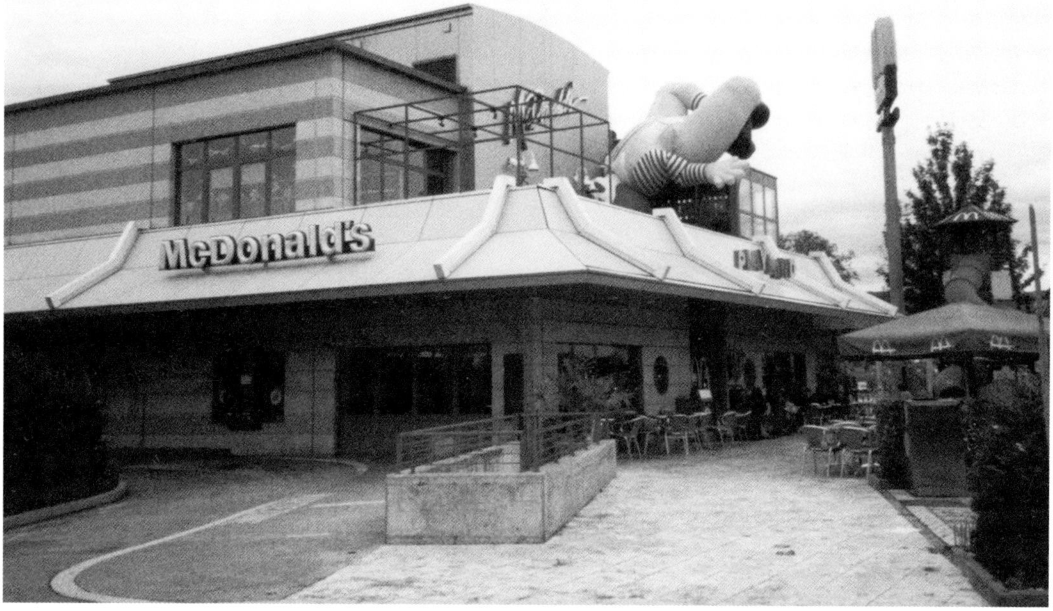

McDonald's

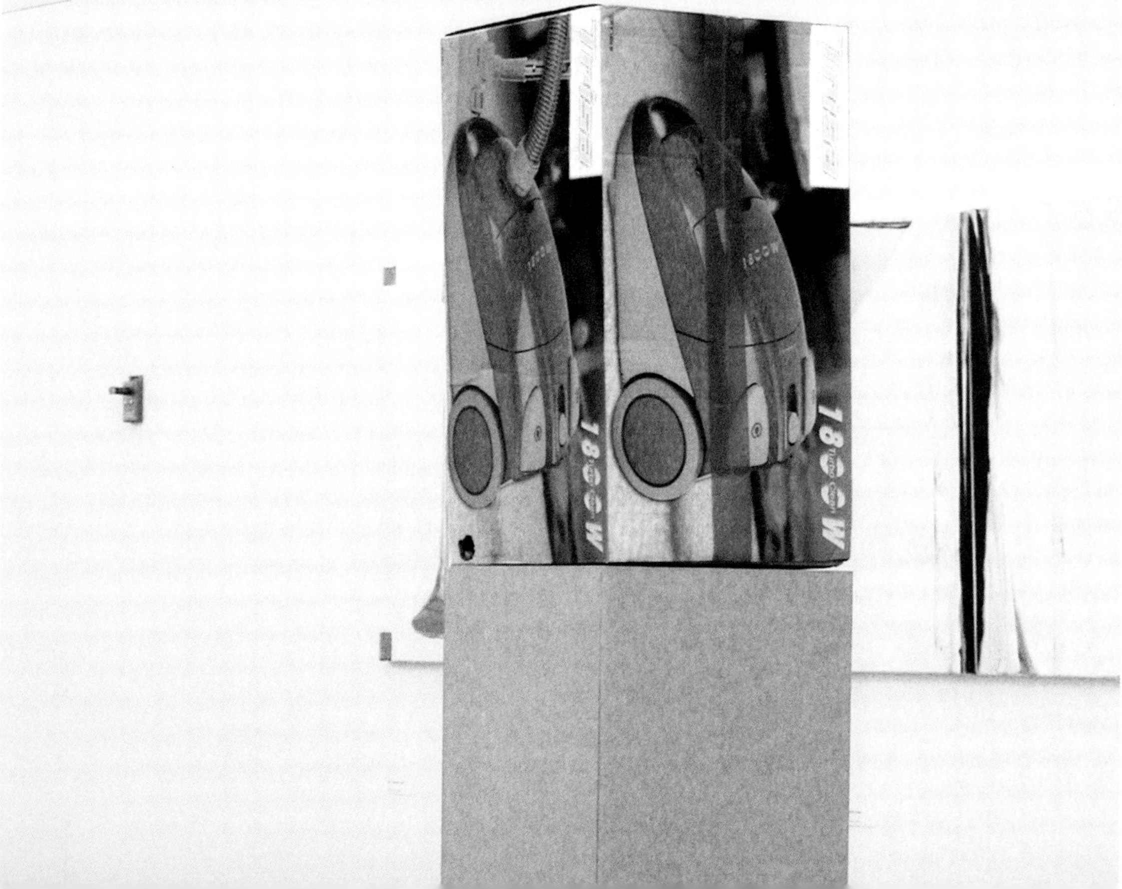

1800W
1800W
18 W

Test

Geschwindig
keit

60 Upm

=

6,6

210"

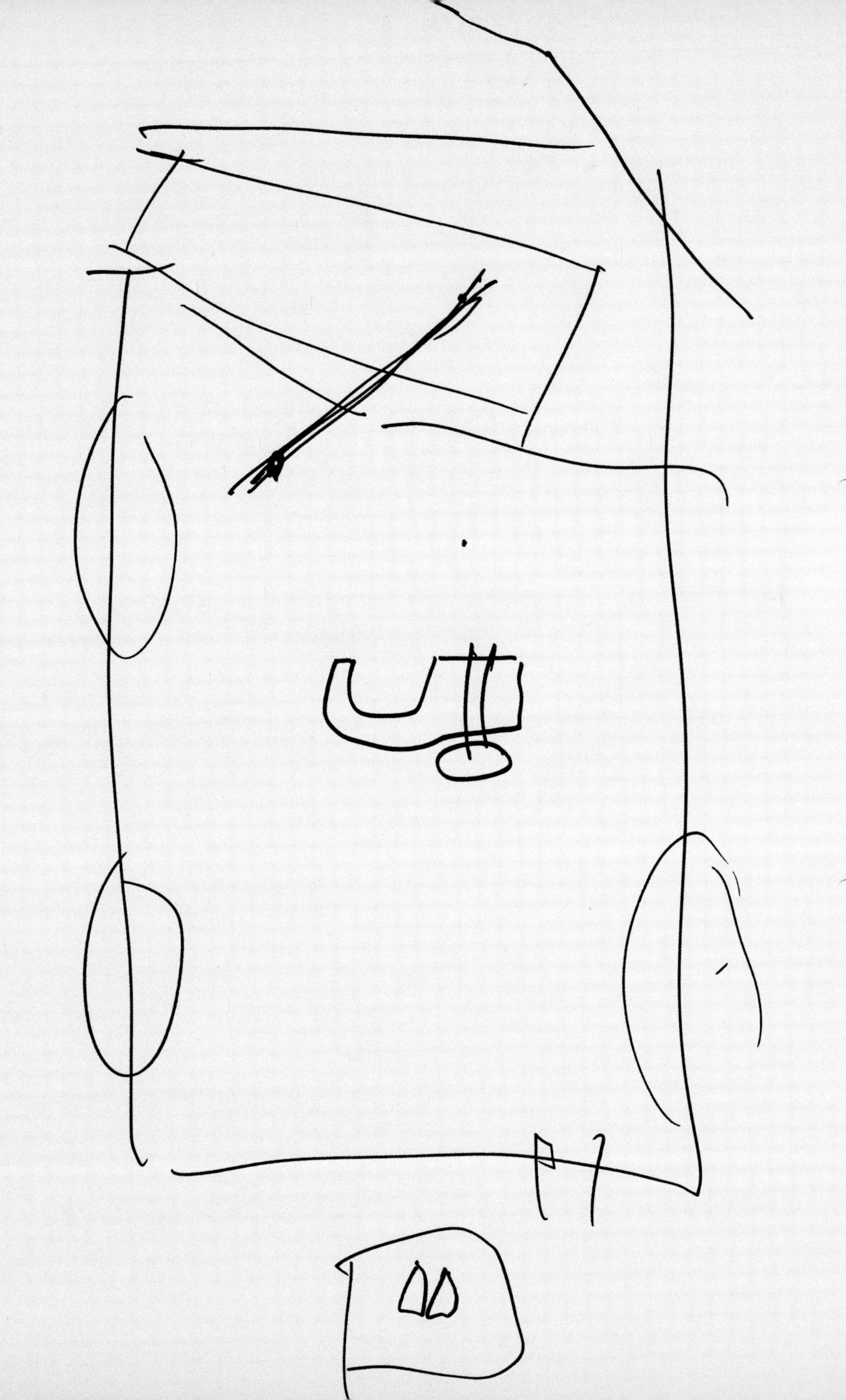

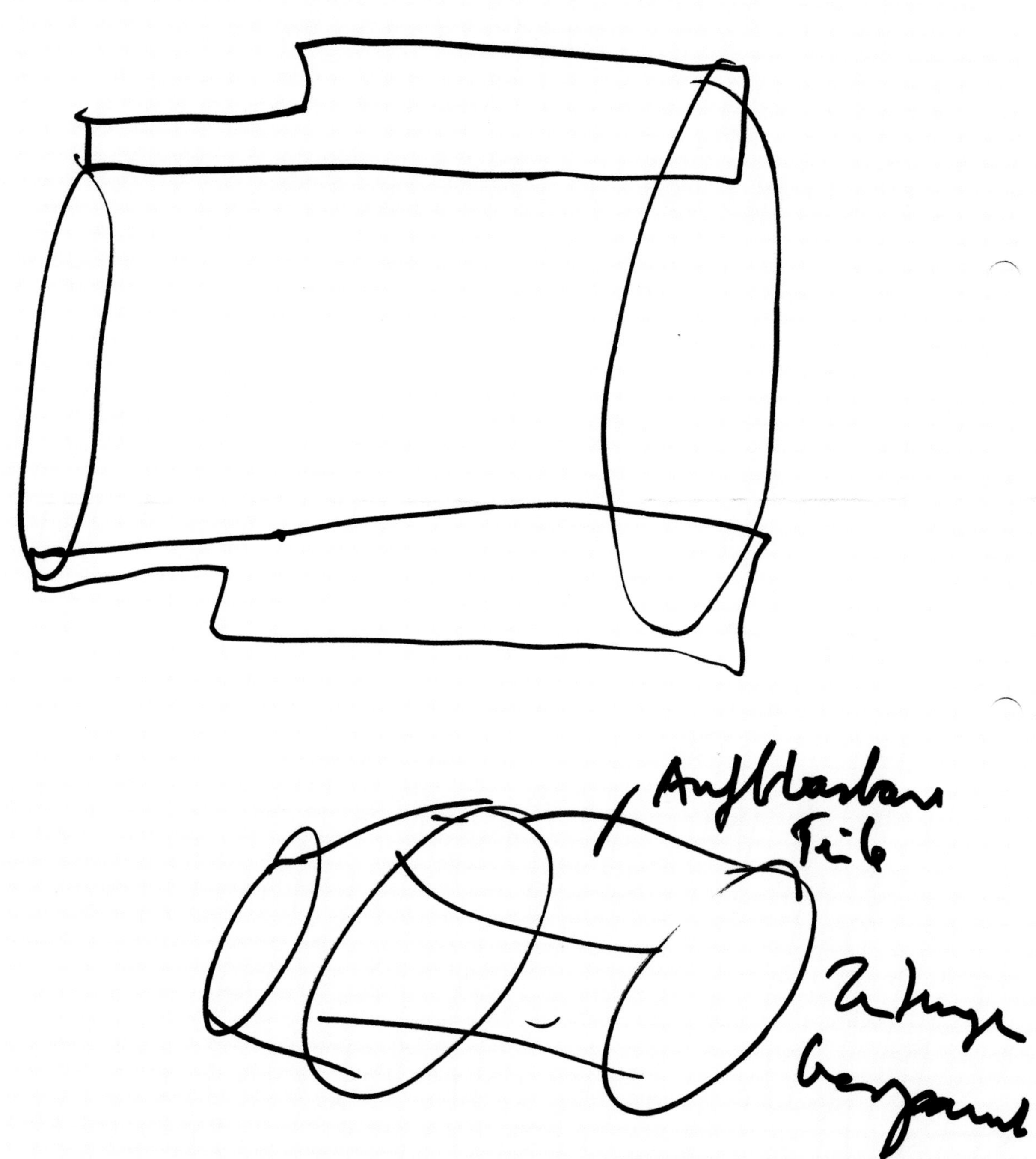

Aufblasbare
Füße
Übergang
Bewegung

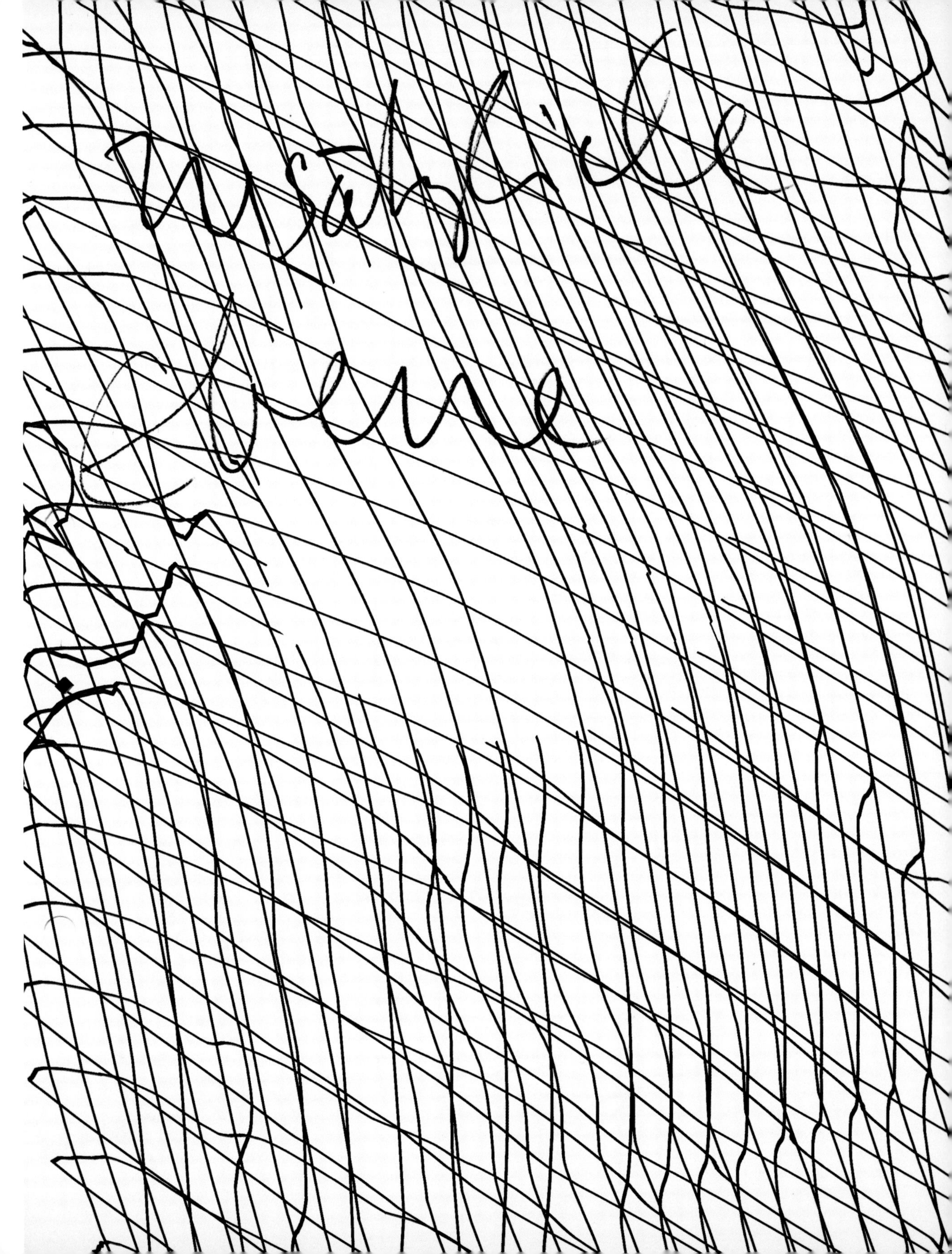

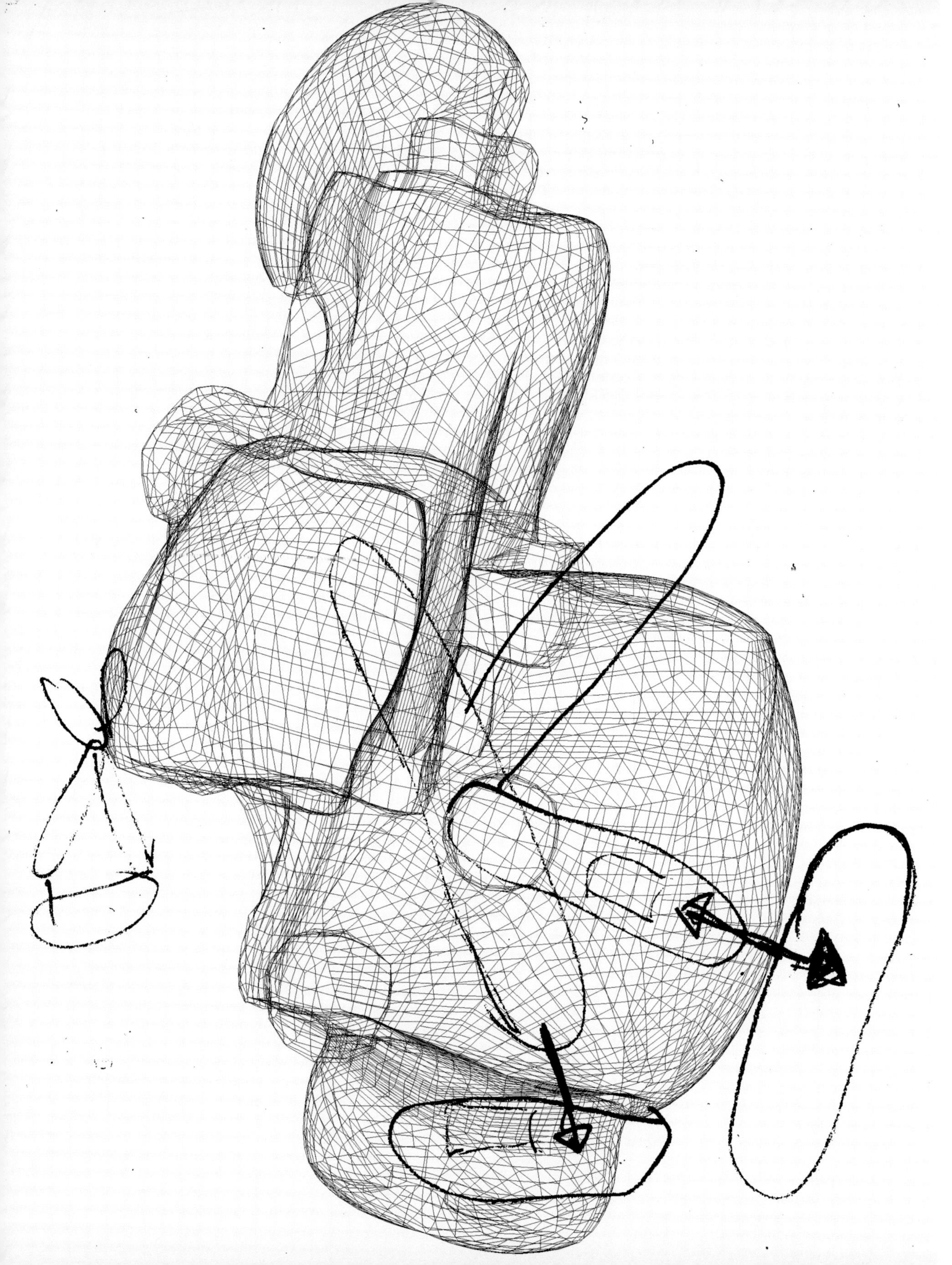

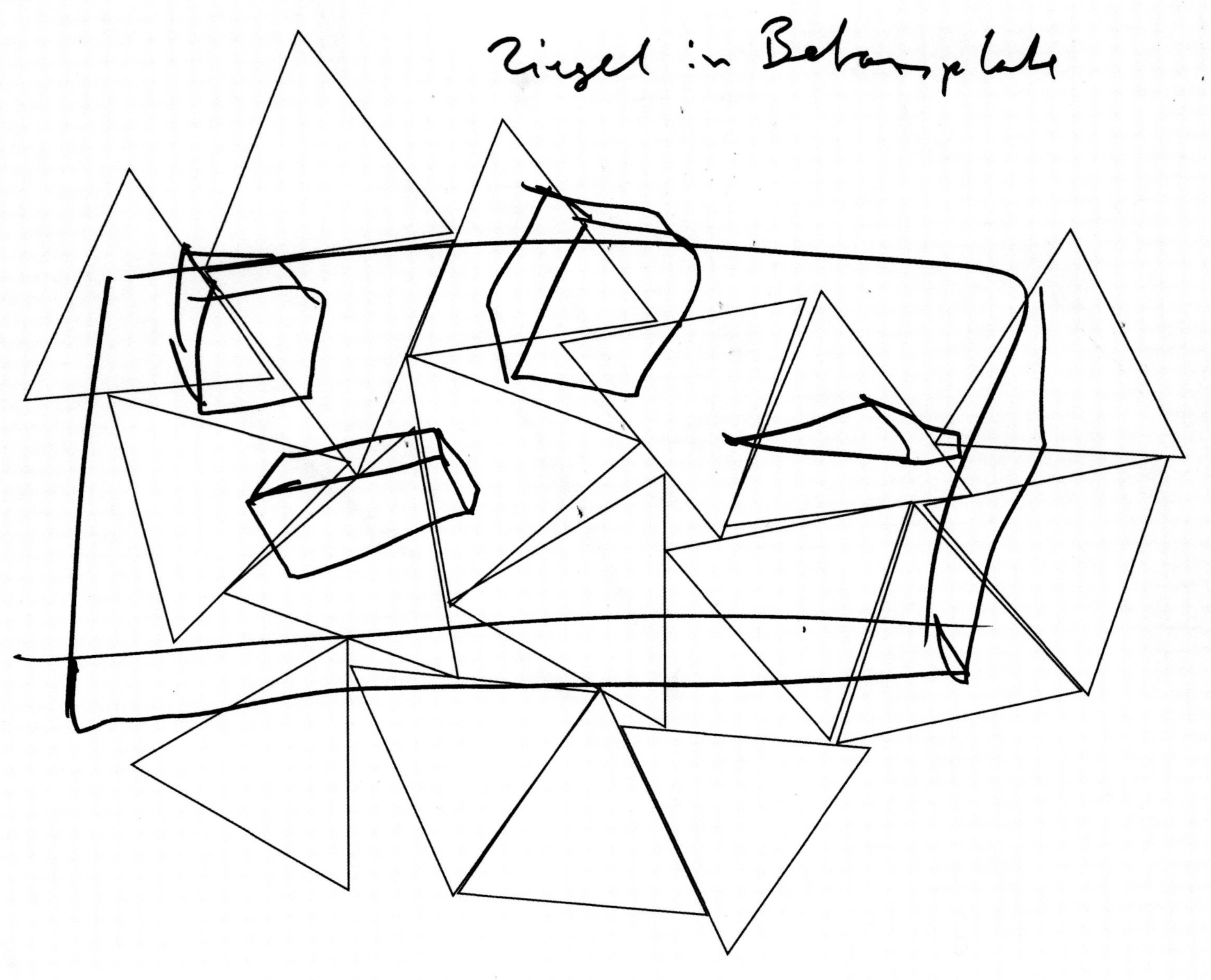

Ziegel in Betonplatte

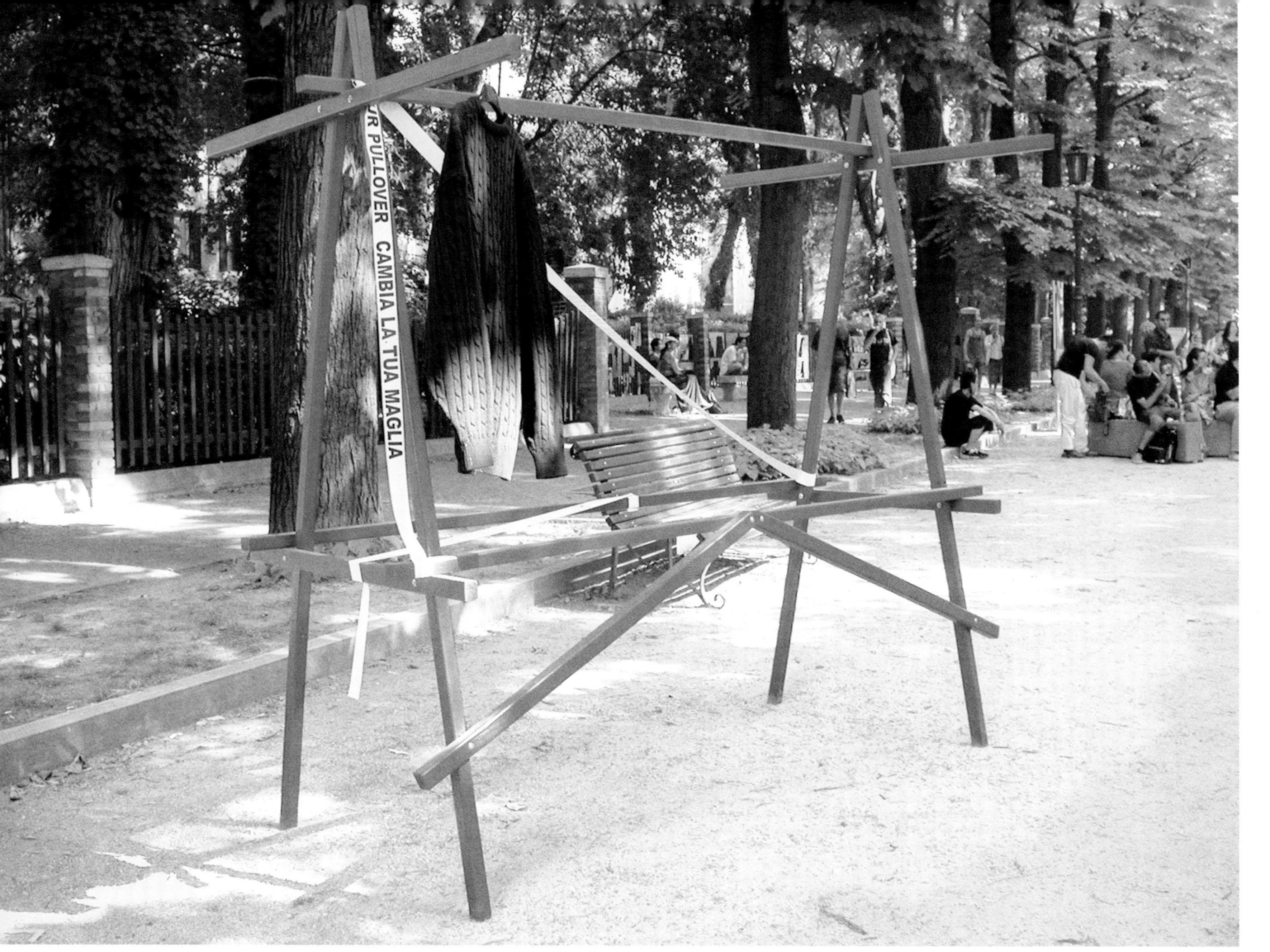
R PULLOVER CAMBIA LA TUA MAGLIA

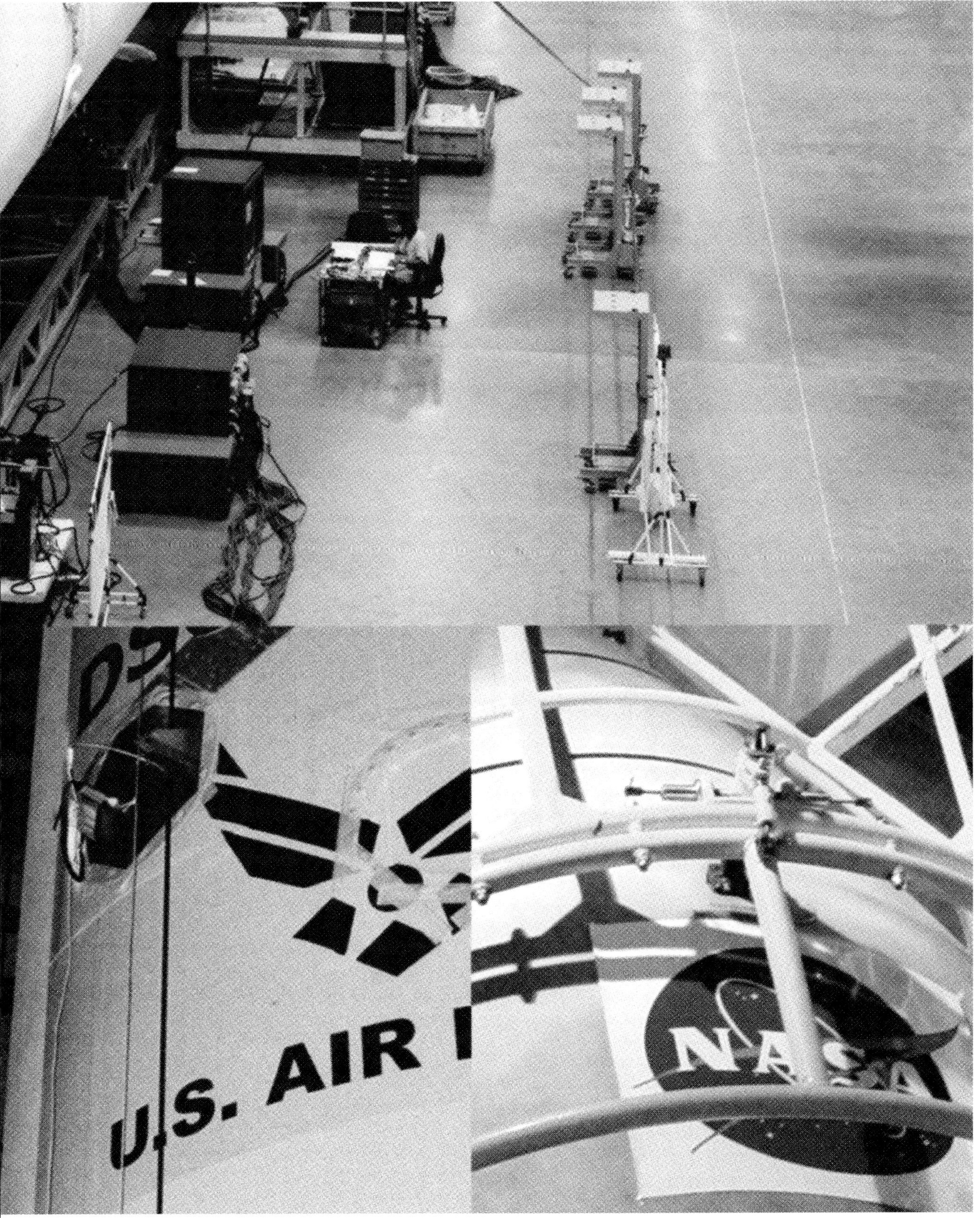
U.S. AIR
NASA

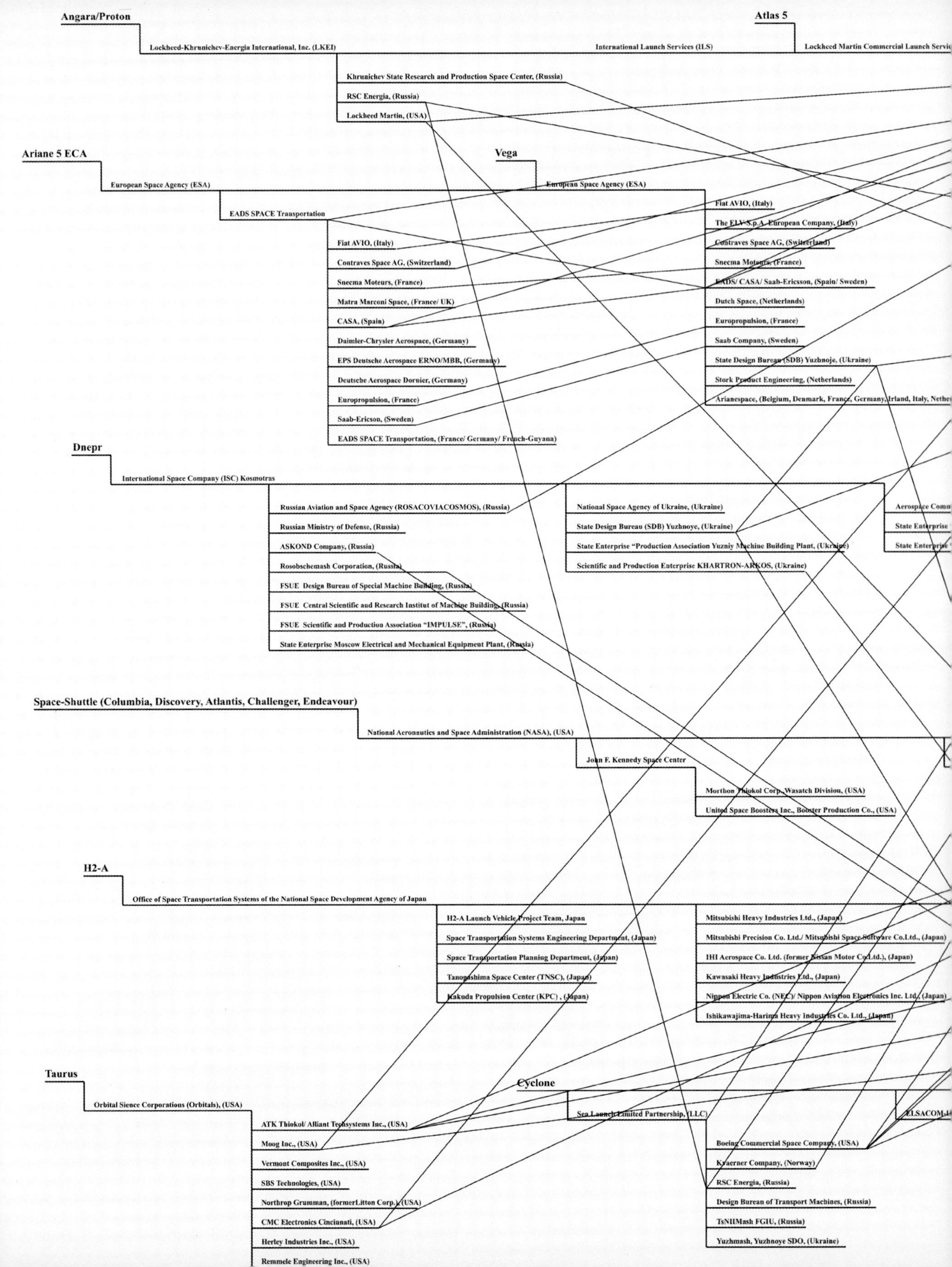

Angara/Proton
Lockheed-Khrunichev-Energia International, Inc. (LKEI)
Khrunichev State Research and Production Space Center, (Russia)
RSC Energia, (Russia)
Lockheed Martin, (USA)

Atlas 5
International Launch Services (ILS)
Lockheed Martin Commercial Launch Services

Ariane 5 ECA
European Space Agency (ESA)
EADS SPACE Transportation
Fiat AVIO, (Italy)
Contraves Space AG, (Switzerland)
Snecma Moteurs, (France)
Matra Marconi Space, (France/ UK)
CASA, (Spain)
Daimler-Chrysler Aerospace, (Germany)
EPS Deutsche Aerospace ERNO/MBB, (Germany)
Deutsche Aerospace Dornier, (Germany)
Europropulsion, (France)
Saab-Ericson, (Sweden)
EADS SPACE Transportation, (France/ Germany/ French-Guyana)

Vega
European Space Agency (ESA)
Fiat AVIO, (Italy)
The ELV S.p.A. European Company, (Italy)
Contraves Space AG, (Switzerland)
Snecma Moteurs, (France)
EADS/ CASA/ Saab-Ericsson, (Spain/ Sweden)
Dutch Space, (Netherlands)
Europropulsion, (France)
Saab Company, (Sweden)
State Design Bureau (SDB) Yuzhnoje, (Ukraine)
Stork Product Engineering, (Netherlands)
Arianespace, (Belgium, Denmark, France, Germany, Irland, Italy, Nether...

Dnepr
International Space Company (ISC) Kosmotras
Russian Aviation and Space Agency (ROSACOVIACOSMOS), (Russia)
Russian Ministry of Defense, (Russia)
ASKOND Company, (Russia)
Rosobschemash Corporation, (Russia)
FSUE Design Bureau of Special Machine Building, (Russia)
FSUE Central Scientific and Research Institut of Machine Building, (Russia)
FSUE Scientific and Production Association "IMPULSE", (Russia)
State Enterprise Moscow Electrical and Mechanical Equipment Plant, (Russia)
National Space Agency of Ukraine, (Ukraine)
State Design Bureau (SDB) Yuzhnoye, (Ukraine)
State Enterprise "Production Association Yuzniy Machine Building Plant, (Ukraine)
Scientific and Production Enterprise KHARTRON-ARKOS, (Ukraine)

Aerospace Comm...
State Enterprise
State Enterprise

Space-Shuttle (Columbia, Discovery, Atlantis, Challenger, Endeavour)
National Aeronautics and Space Administration (NASA), (USA)
John F. Kennedy Space Center
Morthon Thiokol Corp., Wasatch Division, (USA)
United Space Boosters Inc., Booster Production Co., (USA)

H2-A
Office of Space Transportation Systems of the National Space Development Agency of Japan
H2-A Launch Vehicle Project Team, Japan
Space Transportation Systems Engineering Department, (Japan)
Space Transportation Planning Department, (Japan)
Tanegashima Space Center (TNSC), (Japan)
Kakuda Propulsion Center (KPC) , (Japan)
Mitsubishi Heavy Industries Ltd., (Japan)
Mitsubishi Precision Co. Ltd./ Mitsubishi Space Software Co.Ltd., (Japan)
IHI Aerospace Co. Ltd. (former Nissan Motor Co.Ltd.), (Japan)
Kawasaki Heavy Industries Ltd., (Japan)
Nippon Electric Co. (NEC)/ Nippon Aviation Electronics Inc. Ltd., (Japan)
Ishikawajima-Harima Heavy Industries Co. Ltd., (Japan)

Taurus
Orbital Sience Corporations (Orbitals), (USA)
ATK Thiokol/ Alliant Techsystems Inc., (USA)
Moog Inc., (USA)
Vermont Composites Inc., (USA)
SBS Technologies, (USA)
Northrop Grumman, (formerLitton Corp.) (USA)
CMC Electronics Cincinnati, (USA)
Herley Industries Inc., (USA)
Remmele Engineering Inc., (USA)

Cyclone
Sea Launch Limited Partnership, (LLC)
Boeing Commercial Space Company, (USA)
Kvaerner Company, (Norway)
RSC Energia, (Russia)
Design Bureau of Transport Machines, (Russia)
TsNIIMash FGIU, (Russia)
Yuzhmash, Yuzhnoye SDO, (Ukraine)

ELSACOM-I...

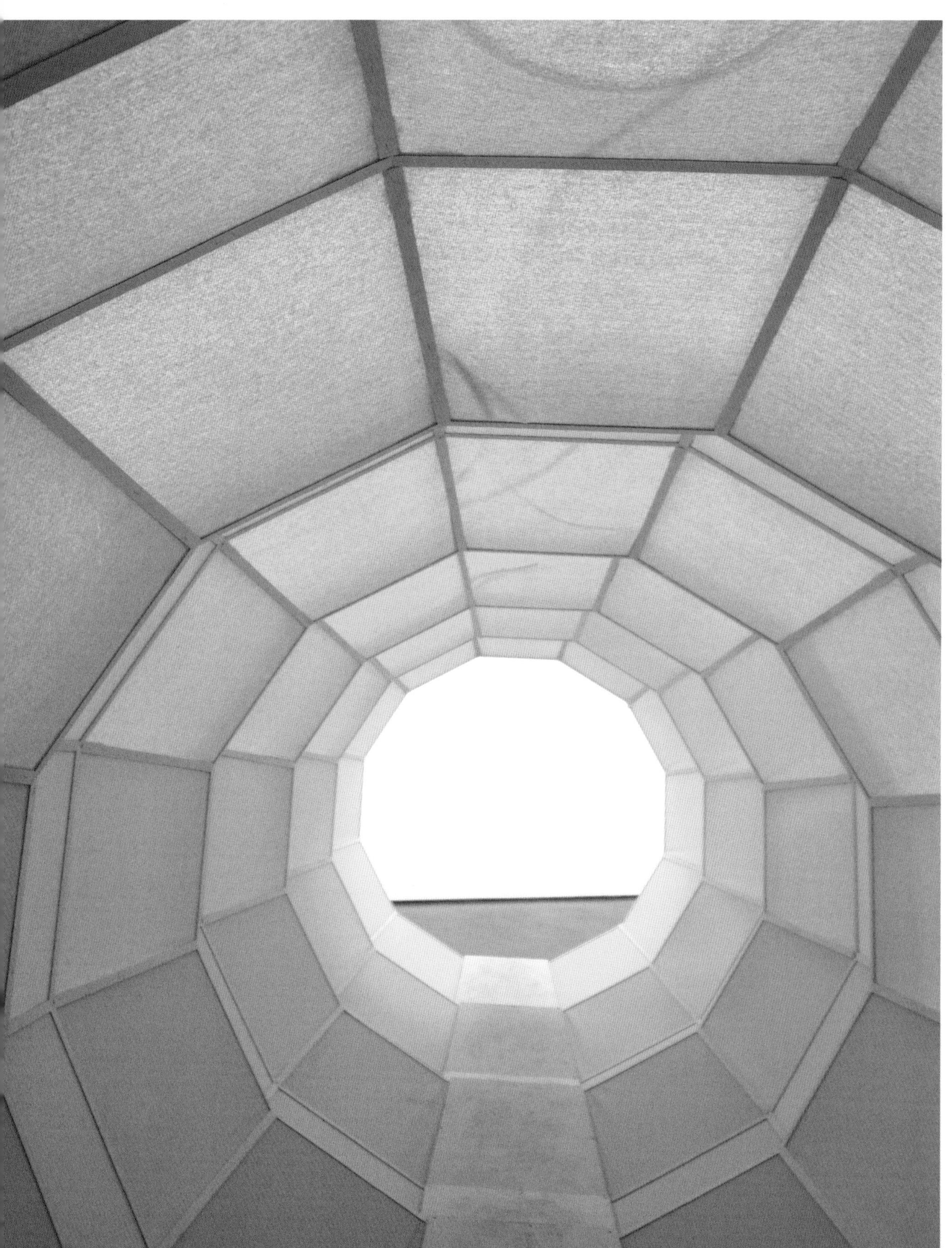

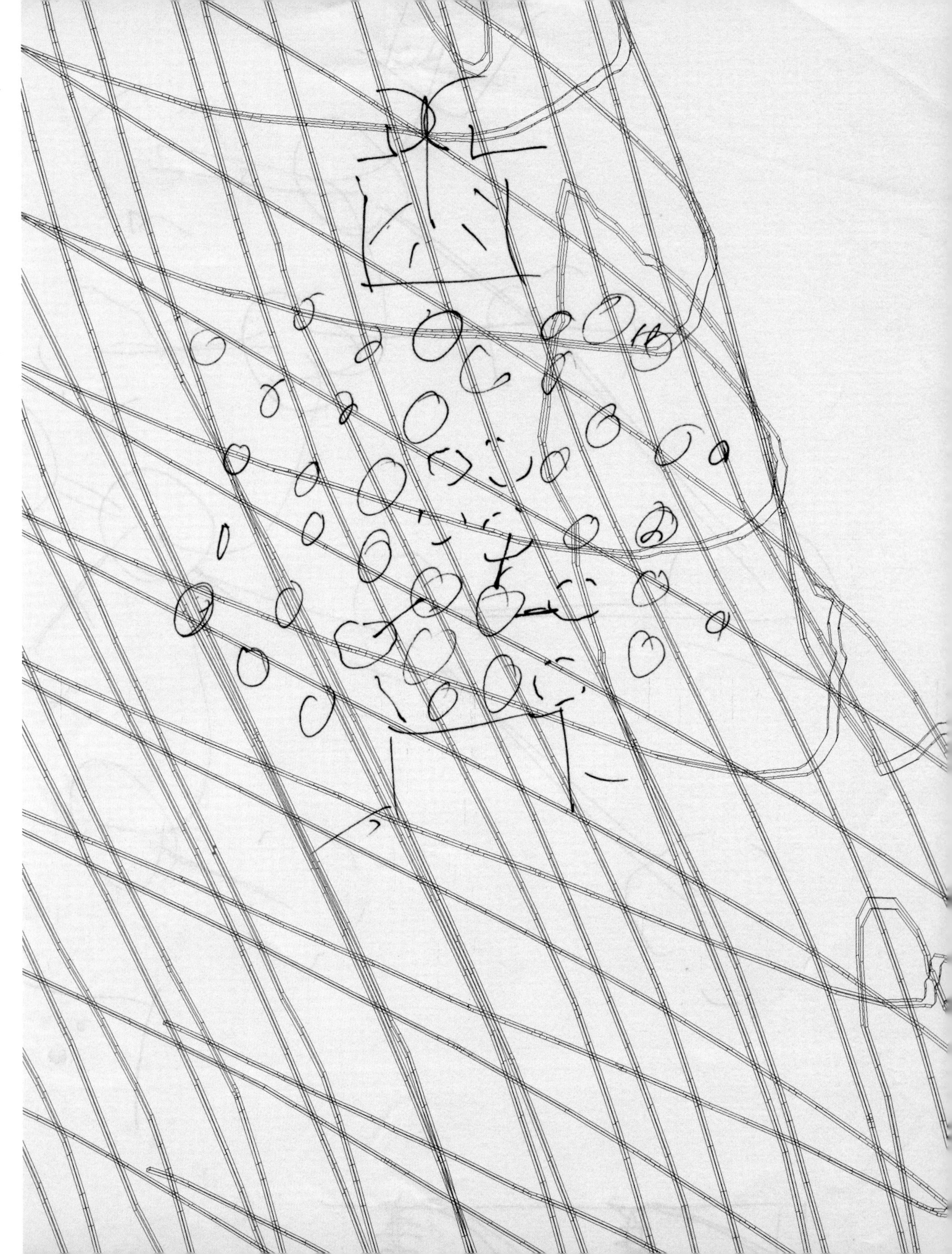

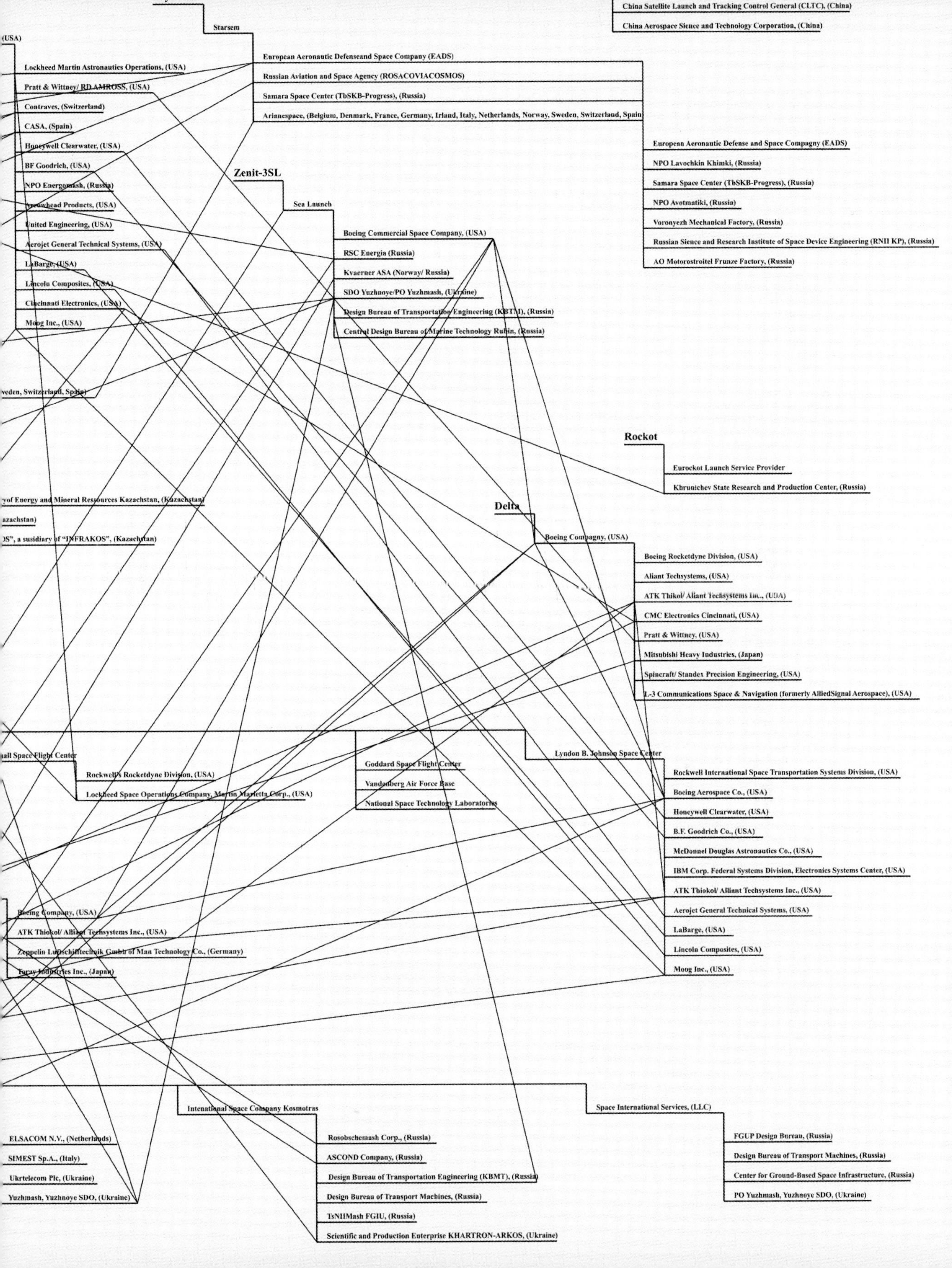
China Satellite Launch and Tracking Control General (CLTC), (China)
China Aerospace Sience and Technology Corporation, (China)
Starsem
European Aeronautic Defenseand Space Company (EADS)
Russian Aviation and Space Agency (ROSACOVIACOSMOS)
Samara Space Center (TbSKB-Progress), (Russia)
Arianespace, (Belgium, Denmark, France, Germany, Irland, Italy, Netherlands, Norway, Sweden, Switzerland, Spain
Lockheed Martin Astronautics Operations, (USA)
Pratt & Wittney/ RD AMROSS, (USA)
Contraves, (Switzerland)
CASA, (Spain)
Honeywell Clearwater, (USA)
BF Goodrich, (USA)
NPO Energomash, (Russia)
Arrowhead Products, (USA)
United Engineering, (USA)
Aerojet General Technical Systems, (USA)
LaBarge, (USA)
Lincoln Composites, (USA)
Cincinnati Electronics, (USA)
Moog Inc., (USA)
European Aeronautic Defense and Space Compagny (EADS)
NPO Lavochkin Khimki, (Russia)
Samara Space Center (TbSKB-Progress), (Russia)
NPO Avotmatiki, (Russia)
Voronyezh Mechanical Factory, (Russia)
Russian Sience and Research Institute of Space Device Engineering (RNII KP), (Russia)
AO Motorostroitel Frunze Factory, (Russia)
Zenit-3SL
Sea Launch
Boeing Commercial Space Company, (USA)
RSC Energia (Russia)
Kvaerner ASA (Norway/ Russia)
SDO Yuzhnoye/PO Yuzhmash, (Ukraine)
Design Bureau of Transportation Engineering (KBTM), (Russia)
Central Design Bureau of Marine Technology Rubin, (Russia)
Rockot
Eurockot Launch Service Provider
Khrunichev State Research and Production Center, (Russia)
Sweden, Switzerland, Spain)
yof Energy and Mineral Ressources Kazakhstan, (Kazakhstan)
azachstan)
OS", a susidiary of "INFRAKOS", (Kazachstan)
Delta
Boeing Compagny, (USA)
Boeing Rocketdyne Division, (USA)
Aliant Techsystems, (USA)
ATK Thiokol/ Aliant Techsystems Inc., (USA)
CMC Electronics Cincinnati, (USA)
Pratt & Wittney, (USA)
Mitsubishi Heavy Industries, (Japan)
Spincraft/ Standex Precision Engineering, (USA)
L-3 Communications Space & Navigation (formerly AlliedSignal Aerospace), (USA)
all Space Flight Center
Rockwell's Rocketdyne Division, (USA)
Lockheed Space Operations Company, Martin Marietta Corp., (USA)
Goddard Space Flight Center
Vandenberg Air Force Base
National Space Technology Laboratories
Lyndon B. Johnson Space Center
Rockwell International Space Transportation Systems Division, (USA)
Boeing Aerospace Co., (USA)
Honeywell Clearwater, (USA)
B.F. Goodrich Co., (USA)
McDonnel Douglas Astronautics Co., (USA)
IBM Corp. Federal Systems Division, Electronics Systems Center, (USA)
ATK Thiokol/ Alliant Techsystems Inc., (USA)
Aerojet General Technical Systems, (USA)
LaBarge, (USA)
Lincoln Composites, (USA)
Moog Inc., (USA)
Boeing Company, (USA)
ATK Thiokol/ Alliant Techsystems Inc., (USA)
Zeppelin Luftschifftechnik Gmbh of Man Technology Co., (Germany)
Toray Industries Inc., (Japan)
Intenational Space Company Kosmotras
Space International Services, (LLC)
ELSACOM N.V., (Netherlands)
SIMEST Sp.A., (Italy)
Ukrtelecom Plc, (Ukraine)
Yuzhmash, Yuzhnoye SDO, (Ukraine)
Rosobschemash Corp., (Russia)
ASCOND Company, (Russia)
Design Bureau of Transportation Engineering (KBMT), (Russia)
Design Bureau of Transport Machines, (Russia)
TsNIIMash FGIU, (Russia)
Scientific and Production Enterprise KHARTRON-ARKOS, (Ukraine)
FGUP Design Bureau, (Russia)
Design Bureau of Transport Machines, (Russia)
Center for Ground-Based Space Infrastructure, (Russia)
PO Yuzhmash, Yuzhnoye SDO, (Ukraine)

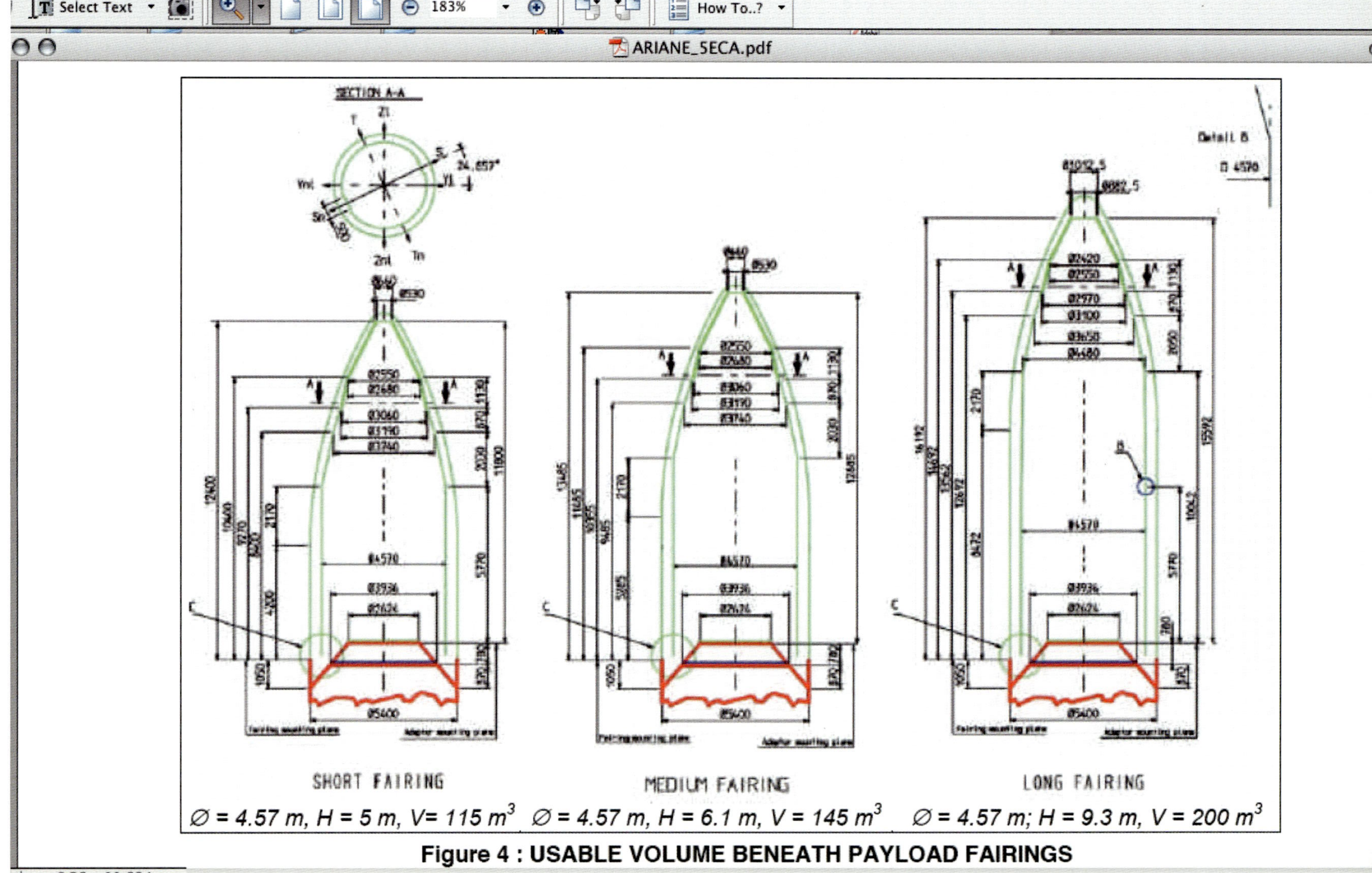

Ø = 4.57 m, H = 5 m, V= 115 m³   Ø = 4.57 m, H = 6.1 m, V = 145 m³   Ø = 4.57 m; H = 9.3 m, V = 200 m³

Figure 4 : USABLE VOLUME BENEATH PAYLOAD FAIRINGS

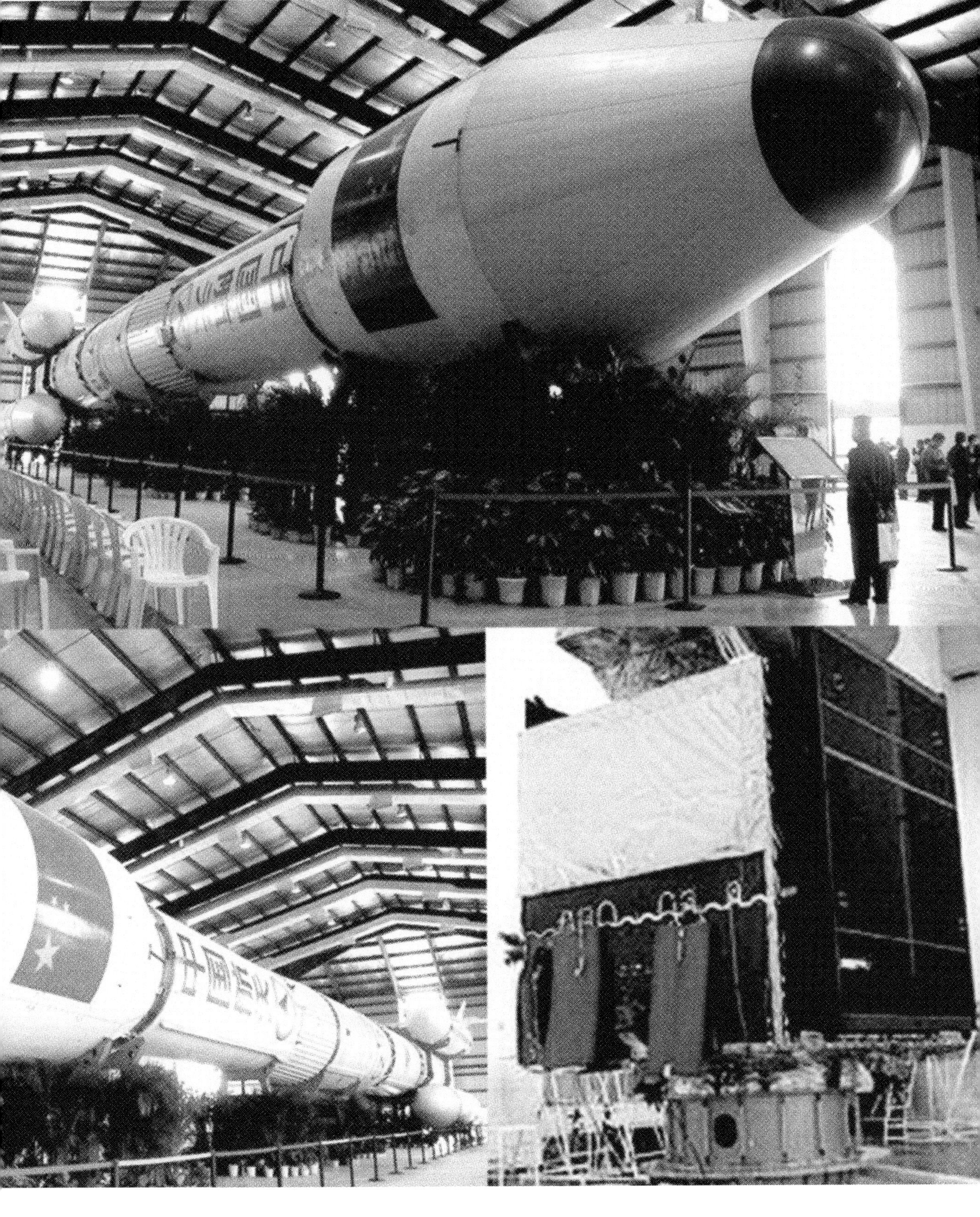

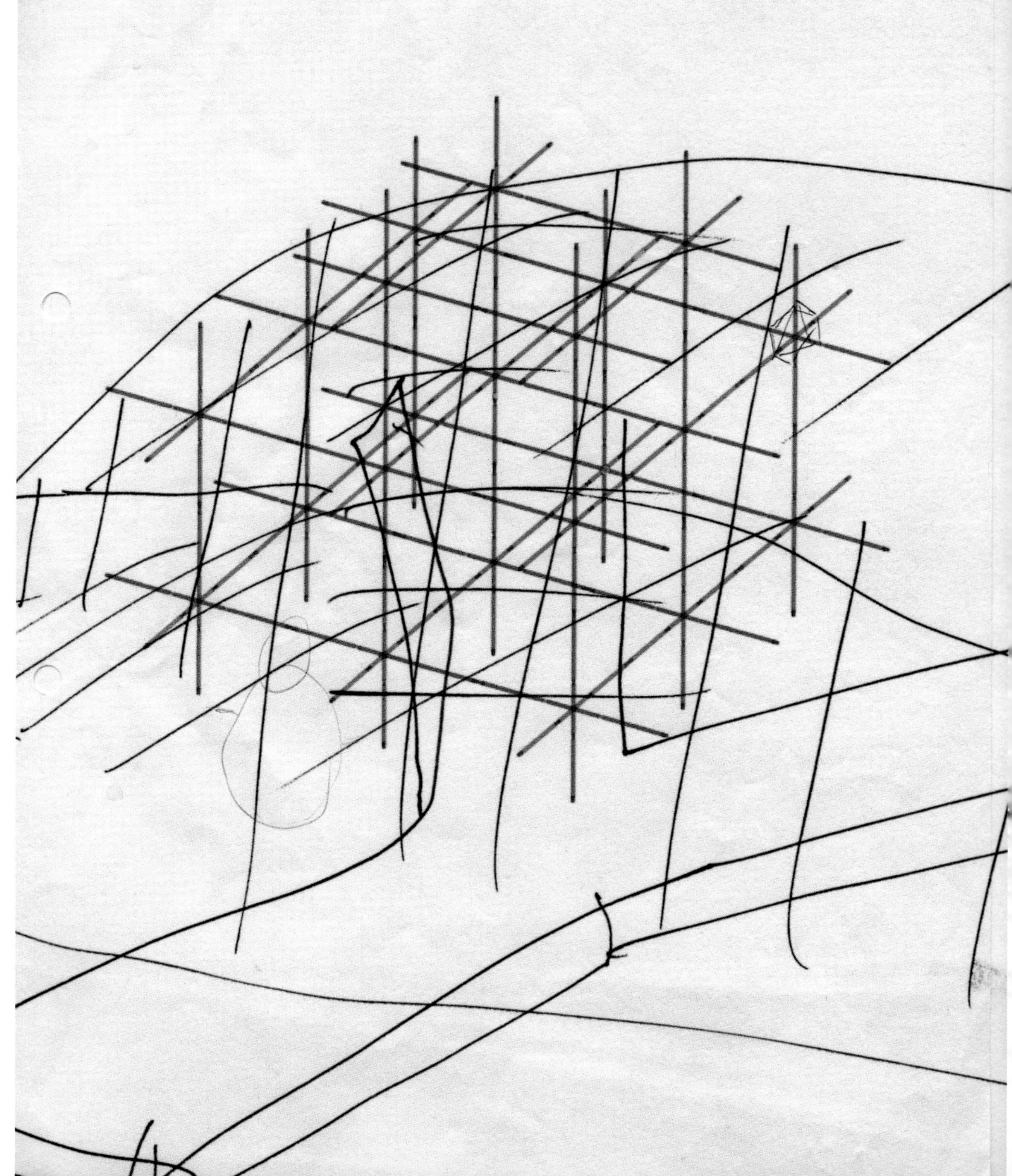

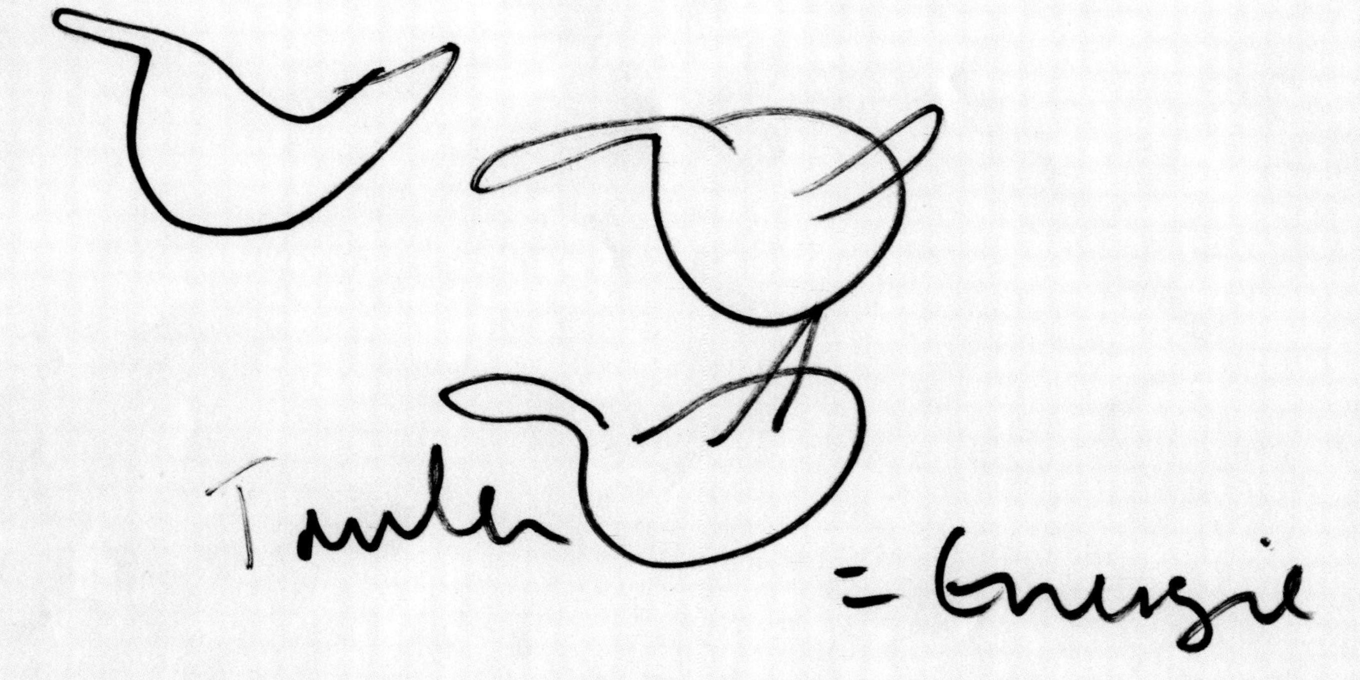
Taulen
= Energie

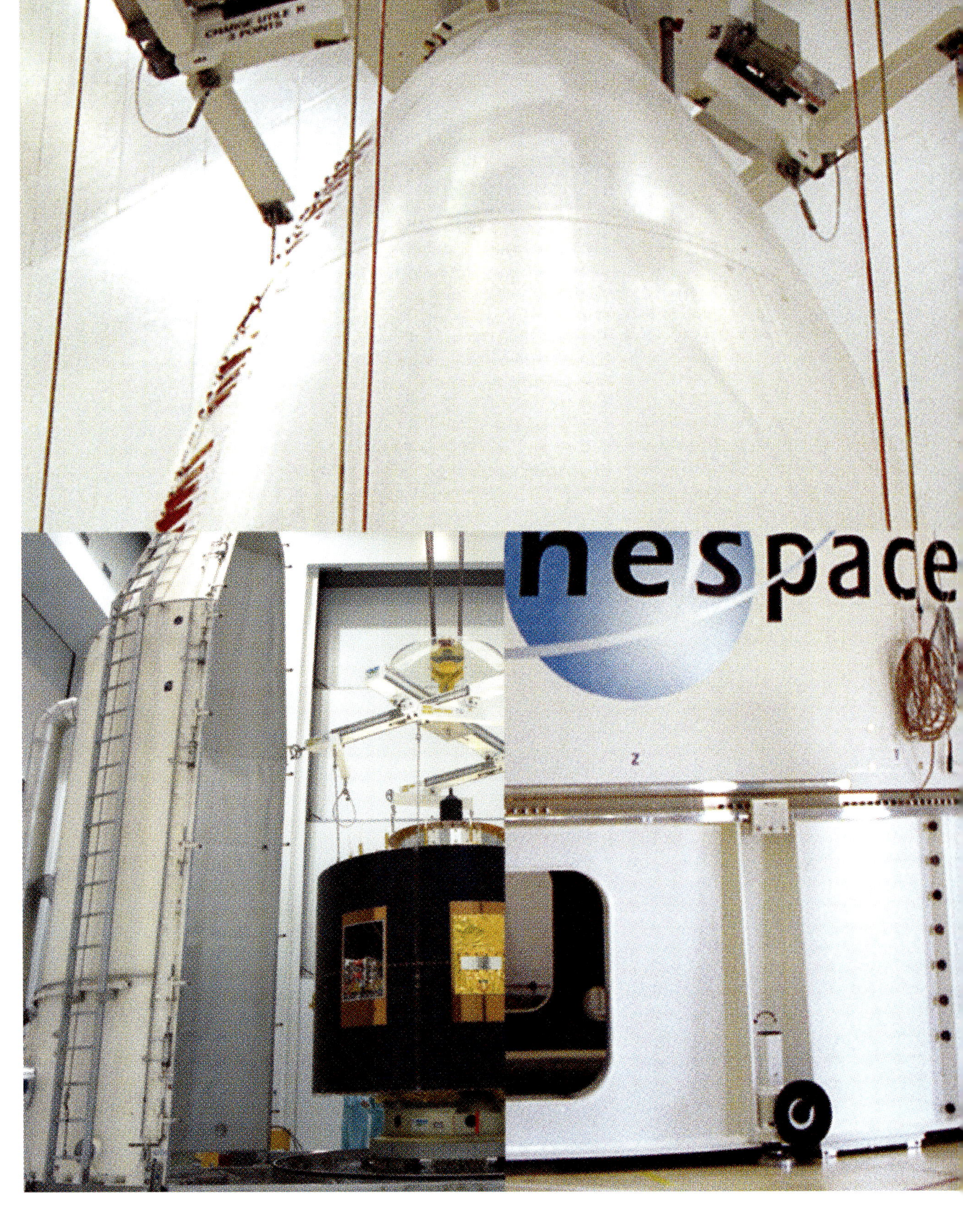
nespace

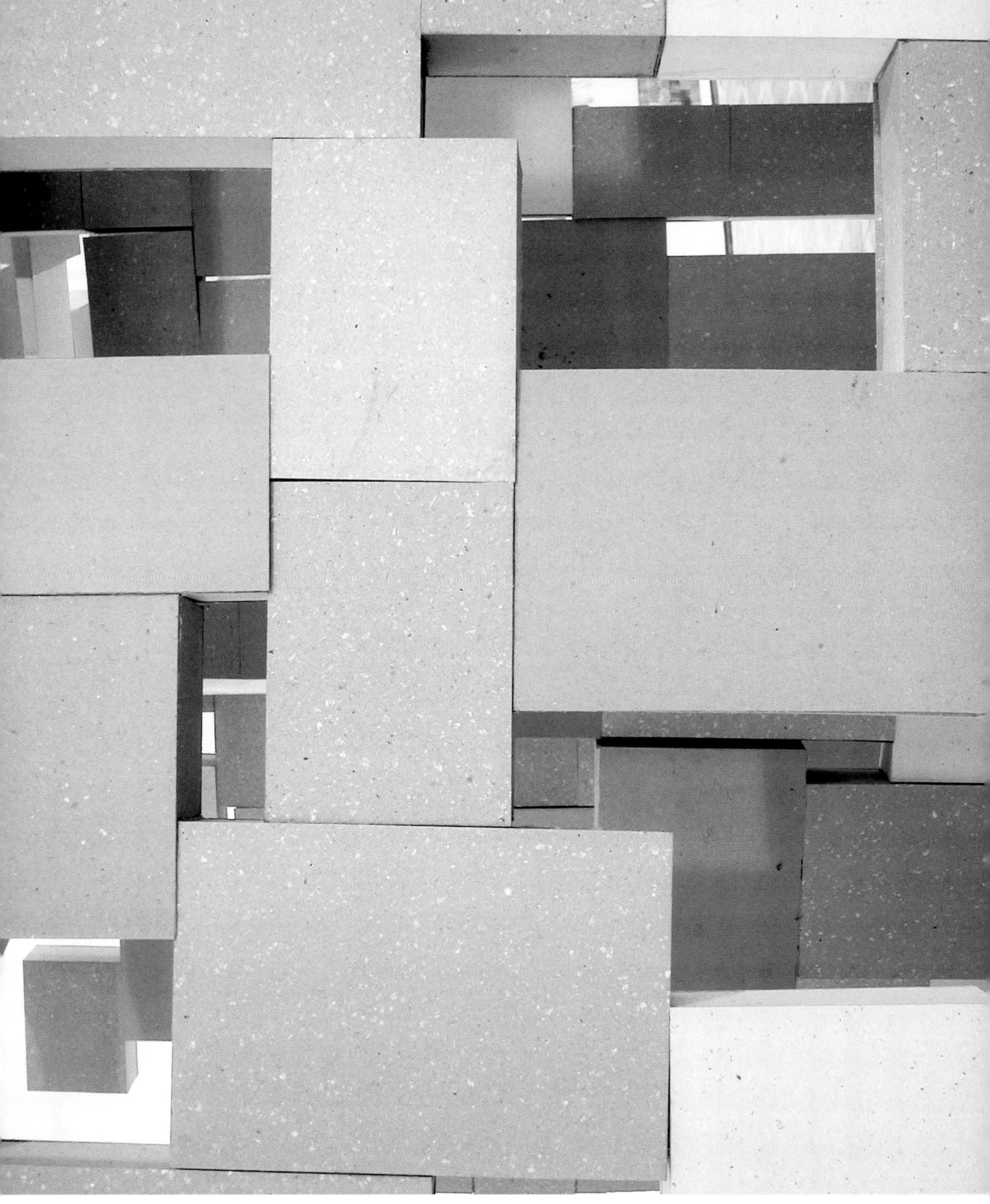

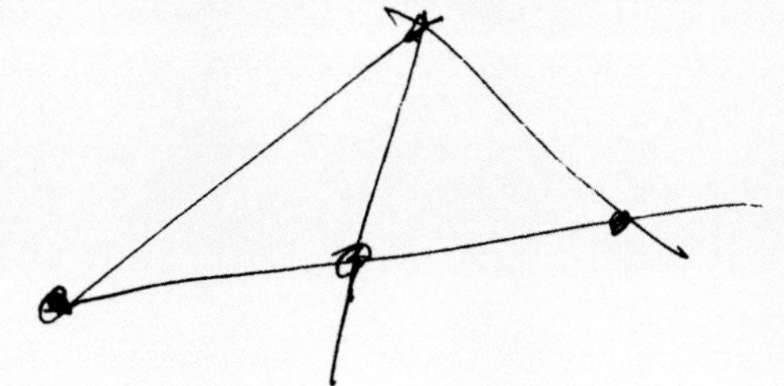

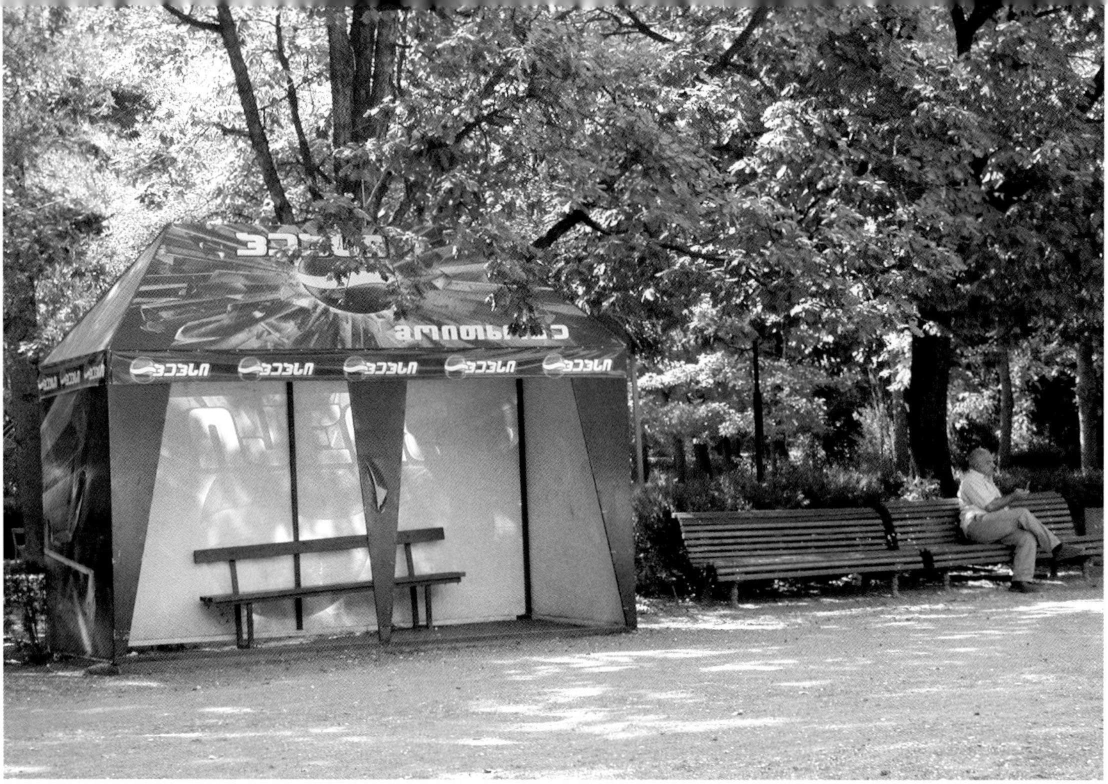

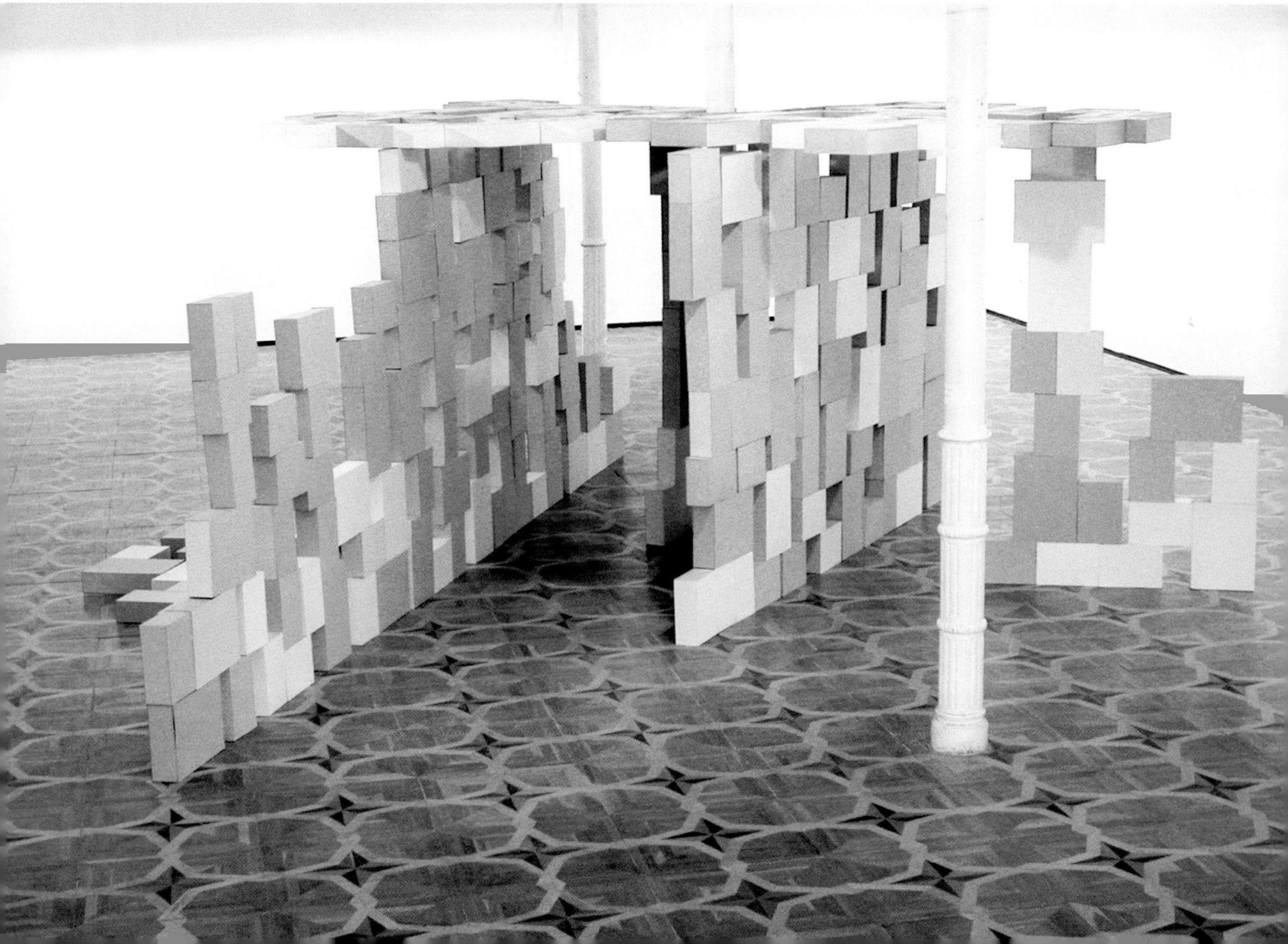

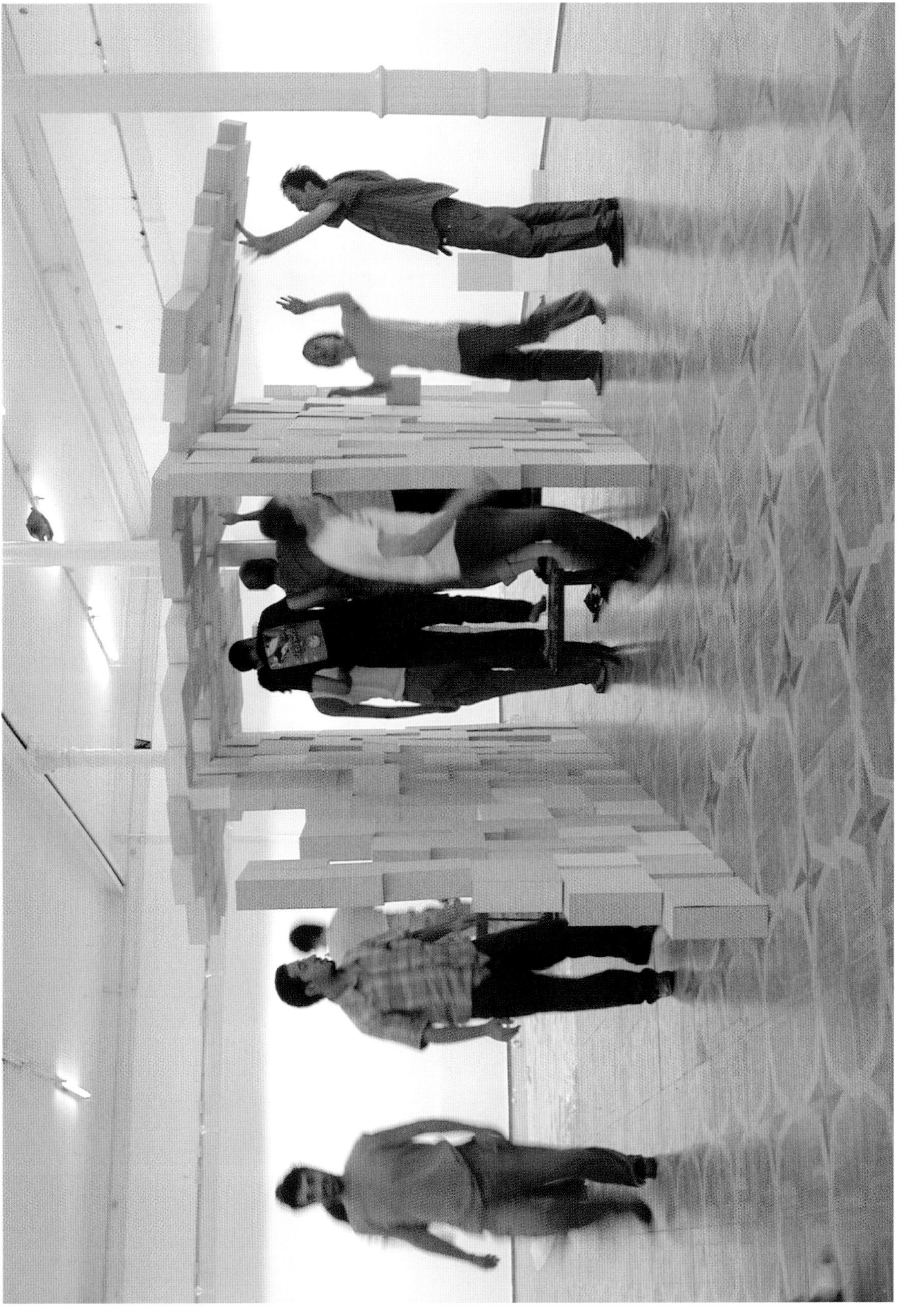

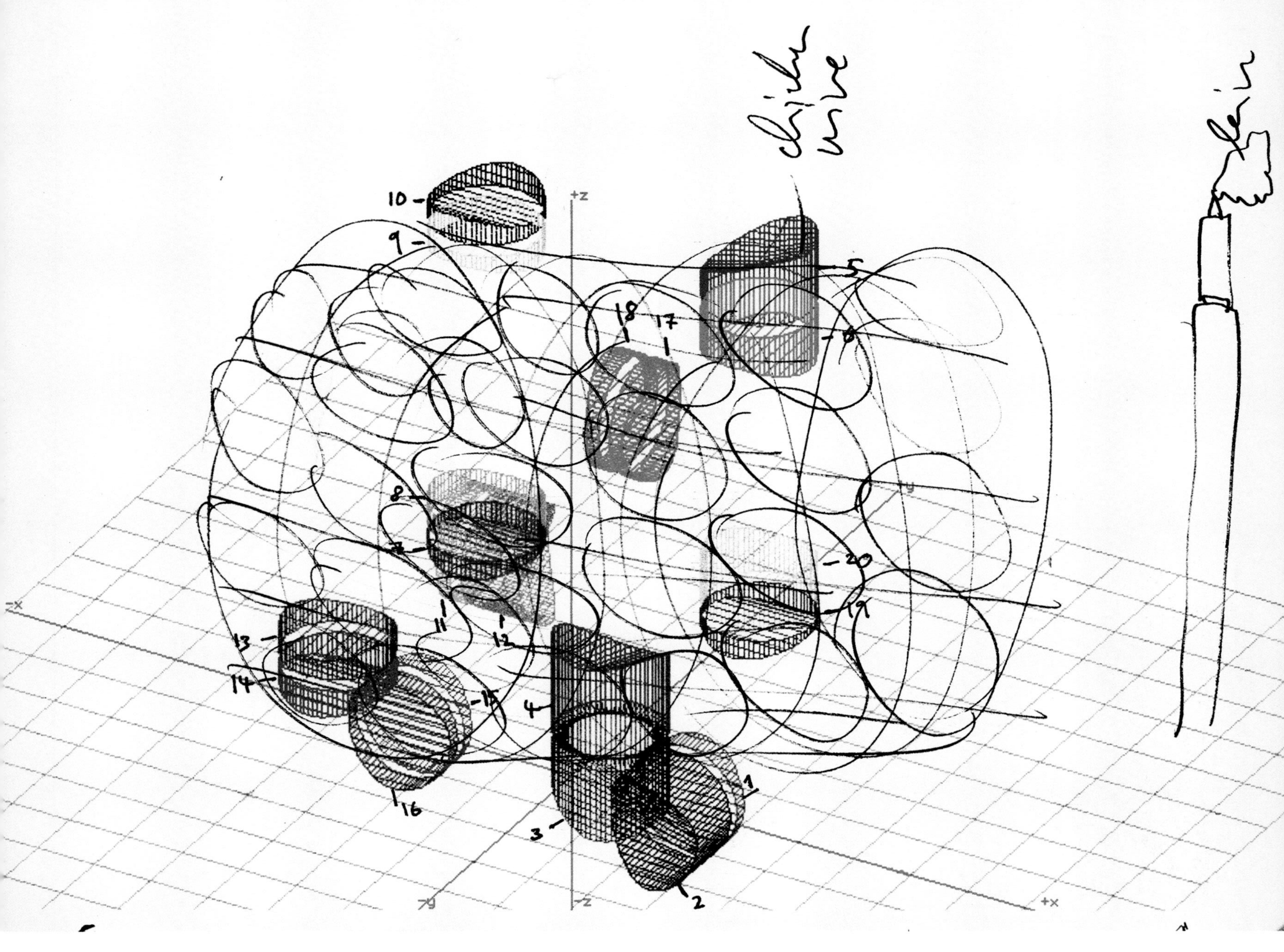

chichen
izre
+z
+x
-x
-z

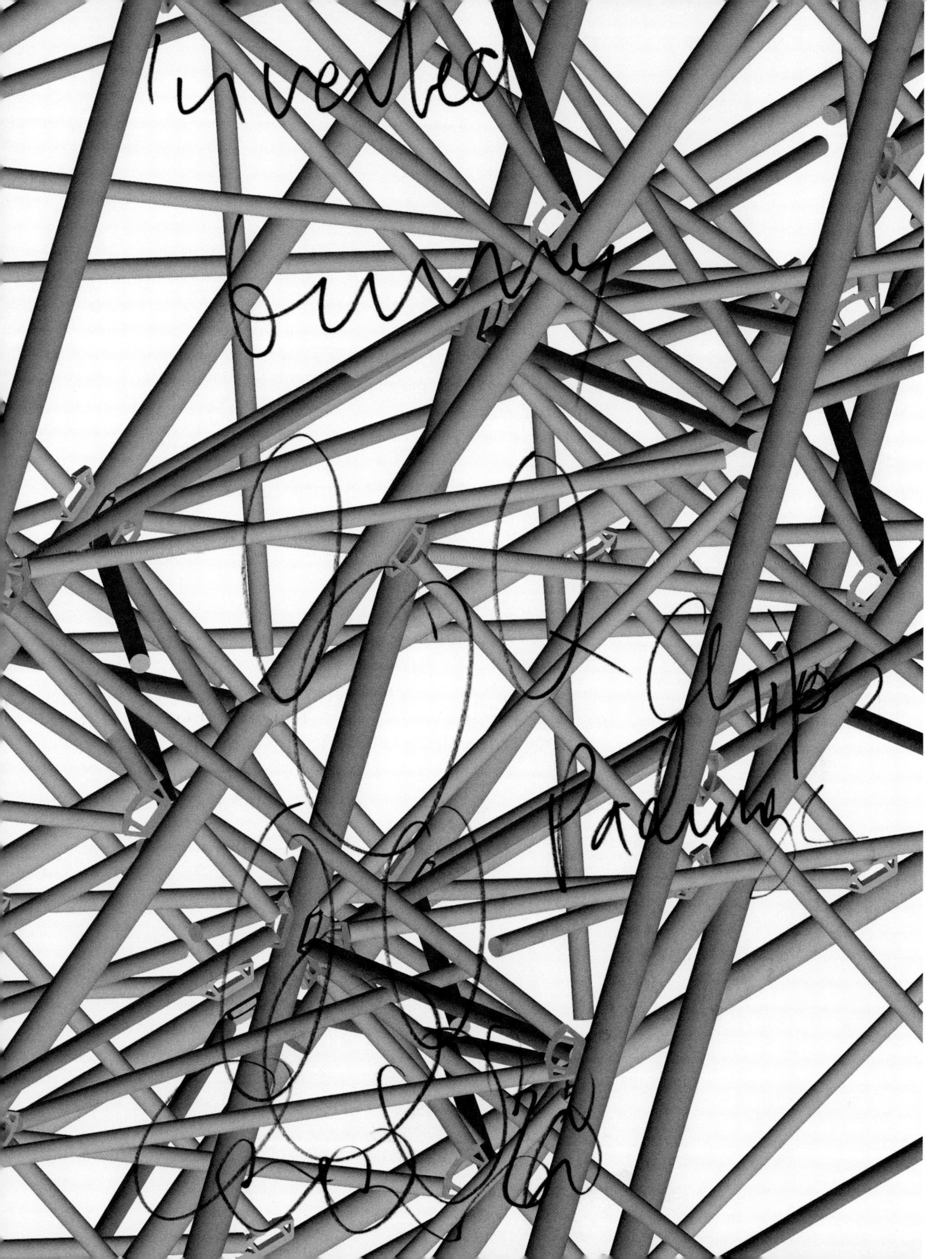

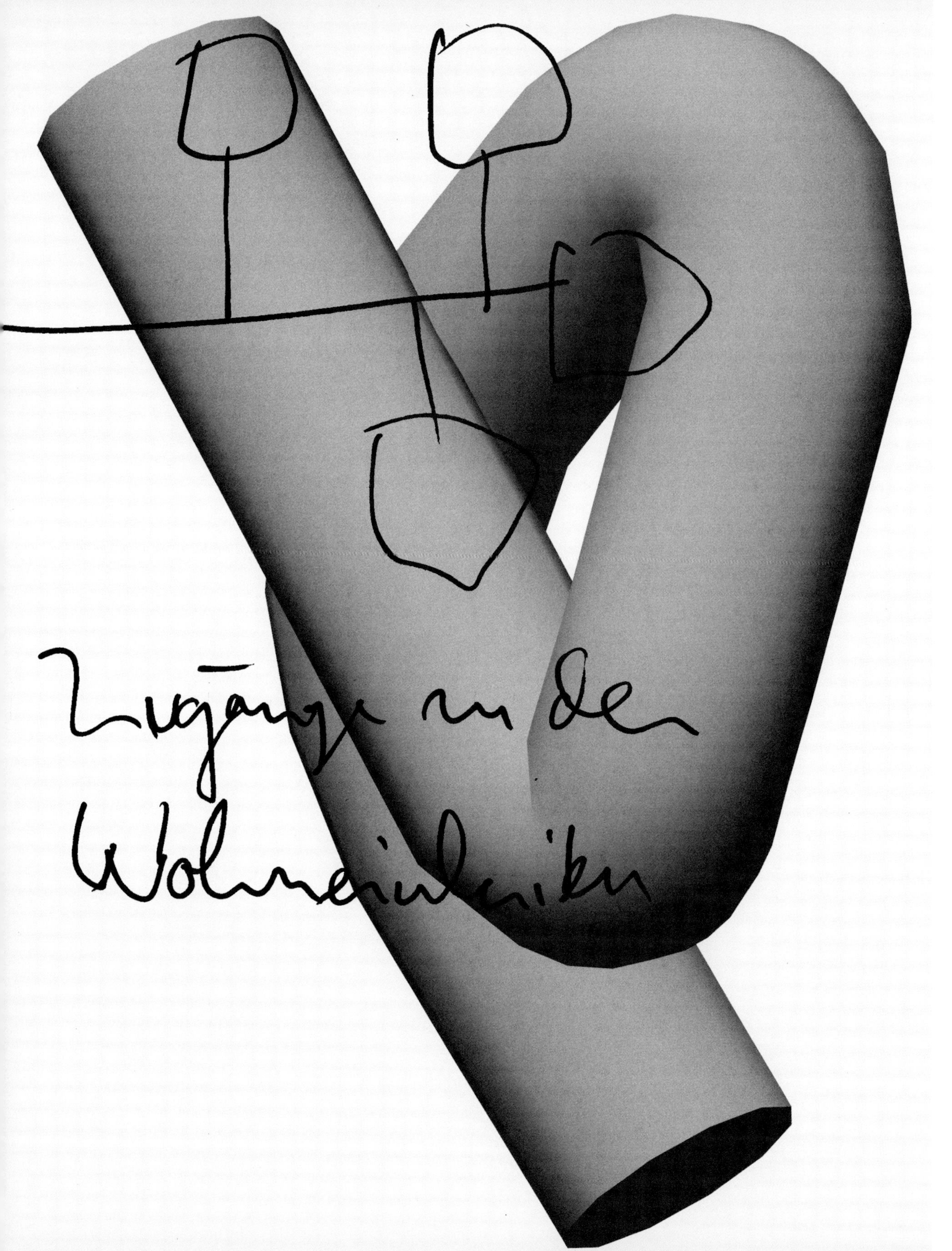

Zugänge zu den
Wohneinheiten

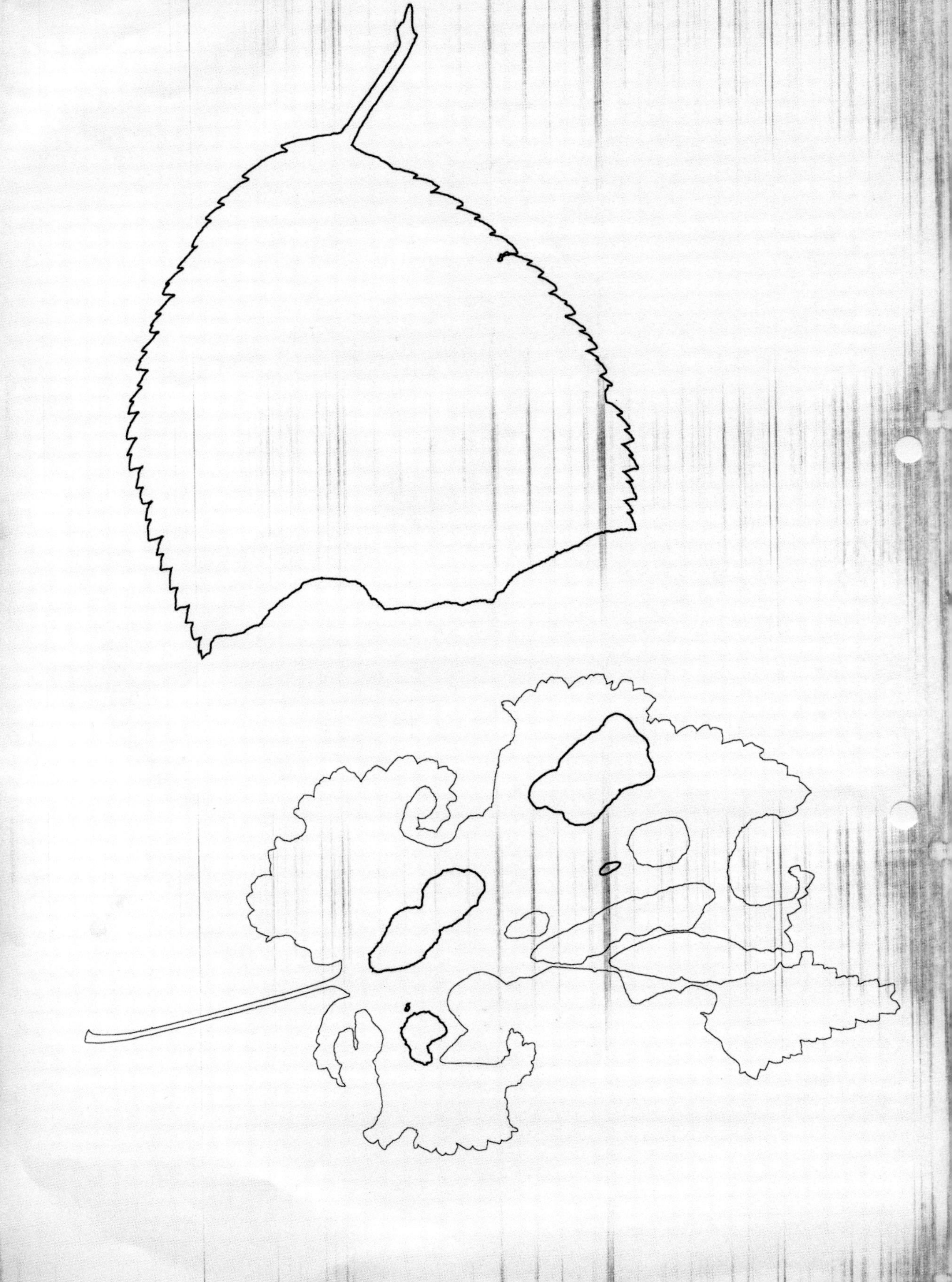

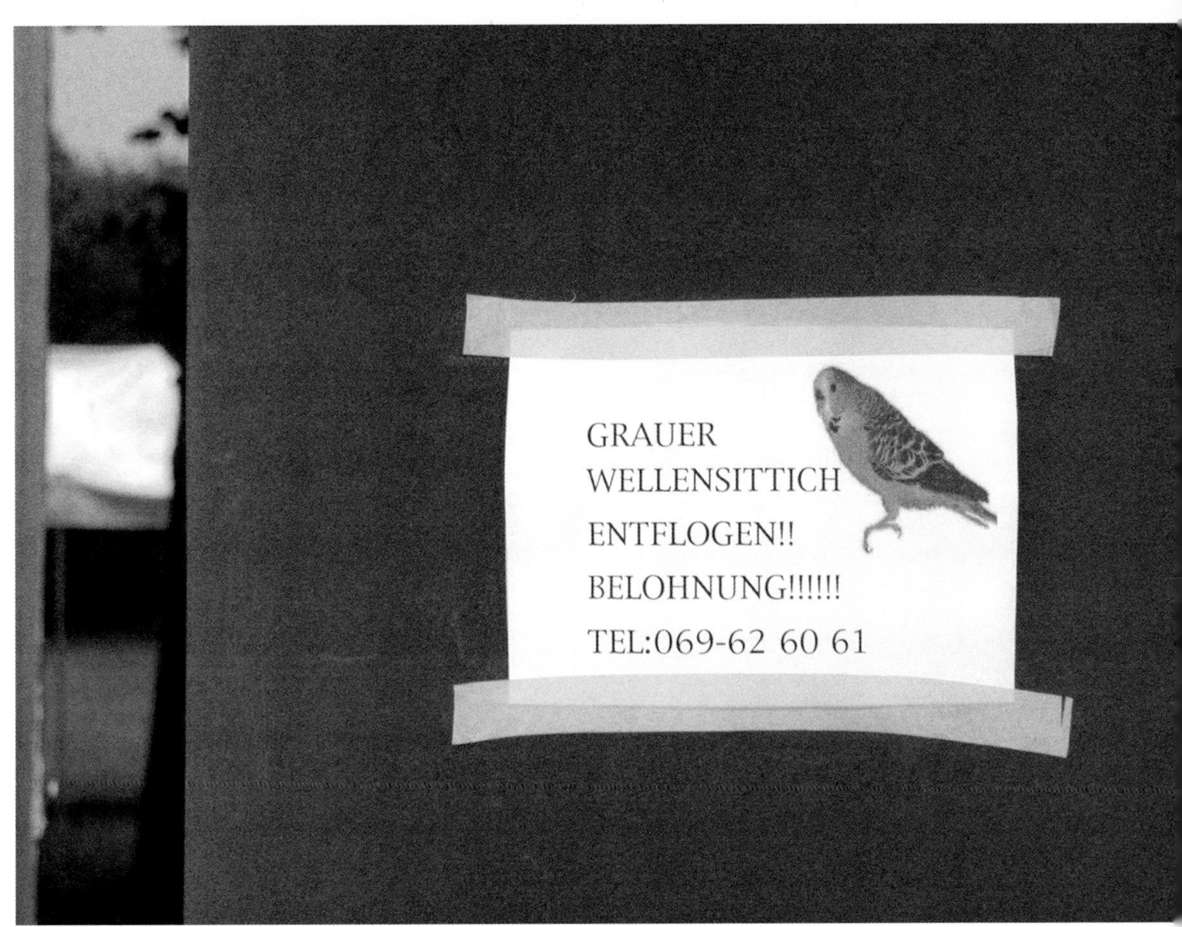
GRAUER
WELLENSITTICH
ENTFLOGEN!!
BELOHNUNG!!!!!!
TEL:069-62 60 61

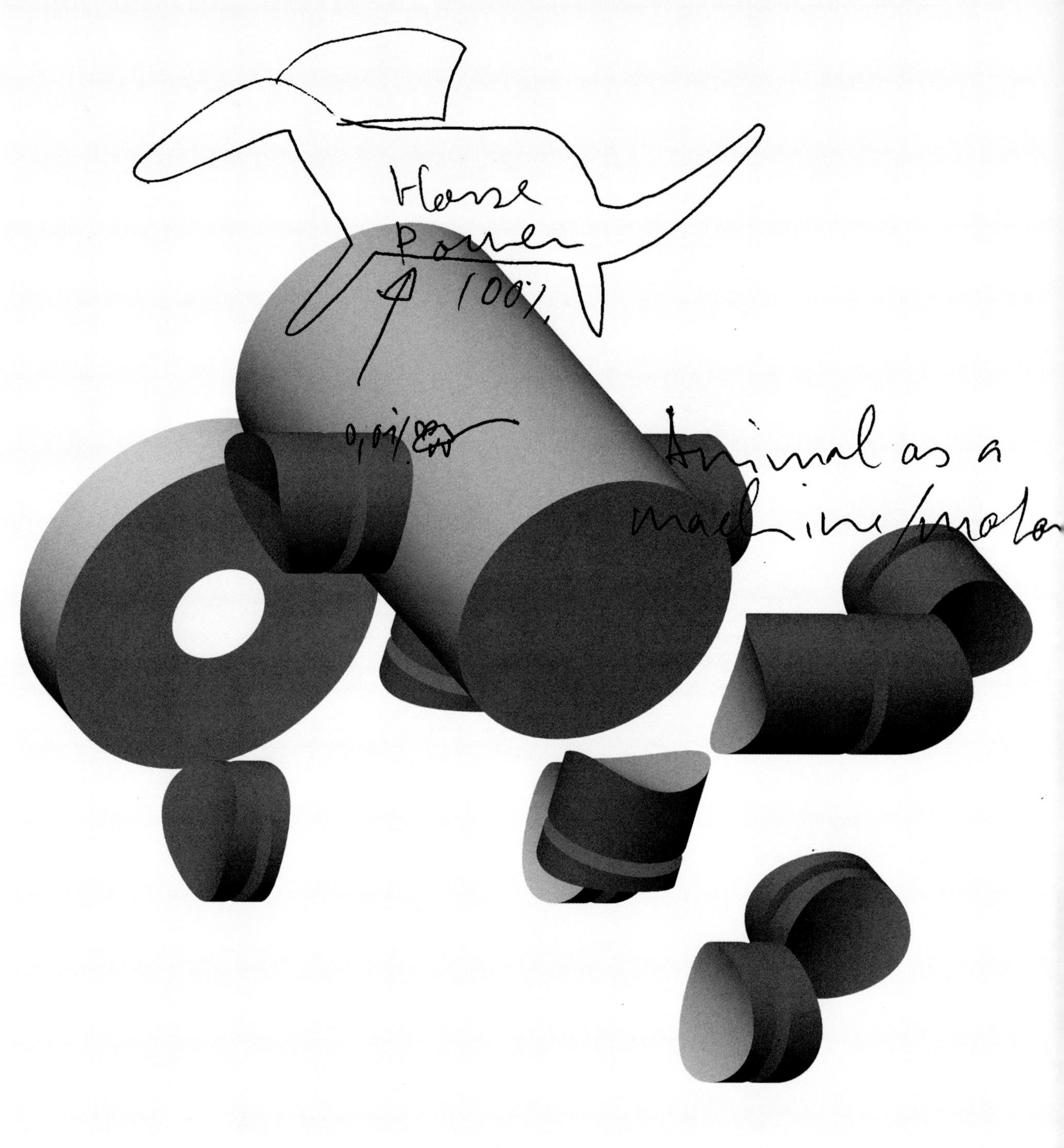

Horse
Power
↑ 100%
0,07%
Animal as a
machine/motor

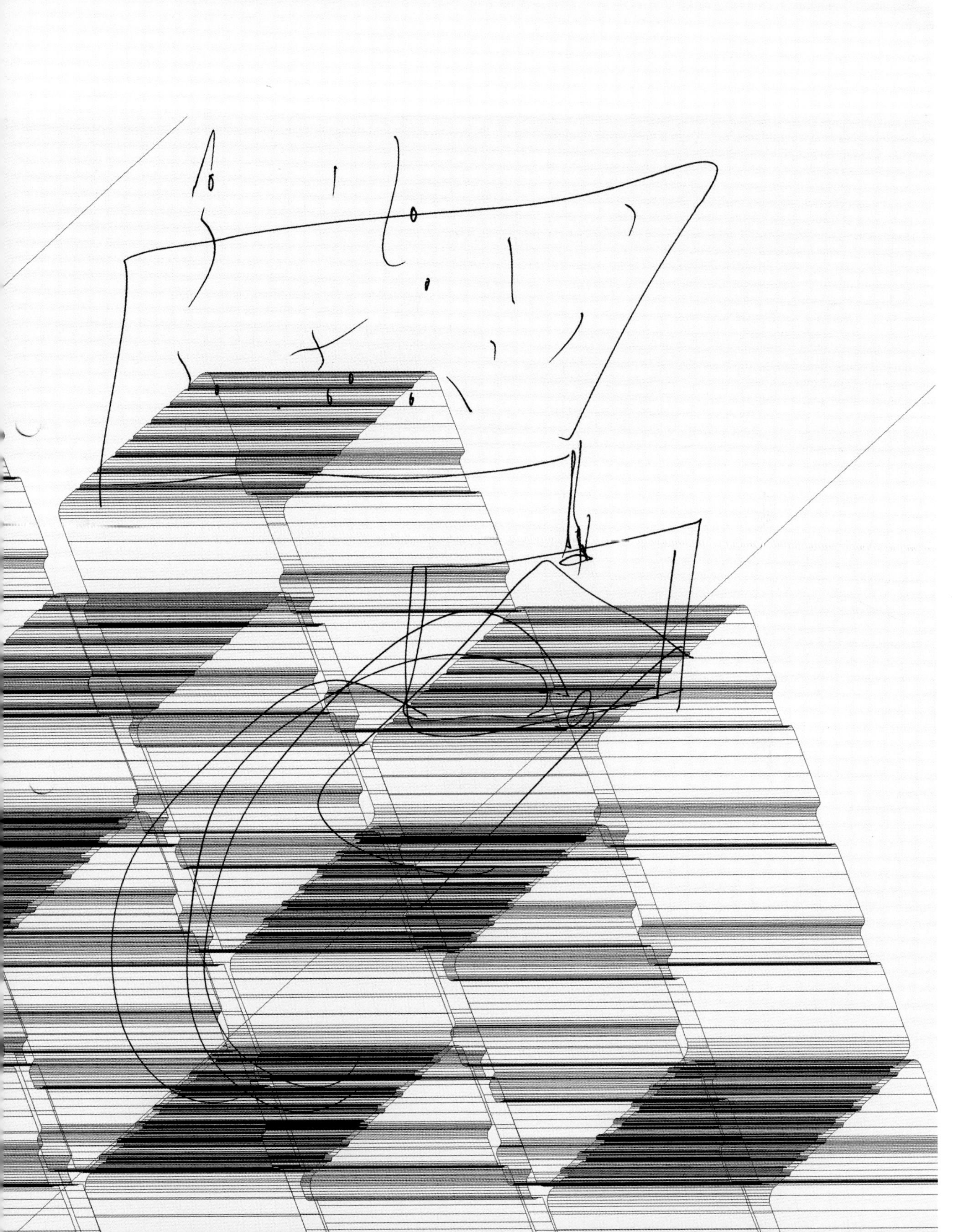

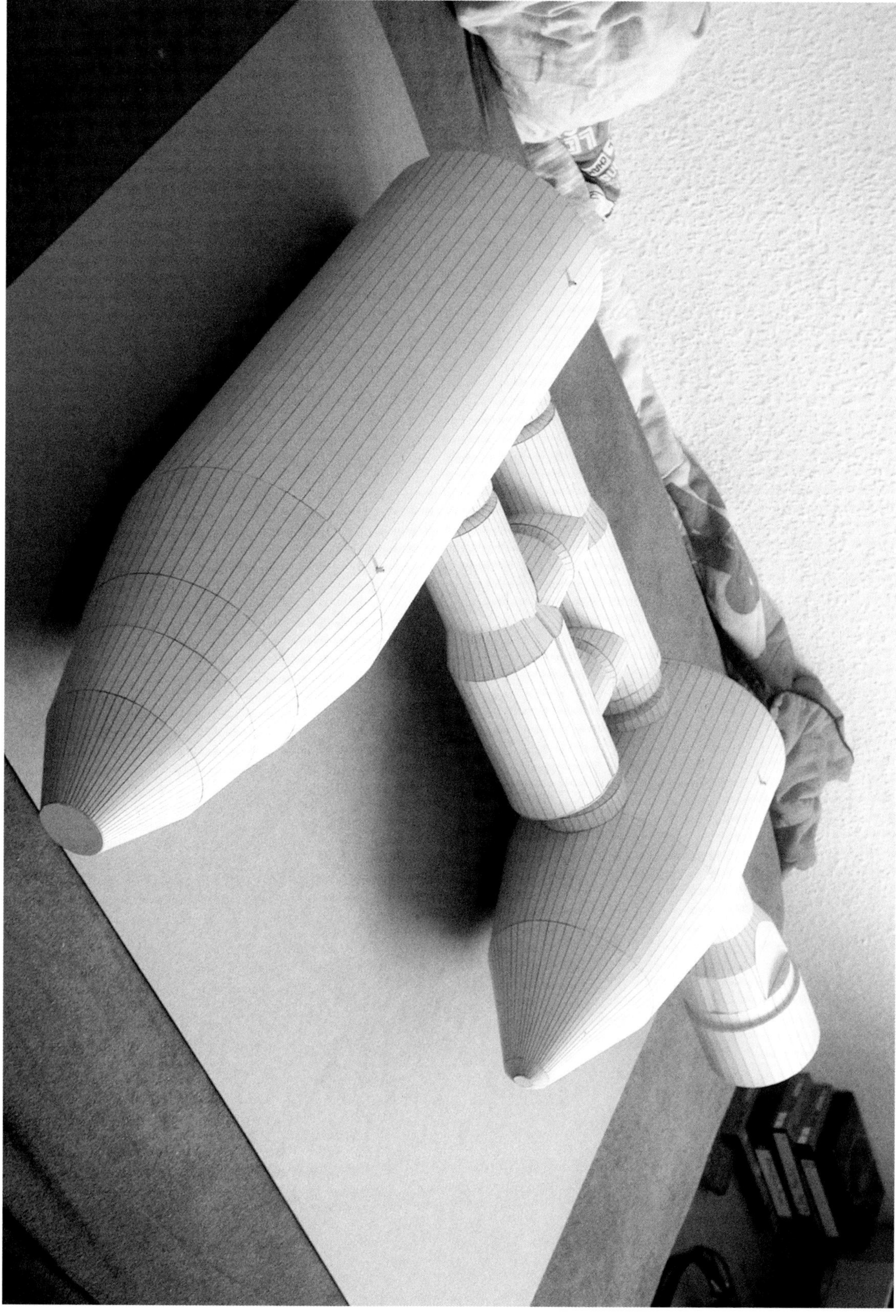

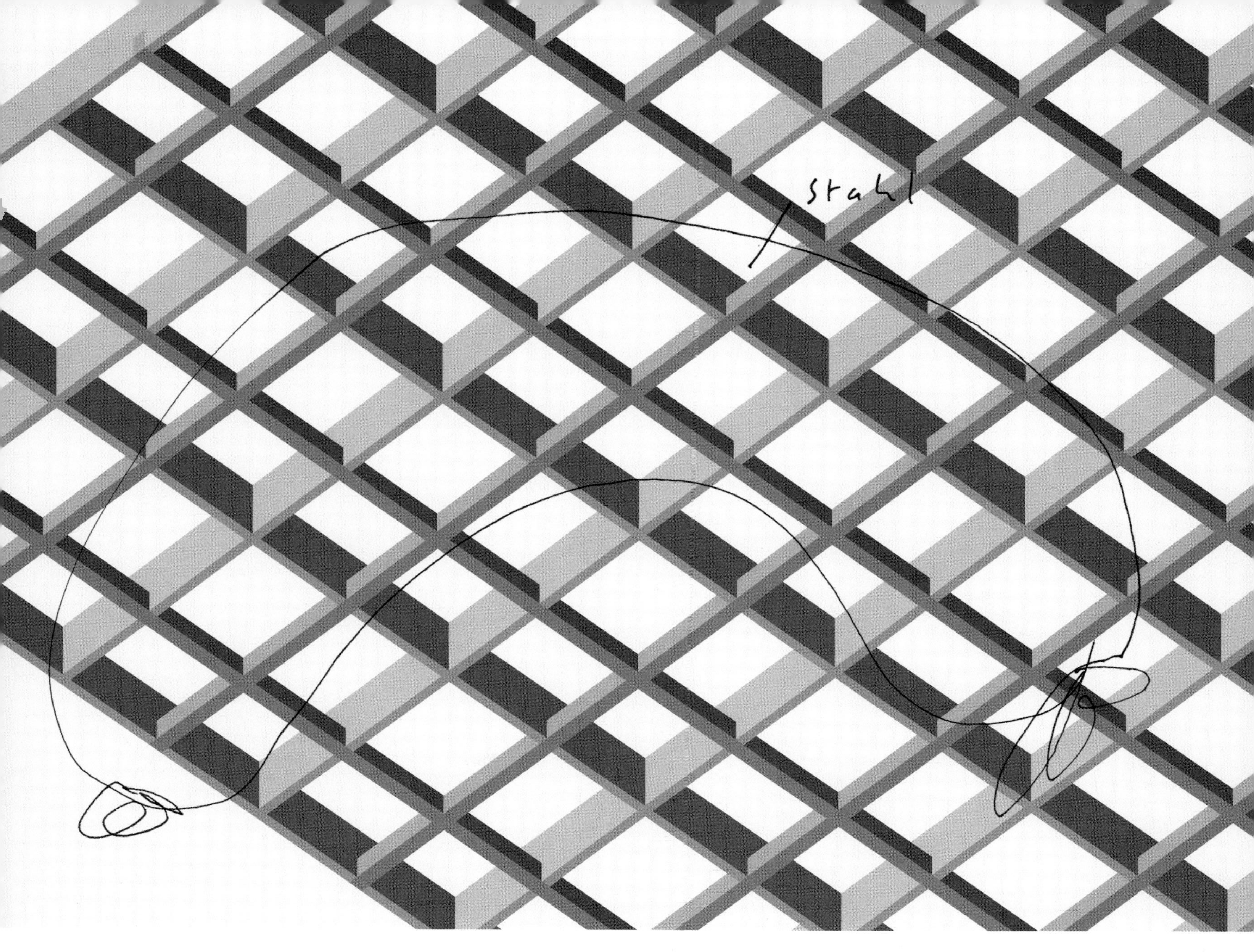
Stahl

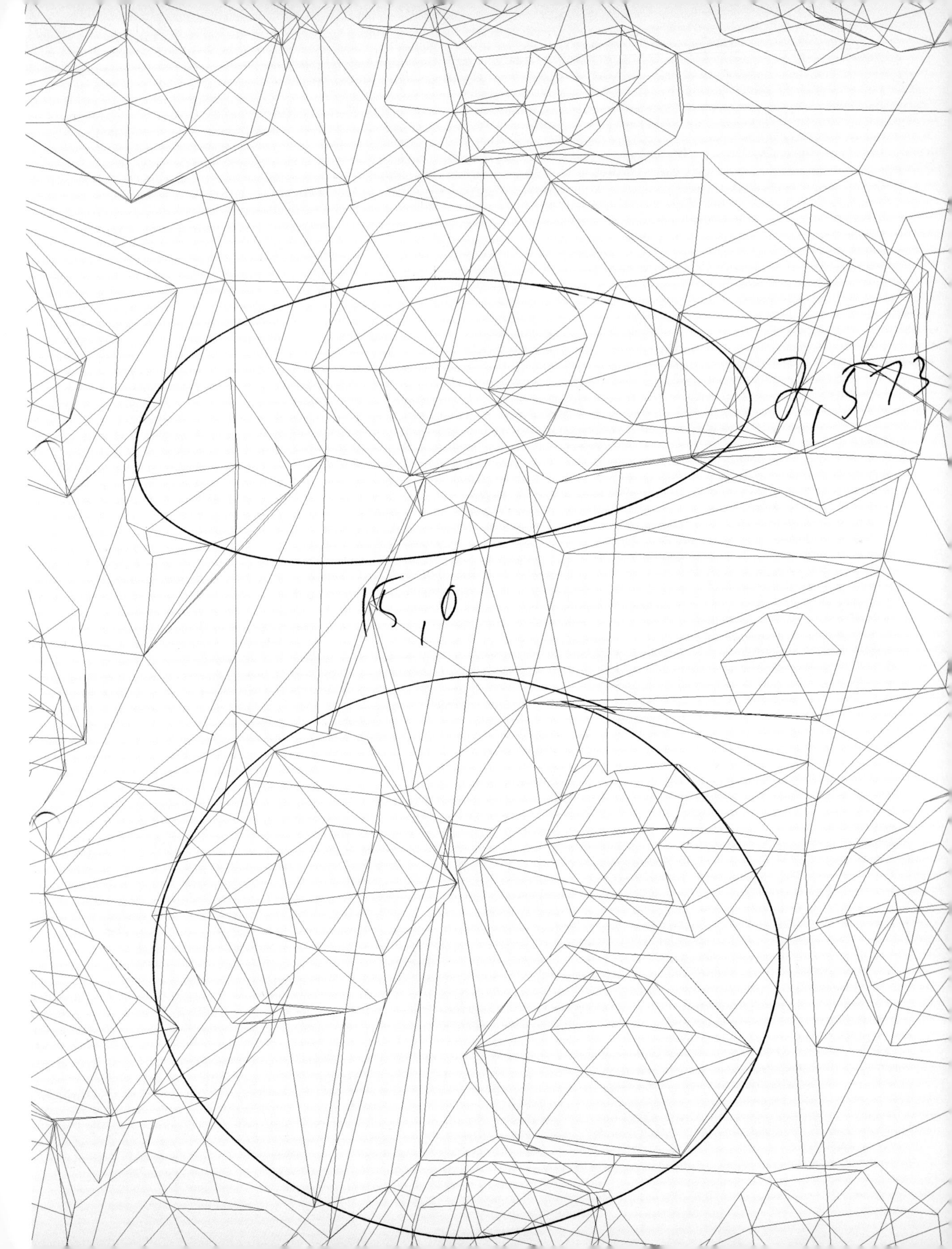

7,573
15,0

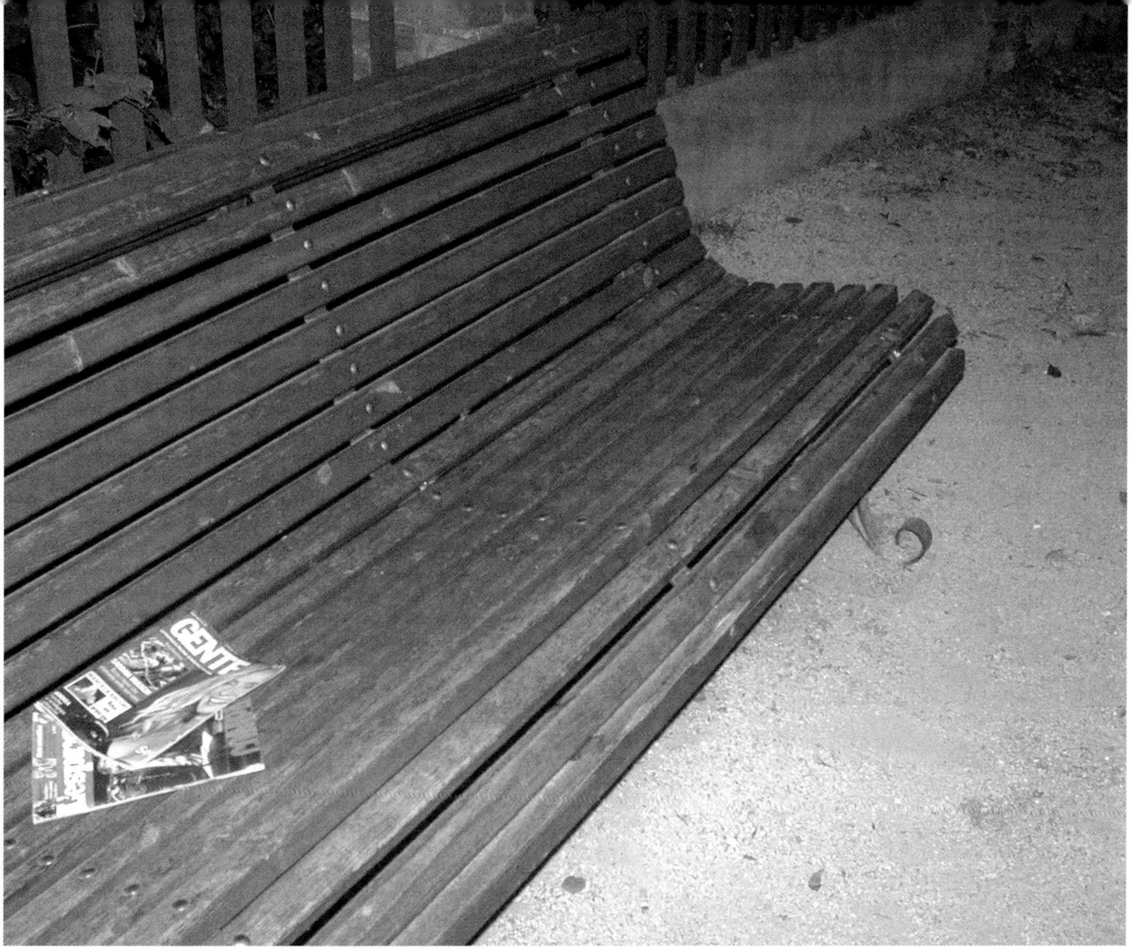

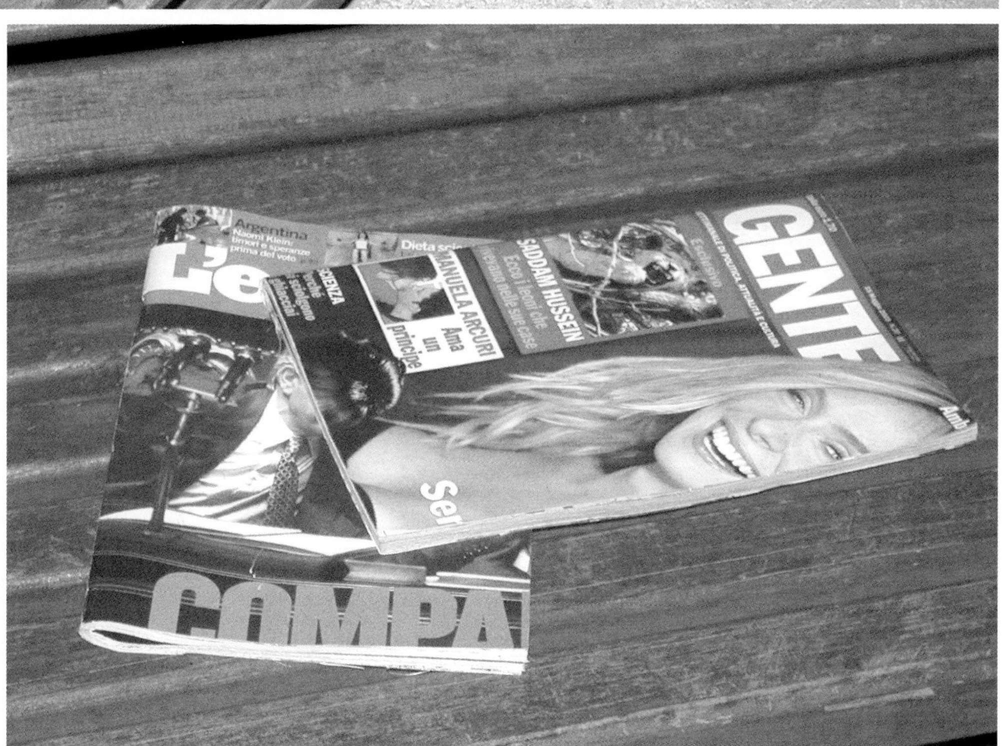
Argentina
Naomi Klein:
timori e speranze
prima del voto
Dieta sci
SADDAM HUSSEIN
GENTE
MANUELA ARCURI
Ama un principe
l'e
COMPA

Brot

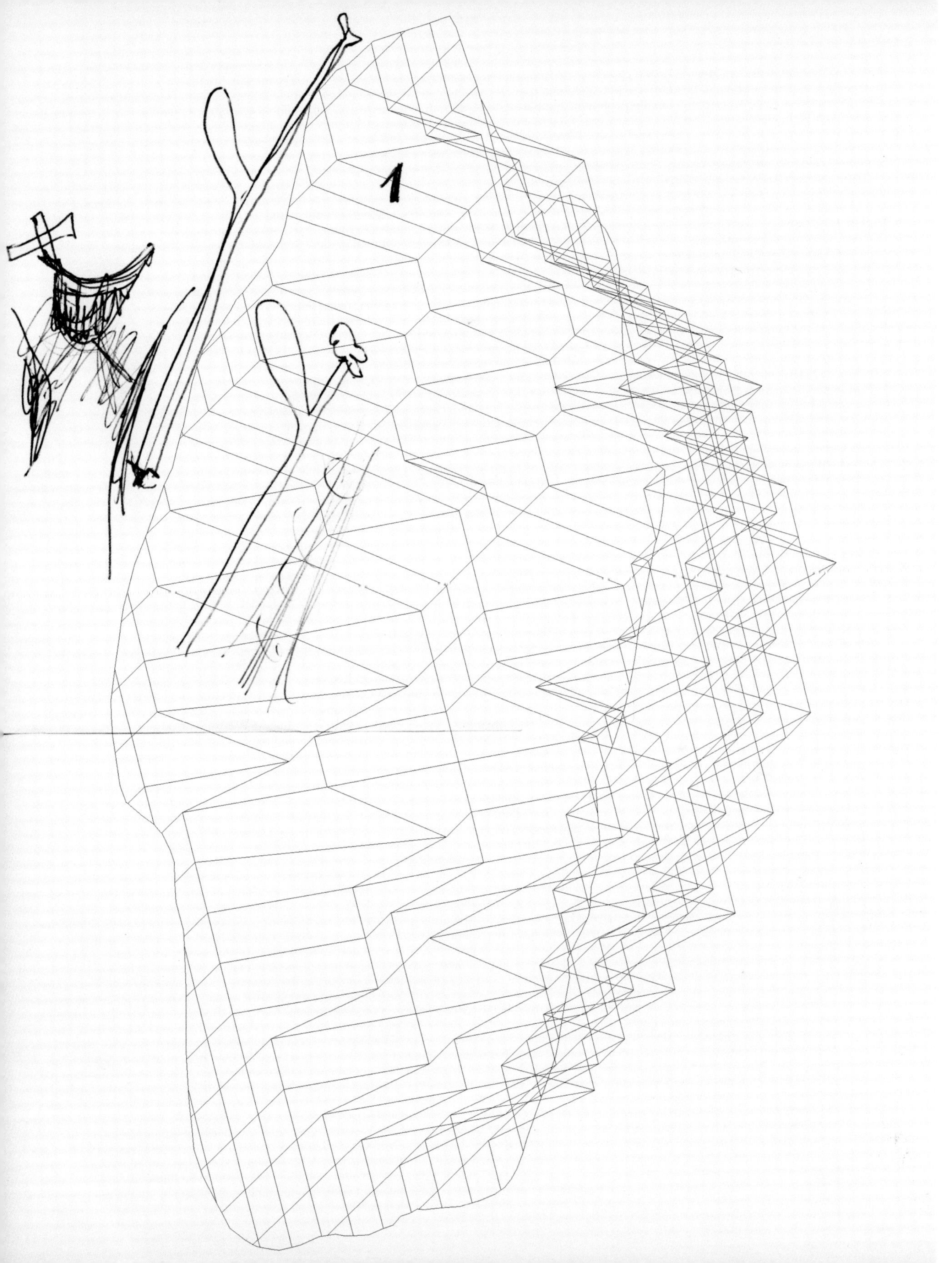
1

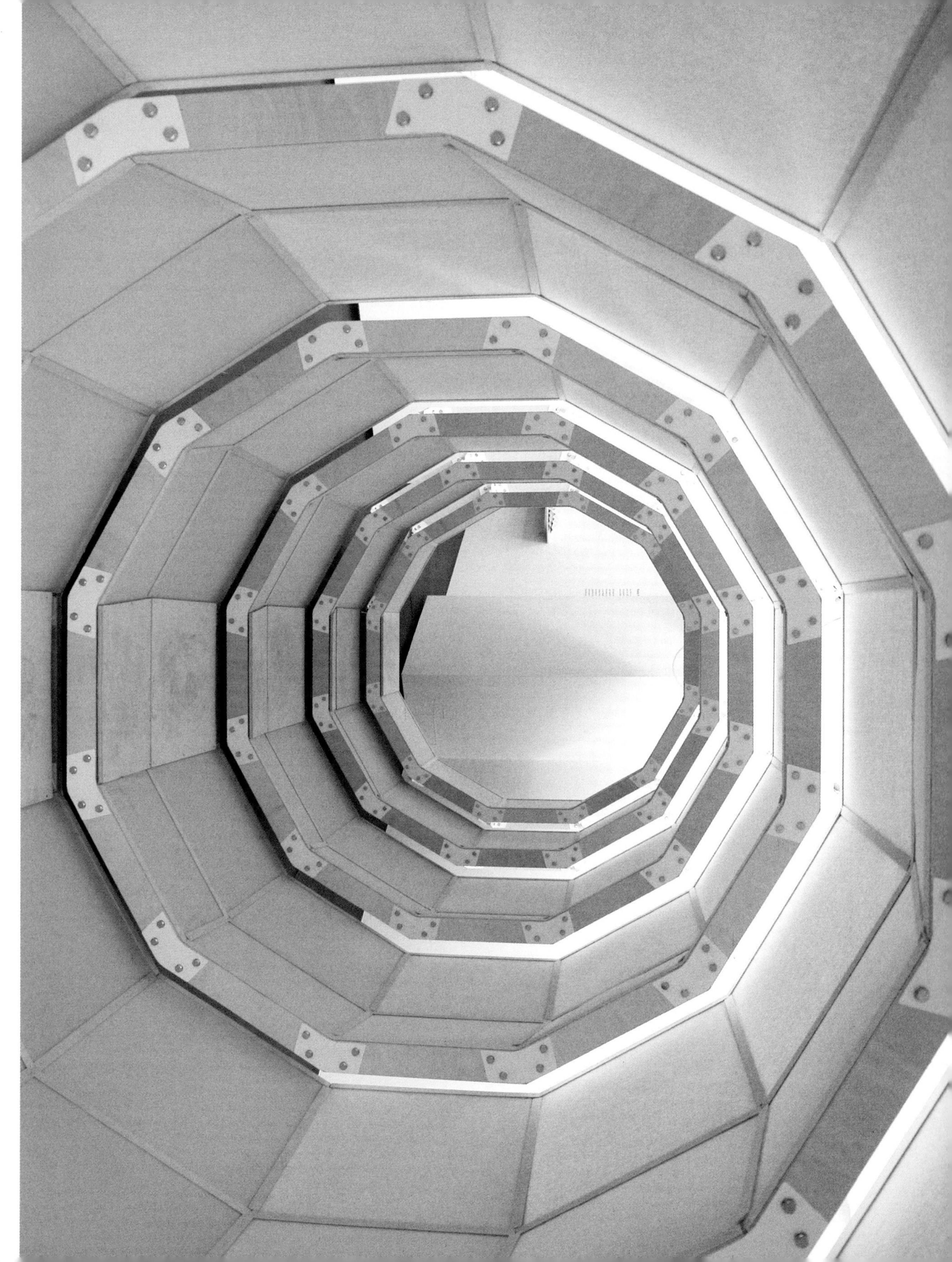

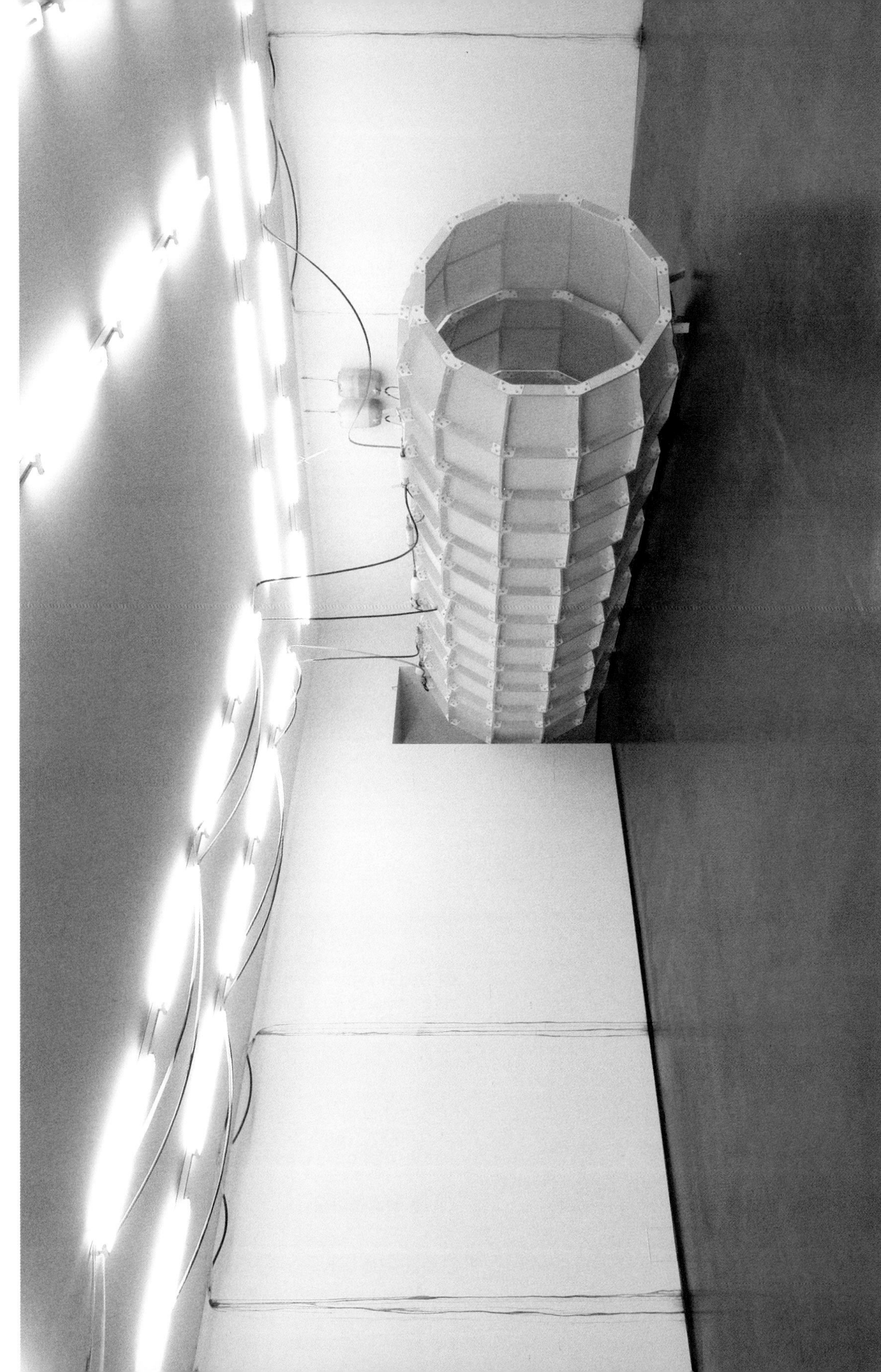

Impressum / Colophon

Diese Publikation erscheint anlässlich der Ausstellung / This book is published in conjunction with the exhibition:
Andreas Zybach, „0-6,5 PS" in / at the Aargauer Kunsthaus, Aarau, 04.05. – 22.07. 2007 kuratiert von / curated by Stephan Kunz.

Herausgeber / Editor:
Aargauer Kunsthaus, Aarau

Gestaltung / Design:
Andreas Zybach

Lithographie / Lithography:
Michael Pfrommer

Übersetzung / Translation:
Judith Raum

Produktion / Production:
Druckerei Otto Lembeck, Frankfurt am Main

© 2007, Andreas Zybach, Aargauer Kunsthaus, Aarau, Johann König, Berlin, Daniel Baumann und / and Verlag der Buchhandlung Walther König, Köln

Erschienen im / Published by:
Verlag der Buchhandlung Walther König, Köln
Ehrenstr. 4, 50672 Köln
Tel. +49 (0) 221 / 20 59 6-53
Fax +49 (0) 221 / 20 59 6-60
Email: verlag@buchhandlung-walther-koenig.de

Die Deutsche Bibliothek – CIP-Einheitsaufnahme
Ein Titelsatz für diese Publikation ist bei der Deutschen Bibliothek erhältlich.

Printed in Germany

Vertrieb / Distribution:

Schweiz / Switzerland
AVA, Verlagsauslieferungen AG
Centralweg 16, Postfach 27,
CH-8910 Affoltern a.A.
Tel. +41 (0) 1 762 42 00
Fax +41 (0) 1 762 42 10
a.koll@ava.ch

UK & Eire
Cornerhouse Publications
70 Oxford Street
GB-Manchester M1 5NH
Tel. +44 (0) 161 200 15 03
Fax +44 (0) 161 200 15 04
publications@cornerhouse.org

Außerhalb Europas / Outside Europe
D.A.P. / Distributed Art Publishers, Inc.
155 6th Avenue, 2nd Floor
New York, NY 10013
Tel. +1 (0) 212-627-1999
Fax +1 (0) 212-627-9484
www.artbook.com

ISBN 978-3-86560-282-4

Dank an / Thanks to:
Ulla Rossek, Kirsa Geiser, Johann König, Stephan Kunz, Daniel Baumann, Judith Raum, Thomas und / and Helke Bayrle, Shannon Bool, Michael Pfrommer, Alex Hanimann

Ausstellung und Katalog wurden ermöglicht durch den „Manor-Kunstpreis 2007".
Exhibition and catalogue were made possible by the "Manor-Kunstpreis 2007".

✿ MANOR

Biografie / Biography Andreas Zybach:
www.johannkoenig.de